Translation Theories Explored

Continuing *Translation Theories Explained*

Translation Theories Explored is a series designed to engage with the range and diversity of contemporary translation studies. Translation itself is as vital and as charged as ever. If anything, it has become more plural, more varied and more complex in today's world. The study of translation has responded to these challenges with vigour. In recent decades the field has gained in depth, its scope continues to expand and it is increasingly interacting with other disciplines. The series sets out to reflect and foster these developments. It aims to keep track of theoretical developments, to explore new areas, approaches and issues, and generally to extend and enrich the intellectual horizon of translation studies. Special attention is paid to innovative ideas that may not as yet be widely known but deserve wider currency.

Individual volumes explain and assess particular approaches. Each volume combines an overview of the relevant approach with case studies and critical reflection, placing its subject in a broad intellectual and historical context, illustrating the key ideas with examples, summarizing the main debates, accounting for specific methodologies, achievements and blind spots, and opening up new perspectives for the future. Authors are selected not only on their close familiarity and personal affinity with a particular approach but also on their capacity for lucid exposition, critical assessment and imaginative thought.

The series is aimed at researchers and graduate students who wish to learn about new approaches to translation in a comprehensive but accessible way.

Theo Hermans
Series Editor

Representing Others

Translation, Ethnography and the Museum

Kate Sturge

St. Jerome Publishing
Manchester, UK & Kinderhook (NY), USA

Published by

St. Jerome Publishing
2 Maple Road West, Brooklands
Manchester, M23 9HH, United Kingdom
Telephone +44 (0)161 973 9856
Fax +44 (0)161 905 3498
stjerome@compuserve.com
http://www.stjerome.co.uk

InTrans Publications
P. O. Box 467
Kinderhook, NY 12106, USA
Telephone (518) 758-1755
Fax (518) 758-6702

ISBN 978-1-905763-01-6 (pbk)
ISSN 1365-0513 (*Translation Theories Explored*)

Printed and bound in Great Britain by
T. J. International Ltd, Padstow, Cornwall, UK

Typeset by
Delta Typesetters, Cairo, Egypt
Email: hilali1945@yahoo.co.uk

British Library Cataloguing in Publication Data
A catalogue record of this book is available from the British Library

Library of Congress Cataloging-in-Publication Data
Sturge, Kate.
Representing others : translation, ethnography, and the museum / Kate Sturge.
p. cm. -- (Translation theories explored)
Includes bibliographical references and index.
ISBN 978-1-905763-01-6 (pbk. : alk. paper)
1. Translating and interpreting. 2. Culture--Semiotic models. 3. Language and culture. 4. Ethnology--Authorship. 5. Ethnological museums and collections. 6. Museum exhibits. I. Title.

P306.2.S78 2007
418'.02--dc22

2007003005

Representing Others

Translation, Ethnography and the Museum

Kate Sturge

Cultural anthropology has always been dependent on translation as a textual practice, and it has often used 'translation' as a metaphor to describe ethnography's processes of interpretation and cross-cultural comparison. Questions of intelligibility and representation are central to both translation studies and ethnographic writing – as are the dilemmas of cultural distance or proximity, exoticism or appropriation. Similarly, recent work in museum studies discusses problems of representation that are raised by ethnographic museums as multimedia 'translations'. However, as yet there has been remarkably little interdisciplinary exchange: neither has translation studies kept up with the sophistication of anthropology's investigations of meaning, representation and 'culture' itself, nor have anthropology and museum studies often looked to translation studies for analyses of language difference or concrete methods of tracing translation practices.

This book opens up an exciting field of study to translation scholars and suggests possible avenues of cross-disciplinary collaboration.

Kate Sturge teaches Translation Studies and German at Aston University, Birmingham, UK.

Contents

List of Figures

Acknowledgements

For their support, inspiration and practical help at various stages of this book I would like to thank Theo Hermans, Michaela Wolf, Reina Lewis, Allison Brown, Ginger A. Diekmann, Christina Schäffner and my colleagues at Aston University, and especially, with affection, Tanya d'Agostino.

The author and the publishers are grateful to the copyright holders of the following material for permission to reproduce images and excerpts from translations: University of Nebraska Press for "Coyote and Junco", reprinted from *Finding the Center: The Art of the Zuni Storyteller*, translated by Dennis Tedlock, copyright 1999 by Dennis Tedlock; Simon & Schuster Adult Publishing Group for *Popol Vuh*, translated by Dennis Tedlock, reprinted from *Popol Vuh: The Definitive Edition of the Mayan Book of the Dawn of Life*, copyright 1985/1996 by Dennis Tedlock; *Journal of Education* & Boston University for "Andrew Peynetsa's 'Coyote and Junco'", retranslated by Dell Hymes, from 'Narrative Form as a "Grammar" of Experience: Native Americans and a Glimpse of English', 1982; University of New Mexico Press for "The 13th Horse Song of Frank Mitchell (White)", by Jerome Rothenberg, in *Shaking the Pumpkin: Traditional Poetry of the Indian North Americas,* copyright 1986 by Jerome Rothenberg; Cambridge University Press for "A man of the Akar-Bale tribe", A.R. Brown [=Radcliffe-Brown], *The Andaman Islanders*, 1922 (Figure 1); Oxford University Press for E.E. Evans-Pritchard, *The Nuer*, 1940 (Figure 2); Government Printing Office/Smithsonian Institution for Franz Boas, *Kathlamet Texts*, 1901 (Figure 3); The Pitt Rivers Museum, University of Oxford, for 'The Museum Court in about 1910' (Figure 5) and 'Magic and Trial by Ordeal' (Figure 6); The Horniman Museum, London for 'Label to Yoruba Epa mask' (Figure 7) and 'Bronze plaques with labels by Joseph Eboreime' (Figure 8).

1. Introduction

Let's begin at the deep end, with a decontextualized piece of translated conversation:

> *What would make you decide to bring her back?* – She must open her mouth and say, "They did this to me, they did this, and this." In front of the Bukhensha family, in front of them! So that I know, so that their errors appear to my eyes too. Otherwise,... perhaps she is playing with me, and with them, with the both of us. That couldn't be. (Dwyer 1982:161)

How did these English words, published in an ethnographic account of Moroccan life, come into existence? Were they mechanically generated by the Arabic words in which the interview took place? Do they amalgamate or paraphrase or reflect or explicate, are they literal or free or do they deliberately exoticize? Under which conditions were their preceding Arabic words spoken, and under which do they reach an anglophone audience on the page? This book attempts to explore some of the questions such a passage might prompt. It does so by tracing those debates in the disciplines of cultural anthropology and museum studies which tackle issues of representation closely connected to translation.

Even without a context, the sample above already indicates that representations of this kind take place within a web of inequalities. On the one hand, the speaker's words are taken into English by a process of selection, editing, reordering into the grammatical and semantic categories of another language, as well as the application of traditions of translating that signal 'literal' faithfulness by using a form of translationese. The speaker himself reports his ex-wife's potential words – both ethnographer and interviewee are engaged in the practice of reporting speech, and in neither case does the reported person get to determine how his or her words are framed. On the other hand, there is a political asymmetry between the two main participants in this conversation: one side initiated the dialogue within the terms of a powerful institution which cannot be accessed by the other; one owns the copyright and 'speaks for' the other in a hegemonic language on an academic stage.

Discussing Marx's use of two German terms, *Darstellung* and *Vertretung*, both translatable into English as 'representation', Gayatri Chakravorty Spivak notes how English combines the notion of *portraying* other people with that of *speaking for* them or in their place, in the parliamentary sense (1988:276-80). The ambiguity in the term 'representation' arises for both ethnography and translation; both claim at once to 'show' others to the domestic audience and to speak the others' words in the language of that audience. As we will see, this is a dynamic which critical voices in anthropology and museum studies have been addressing in detail over the past few decades, and the purpose of this book is to identify areas of thinking that promise to be fruitful for the discipline of translation studies.

Before we start, though, I should identify which strands of translation studies I am working from. In the context of ethnographic translation and the translation of cultures in museum displays, it doesn't make sense to look at translation as a mainly technical process of re-encoding stable meanings into a second linguistic code. We will see that the 'meanings' encoded by ethnographic representation are complex, unstable, hybrid; they are born of the contingencies of the receiving system rather than those of the source. Far from being a potentially reversible bridge-crossing movement, translation in this view is a usually conflictual encounter, one "central to the interface of cultures in the world, part of ideological negotiations and cultural struggles, a form of intellectual construction and creation, a metonym in the exercise of cultural strength: it is a matter of power" (Tymoczko 1999:298).

This line of thinking within translation studies is one that shares many questions with ethnography (understood here in its double sense as the practice of cultural anthropology 'on the ground' and the writing of ethnographic accounts). As Johannes Fabian points out, anthropology used to yearn for 'accurate' representations but is now exploring the implications of an acceptance that representations are not mirrors reflecting pre-existing, separate objects: "the Other is never simply given, never just found or encountered, but *made*" (1990:755), and in recent decades translation, too, has had to face a 'crisis of representation' which undermined positivist notions of fixed 'source texts' capable of objective restatement in another language. According to Talal Asad, anthropology's crisis – feeding into the 'postmodern' turn of the early 1980s – was prompted by shifts in the global political landscape: since the Second World War and with the rise of independence movements, "fundamental changes have occurred in the world which social anthropology inhabits, changes which have affected the object, the ideological support and the organisational base of social anthropology itself. And in noting these changes we remind ourselves that anthropology does not merely apprehend the world in which it is located, but that the world also determines how anthropology will apprehend it" (1973:12). In the same period, he notes, the Western academy was increasingly turning away from totalizing methods in all the social sciences and addressing instead smaller, micro or local histories and geographies (ibid:13; see also Sewell 1999). Moving into the early twenty-first century, we see the growing presence of postcolonial theory, including engagements with globalization and its effect on concepts of 'culture'.

The "experimental moment" in anthropology (Marcus & Fischer 1986) involved increased application to ethnography of the tools of literary criticism – and with this a perspective that fits more closely with studies of literary translation. Thus, ethnographic writing has been examined as fiction and as translation, with more recent critics expanding the notion of translation to cover both such writing and the wider processes of cultural negotiation within which it takes place. These new definitions of translation and of culture itself are discussed in Chapter 2, where we will see that while the 'experimental moment' did much to unpick the 'translation of culture' in the wide sense of filtering and fictionalization, the aspect of interlingual translation of the words of other people, the practical basis of much ethnographic work, has received far less attention. Chapter 3 considers anthropology's long tradition of grappling with the experience and writing of cultural difference: after all, anthropology has always been about "figuring out what went on in people's heads when you couldn't get at it by projecting your own assumptions and experience" (Darnell 2001:xx) and no less so has literary translation. Translation in both forms offers a means of expanding apparently monocultural worlds and drawing out the actual interculturality of the world we all share, but how to do this in practice, without either effacing or "fetishizing" difference (Said 1989), is a thorny question indeed.

In Chapter 4, a historical outline of the rise of 'classical' ethnography will prepare the way for the discussion in Chapters 5 and 6 of counter-moves proposed by the ethnographic experiments of the 1970s onwards. The aim of these chapters is to give a taste of the range of innovative translation techniques being applied by ethnographers, many of which open interesting lines of enquiry for translation scholars.

Chapter 7 looks at ethnographic museums in their capacity as 'translations', for though not written texts, they too are frequently analyzed from a textual perspective. As a genre of ethnographic representation that has a much larger and more diverse audience than the written word alone, museums add an important dimension to our understanding of translation as a practice of representing other people's words, lives and beliefs.

The inclusion of museums makes it even less fair than usual to apply the well-worn accusation 'traduttore traditore' in the critiques that follow. Not only is there no clear-cut object of such translatorial treason once our 'source texts' are no longer printed books with single authors, but even if there were the translator would be bound to betray both it and everyone else involved in the whole process – dialogue participants, institutions, editors, professional colleagues, students, readers. The 'translator's task' I will assume here is not to be 'faithful' but to make principled and if possible accountable choices on how to produce the words and images that will enter the global circuit of cultural representations. This question is the focus of Chapter 8.

Let me close with a few caveats. Firstly, discussing 'there' depends on defining 'here'. In my case that is a white British standpoint, limited to anglophone traditions in order to avoid scattering and diluting the account too far and not because there has been no work done in other languages, other histories. Aside from practicalities, the focus on the English-language tradition also reflects the political impact of this tradition as nurtured by colonialism (for Britain) and internal colonization (for North America). For the sake of consistency of access and because of my own linguistic limitations I have only cited works available in English.

Secondly, the huge spectrum of practices of representing other cultures, most of which could be described as forms of translation in a broader or narrower sense, could include anything from novels and films to travel accounts and translated legal canons. Limiting myself to written ethnographies and anthropological museums is not to exclude these related fields but to invite further investigation of them.

Thirdly, at times my comments will seem only negative, following the hallowed tradition of translator-bashing. But despite the troubled past and present of ethnographic translation – in its harshest formulation, as an imperialistic appropriation into terms of the translating culture – this book starts from the assumption that translation must happen, that, however difficult, it is a necessary move and an assertion of our common ground in being human. Translation must happen, that is, if the alternative is to wait silently until the others adopt our own language and linguistic homogeneity makes translation obsolete.

Finally, this book doesn't claim to offer either great depth or complete coverage of current debates or the state of the art. My aim is to open up curiosity for further work: the next steps are up to you.

2. Translation as Metaphor, Translation as Practice

Applying translation studies perspectives to ethnography means assuming that the work of ethnography is a kind of translation. Before we turn to specific forms and difficulties of 'ethnographic translation', let's first ask what lies behind that assumption. In particular, this chapter explores the metaphor of 'the translation of cultures' and its cousin, 'culture as translation'.

The translation of culture

The concept of ethnography as a translation of culture is nothing new. The tasks of that "pair of inverted twins" (Tedlock 1983:334), the missionary and the anthropologist, were described by Malinowski in 1935 as "translating the white man's point of view to the native" and "translating the native point of view to the European" respectively (in Tedlock, ibid). Talal Asad's important 1986 essay shows that from the 1950s and especially in British social anthropology, the concept of 'translation of cultures' became increasingly common. The alien world of anthropology's objects needed to be reframed in a language which could be understood by the Western academy. As Godfrey Lienhardt put it in 1954:

> The problem of describing to others how members of a remote tribe think [...] begins to appear largely as one of translation, of making the coherence primitive thought has in the languages it really lives in, as clear as possible in our own. (cited in Asad 1986:142)

More recent uses of the metaphor reject the notions of 'remote tribes' and 'primitive thought' but still regard the project of ethnographic writing as a kind of translation: an attempt to "understand other cultures as far as possible in their own terms but in our language, a task which also ultimately entails the mapping of the ideas and practices onto Western categories of understanding" (Tambiah 1990:3).

It is not language in the narrow sense alone – or even primarily – that is to be translated here. Instead, the ethnographic translation proposed by Lienhardt aims to represent the thinking 'behind' language and practices. In his discussion, Asad defends functionalist anthropology's attempt to portray the internal coherence of alien social practices and beliefs, as opposed to approaches that denounced their irrationality and downright wrongness. However, he points out that the search for coherence is not an innocent act. It works on the assumption that the 'natives' cannot know the true meaning of their practices, which must instead be identified by the more skilful and objective outsider; as a result, authorship and agency shift from the people studied to the anthropologist-interpreter. Closely bound up with this point are two issues which will be very important to our discussion: firstly, the 'cultural translation' *constructs* its source text as well as transferring it into a different language in the manner of the traditional translator, and secondly, the production of 'cultural translations' is not the individual business of the ethnographer but a process strongly constrained by the context of institutional power.

To begin with the construction of the source text, Asad notes that although the anthropologist in the field tries to learn to live a different life and think inside the different discourse, when he or she gets home it's time to write a translation "addressed to a very specific audience, which is waiting to read *about* another mode of life and to manipulate the text it reads according to established rules, not to learn to *live* a new mode of life" (1986:159). In other words, life has to be put into textual form. This rules out a range of other possible forms to express what the anthropologist has learned – forms like participation in dance or performance which might try to *recreate* the experience – and foregrounds the written text as a means of verbally *representing* the other way of life (ibid:160). But unlike, say, a literary translator, the cultural translator doesn't simply find the textual form ready made. Not only is there no 'source text' in the physical sense, but people's lives and practices are not necessarily text-like at all. Faced with the complexity of life in the other place, the anthropologist has to "construct the discourse *as* a cultural text in terms of meanings implicit in a range of practices. The construction of cultural discourse and its translation thus seem to be facets of a single act" (ibid).

What is behind this idea of culture as being a text or like a text? Though it was initiated by Paul Ricoeur, we'll focus here on its influential application to anthropology by Clifford Geertz. In his seminal collection of essays *The Interpretation of Cultures*, published in 1973, anthropologist Geertz defined 'culture' as follows:

> The concept of culture I espouse [...] is essentially a semiotic one. Believing, with Max Weber, that man is an animal suspended in webs of significance he has himself spun, I take culture to be those webs, and the analysis of it to be therefore not an experimental science in search of law but an interpretive one in search of meaning. (1973:5)

Geertz goes on to explain that observing behaviour alone cannot tell us enough about 'significance'. He uses (after Ryle) the example of watching somebody close one eye for a second. Is that person blinking, or winking, or indeed rehearsing or parodying a blink or a wink? We can't say anything useful about the behaviour unless we investigate the *meanings* that motivate the blinker/winker and interpret them in terms of a larger, surrounding 'web' of other meanings. This kind of definition, fundamental to Geertzian interpretive anthropology, compares culture to a language (in the sense of a 'semiotic code'), an analogy which has been pursued especially by the linguistics-oriented structuralism prominent in francophone anthropology. But Geertz's own version of the analogy focuses on the process of reading, so that cultural facts are like texts (or "ensembles of texts", ibid:452) which do not stand for themselves but demand complex interpretation. Geertz is trying to demolish the assumption that cultures consist of objective data which simply need to be collected and correctly laid out for analysis. Instead, he says, "what we call our data are really our own constructions of other people's constructions of what they [...] are up to" (9). Such constructions are "fictions" (15), not in the sense of being untruths but in the sense of having been 'fashioned' or 'made'. In Geertz's model the members of a culture themselves make sense of – interpret – their own practices, and the anthropologist in turn attempts to make sense of those interpretations in a kind of 'reading'.

Describing anthropological data as constructions of constructions moves anthropological interpretation very near to hermeneutical literary interpretation – the two activities are intertwined in Geertz's argument. He describes them as "not just cognate activities" but "the same activity differently pursued" (1983:8; for a practical application, see Geertz's famous account of a Balinese cockfight, 1973:412-53). This method provides a more concrete basis for the notion of 'cultural translation' than did the functionalist understanding of the term as described by Asad. If 'translation of culture' can mean the re-framing of meanings from one set of cultural categories to another, the addition of the concept of 'culture as text' brings 'translation of culture' closer to traditional notions of translation. Not only do we now have a 'source text' that is much more textual than in Lienhardt's version of the metaphor, but there is a new interest in the act of interpreting it in an almost aesthetic way and on writting it down. To this extent, the rise of interpretive anthropology in the 1960s and 1970s gave a new lease of life to the metaphor of translation as a way of describing ethnography.

Especially from the 1970s, interest in the literary dimension of anthropology (and specifically of ethnography as its written product) was spurred on by a general climate of questioning within the discipline. As was mentioned in the Introduction, changes in the world order undermined anthropology's self-image and practical basis, but they were accompanied by a crisis in ideas of representation: an attack on the convention that reality existed 'out there' and was merely waiting to be reformulated in a different medium. Instead, it seemed that reality was the product of acts of interpretation. In other words, as Geertz hinted, the writer of ethnography was not unlike a writer of fiction. After all, at the very least the ethnographer creates written artefacts which make use of the rhetorical resources of the receiving language; taken further, the ethnographer actively produces the 'reality' of the culture being studied by means of selection, editing and analysis. From the perspective of translation, the translator makes the source text, not only the target text, and the translation itself cannot claim to be an 'accurate and faithful record' of a static 'original' (a matter discussed in detail by Davis 2001).

This sceptical approach is applied to ethnography as a writing practice in the landmark collection *Writing Culture* (Clifford & Marcus 1986). The *Writing Culture* essays join in criticizing the classical ethnographic tradition, accusing it of representing other cultures by translating their realities into ready-made ideological and rhetorical categories belonging to the target culture, and of disingenuously translating the personal, power-ridden, dialogical complexity of the ethnographer's experience in the field into a written account that seems neutral, objective and timeless. The powerful ethnographic 'authority' of the text subsumes the voices of the original speakers into seamless written English partly by hiding the processes of editing and translation that have gone on (more will be said about this in Chapter 4). Although these critics were influenced by Geertz, it is the textuality of ethnographies, not that of cultures, which they explore.

The 'textualist' stance shares some important ground with translation studies. It assumes that representations are not innocent copies of external reality but are built out of the requirements and presuppositions of the receiving discourse, just as recent thinking on translations sees these as constructs of the target language rather than as glass cases to display a sacred original. Like translators, ethnographers persuaded by this argument face a range of dilemmas when they try to apply it to their writing practice. How can a productive and principled representation of other people (or other people's books) be made once the dream of 'accuracy' and 'faithfulness' has dissolved? We will see in Chapters 5 and 6 that many different responses to that challenge emerged from the broadly 'postmodern' ethnographic experiments of the late 1970s onwards, which searched for textual strategies to undermine the convention of objectivity and the singular authority of the translator's voice.

The emphasis on textuality set by *Writing Culture* has not, though, been without its critics. Contributors to Richard G. Fox's 1991 collection *Recapturing Anthropology*, for example, see the textualist approach as sidestepping the questions of institutional power that underlie ethnographic writing. The terms of the *Writing Culture* debate, with its generous helpings of literary and philosophical jargon, gave a "message of hyperprofessionalism" that cemented rather than undermined the untouchable authority of the academics involved, says Lila Abu-Lughod (1991:152), and the literary approach generally failed to realize that production and reception in the wider world was more decisive for ethnographic writing than any literary manipulation of textual structure, however skilled. In fact, although the *Writing Culture* collection undoubtedly shifted disciplinary attention to textuality, it did not ignore the material and ideological global context of ethnographic writing. Asad's contribution to the collection, as we have seen, explicitly took this line. His focus is on the political and institutional context of cultural translation, discussing the impact of asymmetrical power relations on translation – the kinds of structures of inequality that in translation studies have been called the 'ethnocentric violence' of translation (see especially Venuti 1995, 1998) and their real-world effects. When Malinowski characterized the anthropologist and the missionary in their translation activities, he used a strikingly skewed geometry: as a pair of translators these two characters seem to take up complementary positions (white man–native, native–white man), yet the standpoint of the second 'native' is filled not in fact by a 'native' but by the missionary's compatriot, the anthropologist. In Malinowski's model, ethnography is a conversation *inside* the West *about* the 'native'.

This seizing of the power to define is at the core of Asad's critique of cultural translation by the 'extraction' of implicit meanings. Although traditionally the ethnographer aims to discover the 'native's point of view' (the internal logic and coherence of beliefs and practices), Asad points out that this involves the ethnographer assuming the authority to elicit the underlying truth of what is being said and done – not actually adopting meanings attributed by the meaners themselves. To do the latter would be considered a failure to produce a 'scientific' and objective viewpoint distinct from the subjective one identified with the 'natives'. Translating meanings as perceived within a society into the scientific language of the translator changes the authorship of the 'cultural text', which now belongs to the revealer-producer of the uncovered meanings (Asad 1986:162). Because of the unequal relationship between the cultures concerned, the translation does not remain cordoned off inside some Western ivory tower but instead takes up a powerful position in the practical world: the anthropologist's monograph feeds into dominant 'knowledge' about the other culture and it may also "return, retranslated, into a 'weaker' Third World language" (ibid:163), there to hold higher authority than local knowledge and definitions of the source culture. Not, says Asad, that ethnography is the prime villain, for other forms of Western influence or domination – economic, military and so on – are far more effectual. "My point is only that the process of 'cultural translation' is inevitably enmeshed in conditions of power – professional, national, international" (ibid). Asad's essay closes with serious doubts on the viability of 'cultural translation' in view of the "asymmetrical tendencies and pressures in the languages of dominated and dominant societies" (164).

Asad explores the pitfalls of the 'translation' of culture, but the other half of the couplet is at least as controversial. The notion of 'cultures' itself has been queried by many anthropologists and anthropologically minded critics. Towards the end of his very useful commentary on the term, William H. Sewell sums up the way that traditional anthropological discourse pictured 'other' cultures (anthropology's 'own' cultures never having been considered in these terms): as "neatly coherent wholes" which are "logically consistent, highly integrated, consensual, extremely resistant to change, and clearly bounded" (1999:52). How like a traditional 'source text' that portrait looks, and thus how amenable to translation! But today these assumptions have been widely questioned, and with them the very notion of cultures as distinct units. As Sewell points out, current anthropological thinking focuses on the internal contradictions in cultures, on the inequalities and distinctions that lessen their integration, on their contestation from within, their constant change, and their ever more permeable borders with 'other' cultures (ibid:53-5; see also Brightman 1995).

The acknowledgement of these factors vastly complicates the task of anthropological translation, since it rules out the pretence – beloved of classical ethnographies – that the written representation offered by the ethnographer can be a coherent and accurate synthesis of a coherent and synthesizable whole. Once it becomes clear that cultures are made up of multiple, unpredictable and contingent perspectives, as opposed to a single, accessible though difficult-to-fathom 'native's point of view', the reader of a translation will begin to ask what the translator's perspective was, *which* native points of view he or she was privy to and decided to translate, how those points of view entangle with other, contradictory ones, and so on. That makes the goal of a complete, unified description impracticable, but for the critics of 'cultures' it's also fundamentally misguided. For one thing, says anthropologist Arjun Appadurai (1996), the assumption of clearly boundaried and mutually impermeable cultural units was always an illusion, in view of millennia of contacts both commercial and ideological, both violent and peaceful. But today's world is, he argues, even less easily described in terms of individual, untouched cultural entities, for rapidly increasing communication and migration have set the world in motion to an unprecedented extent. This development has generated the metaphor of 'cultures *as* translation', which we will look at shortly, but it savages the metaphor of 'cultures *in* translation'. As Appadurai explains, the world is made up of interweaving cultural filaments that never stay still and are constantly re-forming and mixing in new diasporic arenas. Rather than 'cultures', we have deterritorialized, shifting "ethnoscapes" that don't allow for a simplistic source/target dichotomy.

If anthropology's traditional concept of culture is inaccurate, in Abu-Lughod's view it is also dangerous. As the "essential tool for making other" (1991:143), the idea of 'cultures' tends to "freeze difference" into uncontestable, dehistoricized forms (ibid:144), brushing aside both divergences within and similarities across the apparent entities of self and other. The emphasis on self/other distinctions, she finds, inevitably brings with it a sense of hierarchy (137) which will always pan out to the disadvantage of the politically weaker side. Historically, the idealization of untouched authenticity in descriptions of cultures has always worked to airbrush out the violence of colonialism and to produce a 'primitive' society in contradistinction to 'modern' ones. Drawing on feminist insights regarding the constructedness of 'selves' and 'others' and the practical consequences of such constructions, Abu-Lughod advises abandoning the very category of 'culture', not just its use as a kind of source text for translation; it could never be so coherent or self-same as to make that possible.

These cautions against understanding translation as an exchange between polarized source and target languages, others and selves, are highly relevant to translation studies. José Lambert, for example, has criticized the widespread concept of translation as being a channel of communication between pairs of distinct, coherently monolingual bodies known as 'nations' – and indeed between pairs of distinct, coherent languages at all. In reality, multiple languages coexist or jostle for space with no regard for the borders drawn on maps (1991). The fallacy of source/target dichotomies is a train of thought that has been followed by translation scholars working on globalization, heteroglossia and hybridity, but not one that has yet gained solid ground in the everyday life of Western translation studies. Anthropology's sophisticated reflections on culture and cultural difference may thus have much to offer the study of translation. Conversely, translators themselves can contribute personal experience of the paucity of self/other dichotomies from their everyday working life. After all, the position of professional translators mirrors that of Abu-Lughod's "halfie" anthropologists – that is, "people whose national or cultural identity is mixed by virtue of migration, overseas education, or parentage" (1991:137). Like translators, these anthropologists live simultaneously in different language-worlds and by doing so not only 'cross', but attack the self-evidence of, the borders between them.

Culture as translation

We have seen that 'cultural translation' has lost its easy claim to source texts and definitive interpretations – but does that mean the metaphor of translation between cultures has nothing more to offer? The currency of 'cultures' as stable units has declined, and in anthropological writing the word is often either replaced by terms like hegemony or discourse (for some criticisms of this move, see Brightman 1995:510) or else retained but recast as process and performance, not product and rule. Yet despite its association with a self/other polarity, the concept of 'translation' in anthropology has not faded quietly away but is enjoying a surge of popularity. The effects of colonial and postcolonial relations have been described as forms of translation, as have migration, travel, and even 'culture' itself.

Translation's concrete role in colonial power struggles has been dealt with by a number of scholars, most notably Tejaswini Niranjana, Eric Cheyfitz and Vicente L. Rafael, all of them extending the term beyond its textual sense to the experience of definition by, submission to and resistance against colonial violence (discussed in Robinson 1997; see also Chapter 4). In the postcolonial context, 'translation' often stands for the alteration of the colonizing language through its mixing with the languages of the colonized and vice versa, a notion of 'hybridity' in both language and identity that has been most fully explored by postcolonial theorist Homi Bhabha. For Bhabha, culture is both "transnational and translational" (1994:5): no longer definable in terms of national borders but constituting itself through 'translation'. This kind of translation refers to the constant exchange and adaptation between linguistic and cultural strands or traditions, especially as it comes to a head in the process of migration. Translation is then not a traffic between wholes but a process of mixing and mutual contamination, and not a movement from 'source' to 'target' but located in a 'third space' between the two, where "conflicts arising from cultural difference and the different social discourses involved in those conflicts are negotiated" (Wolf 2002:190; see also Bachmann-Medick forthcoming).

The spatial aspect of the translation metaphor – *traductio*, or 'carrying across' – is picked up by other critics as well. James Clifford's book *Routes* discusses travel, but not travel as a movement between boundaried cultures; instead, culture itself is the process of travelling and translating. Ideas travel across national borders, and they do so not only as media and commercial products but in the bodies of human beings. Doris Bachmann-Medick discusses Salman Rushdie's frequent references to migration as translation: "I, too, am a translated man. I have been *borne across*", says the migrant narrator in *Shame* (Rushdie 1983:24). Bachmann-Medick concludes that this kind of conceptualization can help to replace "our habituated notion of culture as a location of solid belonging and coherence" with "a notion of culture as translation, transition and unfolding" (Bachmann-Medick forthcoming), something which can help dissolve the hierarchical opposition of self (the scholar) and other (the studied). A persuasive proponent of new metaphorical uses of translation to re-form cultural anthropology, Bachmann-Medick summarizes the potential offered by the concept of cultural translation, but it is a very different cultural translation from that proposed by Lienhardt and criticized by Asad. "For a transnational cultural anthropology, cultural translation can [...] act as an anti-essentialist and anti-holistic metaphor that aims to uncover counter-discourses, discursive forms and resistant actions *within* a culture, heterogeneous discursive spaces within a society" and enable "a dynamic concept of culture as a practice of negotiating cultural differences, and of cultural overlap, syncretism and creolization" (2006:37). Here translation is equated with negotiation and mutual alteration between cultural groups, not necessarily in written form.

How do these metaphorical reconceptualizations of culture and translation feed into the idea of cultural translation? They certainly don't push actual translation practices off the stage; on the contrary, it becomes clear that the importation and adaptation of meanings and practices from other places is the very basis of the hybrid cultures we inhabit today. Unpicking the assumed monolingualism and monoculturalism of 'cultures' hugely multiplies the requirement for and the complexity of translation, abolishing the 'source'/'target' model and bringing translation into almost infinite permutations across a social space. It also makes ordinary people into constant translators of culture, questioning the authority of the professional describer – Malinowski's anthropologist 'translating the native's point of view to the white man'.

Translation without language difference?

But something has gone largely unmentioned in the account so far, especially in the more metaphorical explorations – something, in fact, one wouldn't expect to find missing in a discussion about translation, and that is language difference. This is where translators may well baulk at the metaphorical uses of the word 'translation', which sometimes proliferates as a general label for any kind of mediation, change or confrontation with difference, and at worst for any kind of communication breakdown, failure and loss. There is a striking lack of attention in practical handbooks of anthropology to the requirements of translation. Even when issues of representation are covered in detail, such textbooks often subsume translation under their advice on transcription technique, or do not mention it at all. Yet as Paula Rubel and Abraham Rosman point out in the introduction to their important collection *Translating Cultures*, translation is a practical skill required by all ethnographers working in more than one language, quite apart from the theoretical issues it inescapably brings with it. They enumerate the stages of interlingual translation during anthropological fieldwork:

> Anthropologists going to do fieldwork in a culture foreign to their own usually try to ascertain which language or languages are spoken in the area of their interest and begin to learn these before they leave their home base or immediately upon arriving at the field site. Field assistants or interpreters may need to be used at first, and it is their translations upon which the anthropologist relies. Data that the fieldworker records, what

> people recount to him or her, words associated with rituals or conversations and observations may initially be written in the native language to be translated into their own language – English, German, etc. – soon after or in a procedure which combines both [the local language and the researcher's own language]. (2003:4)

To any language learner, this process will sound most daunting, yet as a rule the introductions to ethnographic texts refer to it only laconically. A few months' study are mentioned, or the language is picked up on the job ("with [the children's] help I mastered a rudimentary Lacandon vocabulary by the end of the summer", says McGee, 1990:10). As for the contribution of the interpreters, we'll see in the case studies later on that they are downplayed to the point of near invisibility, and likewise the task of translation is almost never discussed in detail.

We could certainly interpret the dearth of comment on language and translation as a tacit agreement not to reveal the possible gaps in comprehension or the experience of language-shock, an aspect dealt with more commonly in recent, confessional-style ethnographies. For 'insider ethnographers' the fact that their own linguistic competence may not match uses of the 'same' language in the field could also threaten identity and authority (see Chapter 5). At the same time, though, silence on this matter acts as a repression of language difference, repressing too the inequalities of languages in the world system and the implications of the choices made by the ethnographer-translator. This point will be pursued in the following chapters, but first we should mention some major exceptions to the silence. Not only have individual ethnographers thought carefully about translation – Malinowski's reflections will be discussed in Chapter 3 – but since the 1960s the 'ethnography of speaking' (also known as 'ethnography of communication') has addressed itself to language in use, inevitably raising issues of great importance to translation.

The ethnography of speaking was initiated by the anthropologist and sociolinguist Dell Hymes in the early 1960s. Hymes called for anthropologists to study the ways people speak in societies – the specific functions and regularities of speaking in specific contexts, among groups which he categorized not as 'cultures' but as smaller and less fixed 'speech communities'. The approach bridges linguistics and anthropology and relies heavily on verbatim transcriptions of data, which could be from another language or in the 'same' language as the researcher but with a special focus on the meaning of distinctions between varieties and styles of that language. For example, several essays in the influential collection *Explorations in the Ethnography of Speaking* (Bauman & Sherzer 1974/1989) ask what is 'pointed to' by a person's use of a particular language or style from their linguistic repertoire in a particular situation. Rather than examining sentences alone or the social structure alone, ethnographers of speaking try to identify the ways that language is used as an "instrument of social life" (ibid:5); rather than predictable expressions of rules, speech events are considered performances with particular actors and audiences. And as language is not a set of idealized rules, so cultures are not static units but "emergent", "not rigidly determined by the institutional structure of the society, but rather largely created in performance by the strategic and goal-directed manipulation of resources for speaking" (ibid:8).

For this branch of anthropology, then, language is not simply a medium, the 'clothes' of the foreign which can be stripped off and replaced by a new code, but is at the heart of human practices. That brings translation to the fore in several useful ways. For one thing, when speech is prioritized as an object of study, translation of it can be prioritized as a methodology. Examples will be discussed in Chapter 6 with reference to Sherzer's work on Native American verbal art, which makes translation a means of appreciating the rich and crucial roles of spoken language. Secondly, the approach highlights the moments when people switch between different components of their own language repertoire in situations of negotiation and sometimes conflict. This fits well with Bachmann-Medick's vision of translation as a potential battleground or hothouse for languages and identities, and in practical terms it is also a matter which has long concerned translators trying to work with a multiplicity of voices and sometimes of languages within their source texts (see, for example, the essays collected in Dingwaney & Maier 1995b). And as the ethnography of speaking tries to trace the positions that speaking takes up in societies, it offers a useful basis for a future 'ethnography of translating', a project currently under construction by translation sociologists (see, for example, Inghilleri 2005, Wolf 2006). James Siegel's study of an Indonesian city (1986) is an inspiring example of ethnography addressing the act of translating as the central node of a whole range of social and ideological practices, and despite the famed reluctance of anthropologists to anthropologize themselves (see Fox 1991) there is clearly room for an anthropological approach to translating 'at home' as well.

We have seen that the 'translation of culture' is not an easy term. The collapse of the concept of coherent, separate language-cultures means the opposition 'source' and 'target' culture or language has to be rethought or at most used cautiously as a label of convenience, for in reality such discrete spheres do not exist; nor can the designation 'translator' be used as if it were completely equivalent to the translator of written texts. But as Robert Brightman points out, since representation takes place, being sceptical about its basis shouldn't mean ignoring it or assuming that there are no grounds for making judgements about how it is done in any one case (1995:525). Instead, we can use the attacks on 'cultures as entities' as a way of formulating some questions directed at representations – here, ethnographic texts and their multimedia counterparts in museums – that seem to 'translate' others. For example, we might ask how such texts deal with plurality and specificity, heteroglossia and power differentials within and between the local and the receiving languages. Another relevant question will be how they envisage the role of the translator, as an innocent purveyor of reality or an agent of intervention, as an invisible hand or an active rewriter. How does the form of translation chosen arise from and play into global power relations? Finally, we could ask what concept of linguistic-cultural difference the translator is proposing. Does the translation method used imply the language gap is a superficial difference, reasonably easily overcome and fairly ignored, or does it argue that difference is overwhelming in scale and impossible to overcome? This question of difference is what we will turn to next.

3. The Translatability of Cultures

The previous chapter discussed ethnographic representation as a kind of translation and the objections to that metaphor, bearing in mind that even if we don't accept the metaphorical use of 'translation', ethnography still relies on translation in the narrower, practical sense. In both senses, translation is faced with a controversial question: how 'translatable' are language-cultures? In other words, is there or is there not enough common ground between human cultures to enable meaningful translation?

The issue of cultural difference and its role in translation practice figures strongly in 'how-to' manuals of translation. Trainee translators are warned that culturally specific items may not have straightforward equivalents in the target language and will need to be substituted, or glossed, or generalized, or deleted. In the face of rather similar practical difficulties, anthropological discourse has tended to take things to a far more radical level, discussing the incommensurability of language worlds and the chances of calibration between them. To be sure, whether or not things are untranslatable, translation still happens – and so we will look here not only at the debates around translatability but also the ways that ethnographer-translators have handled the issue of proximity and distance, sameness and difference, in their work.

Translatability, untranslatability and relativism

The discipline of anthropology is crucially interested in difference; the detail of distinct and particular cultural practices has been its daily bread over the past hundred years. To a greater or lesser extent (and the precise extent is fiercely debated) Anglo-American anthropologists start from a relativist, not a universalist, position.

In the United States in the late nineteenth century, relativist anthropology as championed by Franz Boas arose as a stand against evolutionist racism, countering the idea that the world's cultures were located at different points on a ladder of evolutionary development which culminated in European civilization. Boas and his followers argued that being different from the Western norm was not an indication of inferiority; instead, each culture was of equal value, and highly developed in its own terms. Specifically, since these anthropologists were interested above all in language, each language was of equal value and highly developed to express all the meanings needed by its speakers. The diversity of cultures was an expression of different interpretations of the world but not of less or more accurate interpretations of it. Aside from the question of superiority/inferiority, the proponents of linguistic relativism in the early part of the twentieth century, especially the Boasian-trained Edward Sapir and his student Benjamin Lee Whorf, were interested in the idea that difference in language brought with it a different experience of the world. Boas himself kept to the idea that linguistic differences reflected different interests, often enforced by environmental factors (he is the source of the well-known note on the multitude of Eskimo snow terms, 1911:25-6), while Sapir and Whorf went further in their view of linguistic patterns as a strongly influential or even determining factor in cognition. The common theme of the Boasian cultural and linguistic relativists, though, was the absence of one naturally given, absolute or inherently superior version of the world and people's experience of it – a familiar claim in our anti-positivist climate a century later.

Taken to its extreme, strong cultural relativism would allow little chance of cultures understanding each other's realities, because those different realities would be not just distant but fundamentally incompatible. In this view, there is no general reality at all, only particular realities located in particular cultural settings. Rather than being different perspectives on a shared or universal human world, people's outlooks are themselves different worlds and there is virtually no common point of reference; it is culture, not nature, which determines what we see. As a result, beliefs and customs cannot be judged against a universal standard of reality, rationality or rightness, but only on their own terms, and two conflicting beliefs can both be true. More common, milder versions of cultural relativism would allow that we are all looking at what is biologically the same world, but from culturally mediated or 'situated' perspectives that differ and that must be examined on their own terms, not in terms of their conformity with or divergence from an ideal, universal truth. Thus, the natural world may be the same, but the grids we use to make sense of it will differ widely:

> this theory assumes an unorganized, but still pre-given reality, which, however, only takes on a coherent form by the imposition of the mental categories supplied by the language, culture, or theory. Because the categories found in various languages or cultures obviously differ, it then follows that each language or culture will impose different coherent orders, resulting in contrastive ranges of sensible experiences for the Natives of these languages and cultures. (Foley 1997:170)

If we take translation to be the recasting in one set of categories of a reality experienced in another set, then relativist arguments about the distance between categories are going to be very important. They force us to ask whether meanings that are generated by one grid are transportable at all: is there enough 'commensurability' between knowledge systems to enable cross-cultural communication?

Todd Jones (2003) examines this question in some detail. He starts from the difficulty which we have even within our 'own' cultural setting in interpreting other people's actions and words. While it's relatively easy to make sense of outward actions, unobservable states of mind are much harder to fathom, and we have a limited number of means at our disposal as we try to work out what someone else believes. We can try to infer what they must be thinking based on the situation surrounding them (in Jones's example, if we see a person and an attacking dog, we could infer that the person believes he or she is being attacked by the dog), or based on the other person's behaviour (so if we see the person running away from the dog with a frightened look, we could infer that he or she believes she is being chased). This kind of judgement, based on our knowledge of the network of prior beliefs which feeds into the belief of the moment, is not foolproof, but for cultural insiders it normally gets the job done well enough – because it can be backed up by an introspective 'simulation' where we put ourselves in the shoes of the other person and see what *we* would believe in an analogous situation.

As Jones puts it, "if others really are like us, we can use ourselves as models both of what prior beliefs exist and which beliefs get formed in certain circumstances" (2003:51). For cultural outsiders like most ethnographers, however, this introspective approach is fraught with difficulty. What if 'exotic' others are *not* really like us: in that case inference based on our own probable reactions carries a high risk of misinterpretation. There are too many potential hypotheses to explain what people say and do, and for an outsider it is difficult to restrict that potential to a manageable size. This is the problem addressed by Quine in his essay on indeterminacy in translation (1959/2000). Famously, Quine imagines a situation where, on seeing a passing rabbit, a native remarks "Gavagai". The watching anthropologist puts two and two together: the stimulus is clearly "a rabbit", the word uttered is "gavagai", hence the native word for rabbit (or for 'Lo, a rabbit!') must be 'gavagai'. But, Quine warns, in fact the same stimulus could produce different meanings. The word 'gavagai' might refer to temporal stages in rabbithood, or to undetached rabbit parts, or to universal rabbitry, or to generally rabbit-like stuff. Physical reality is capable of different theoretical interpretations, and different or even incompatible translations (translations being positings of the 'meaning' of a thing or event) may each be valid. Without knowing absolutely that the other person's categories are the same as our own – and this is impossible even for members of the 'same' culture – we can't make an absolute statement about equivalence in meaning, even for such an apparently innocuous item as Quine's imaginary rabbit.

We are left with a large degree of inscrutability, of doubt about the referents of words and the intentions of people speaking them. But Jones notes that the problem for translators doesn't end with uncovering other people's beliefs (in other words, 'comprehension'). The translator is also faced with communicating them (in other words, 'reformulation' or 're-encoding'), and this raises a new set of issues. For what makes a particular mental state the 'belief that p' is the way this belief interacts with the surrounding beliefs and with the surrounding perceptions and behaviour of other people. Once this 'belief that p' is transplanted into a different network of beliefs, perceptions and behaviour, then it "does not count as the belief that p" – for being defined interactively by its relationship to its surroundings, without those same surroundings it cannot survive as the 'same' belief (Jones 2003:53). And as soon as we give this belief a name in English, we summon up the whole network of beliefs which underlies the English-named belief, a network likely to be very different from the one found in the source culture's 'cognitive economy'. The original utterance is reengineered to fit its new setting, or else its logic may dissolve completely.

If that original logic disappears, and if it is not replaced by a (perhaps spuriously) 'equivalent' logic in the receiving language, the result is often an impression that the foreign culture must be rather irrational. After all, these foreigners believe that, for example, 'twins are birds' or that 'we are red macaws' (ibid:55), and how can that be right? The question of what to do with beliefs that are impossible to reconcile with our own is tackled by Tambiah (1990), writing on Western attributions of rationality and irrationality to alien beliefs as translated into Western languages. In his chapter on translation, Tambiah distinguishes between anthropological proponents of a single rationality and proponents of multiple possible rationalities: 'lumpers' and 'splitters', as he puts it (1990:115-16). For the lumpers, the scope of universal meanings is large and translation is perfectly feasible because it can work with formal switches inside a shared universe. For the splitters, translation is much more problematic, since it cannot assume that meanings are the same or even commensurable across cultural boundaries. In either case, the key issue is the extent of the shared ground between cultures, the 'bridgehead of understanding' which is needed in order for any intercultural communication to take place at all. This bridgehead is the basis for comparisons to be made that allow us to approach, even if cautiously and incompletely, an understanding of other people's realities from their own point of view. Tambiah joins the splitters in warning against the imposition of the ethnographer's own categories onto other people's ideas, but argues that ethnographic investigation of the other's point of view can stretch those categories and enlarge the bridgehead of understanding. In the following we'll work with this image of the bridgehead, even though anti-culturalist attacks on the notion of strictly bordered cultural entities, as discussed in Chapter 2, might in the end force us to abandon the notion of separate cultures with identifiable overlaps between them.

Incompatible terms

Let's look at the issue of commensurability in the context of a concrete problem in ethnographic translation and one of anthropology's favourite lines of enquiry: kinship. Abraham Rosman and Paula Rubel (2003) explain how kinship is traditionally investigated by searching for a structure of terminology; working from the relativist position discussed above, terminological categories are presumed to be categories of thought and thus of cultural experience of the world. Because kinship terms articulate a specific structure which is, if at all, only minimally shared between different societies, putting them into English immediately confronts the writer with doubts about translatability. As Rosman and Rubel explain, the first difficulty arises when collecting information on kinship terms, especially if English prompts are used. For example, requesting the word for 'father's sister's son' may elicit the local-language translation of 'father's sister's son' rather than the lexical item which would be used for this category in the local language itself (ibid:270). It is also problematic to translate categories into English categories which are quite differently structured. Thus, some anthropologists have assumed that there are 'fundamental', biologically determined categories (father, mother, child, husband, wife), into which the various local terminologies can be fitted. But while biological relationships clearly exist, they do not determine, and only weakly limit, the huge range of permutations of kin relationships that can be categorized in any language. That means biology doesn't offer enough help to the translator of kinship terminologies. For example, Rosman and Rubel cite the possessive affixes in Melanesian languages which distinguish between 'inalienable' possession – something that can't be lost or severed – and 'alienable' for "ownership and temporary possession" (ibid:272). Having that distinction is as little biologically determined as not having it, but it needs to be accounted for in translation: the use of these affixes in Melanesian kinship terms adds crucial information, as most kinship terms involve 'inalienable' possession, while husband and wife are marked with the 'alienable' possession marker. The grammatical information in these terms has to be made available in the English version without the aid of a convenient 'equivalent' in English grammar.

Trickier is the problem of category match (ibid:274-5). If in the Trobriand language, for example, one word covers the English 'father's sister', 'father's sister's daughter' and 'all the women of the father's clan', a categorization is at work which can't be expressed within the generation-oriented categorization of the language Boasian linguists called 'Standard Average European'. When he found that a form of the same Trobriand term also covered 'ancestor' and 'descendant', the ethnographer Malinowski was tempted to consider the uses simply as homonyms – only coincidentally the same – and to interpret apparently incongruous uses as being metaphorical or anomalous. However, say Rosman and Rubel, in fact these uses are all members of one category, a category quite foreign to the target language and not sayable in it, or at least not in the form of a category but only in the form of pointers to the fact that in the source language there *was* such a category (ibid:280).

Faced with this kind of difficulty, Rosman and Rubel conclude optimistically that kinship terminologies *are* translatable, by means of a focus on the internal logic and a system of comparative mapping across cultures (ibid:282). Jones, too, is interested in the 'mapping' approach. He argues for a description of mental states that sidesteps the familiar method of comparison with our own experience of our own mental states, a comparison which is implicit in the use of one-word English translations such as 'afraid' (actually a shorthand to mean '*like our* state of being afraid'). Instead, description should address such states in terms of their "roles in the *native* cognitive economy" (Jones 2003:58). The idea of tracing other people's sets of concepts from the inside is known as the 'emic' approach, as opposed to the 'etic' approach which aims to find a larger, abstract reality against which those concepts can be calibrated. Just as phon*etics* refers to the physically possible spectrum of sounds in language and phon*emics* to the distinctions which speakers of a language make between them, an emic investigation of meaning focuses on meanings as a set of contrasts and complementarities that structure the world in another person's experience (for a detailed philosophical discussion of this and related issues around 'meaning', see Feleppa 1988; the work of anthropologist Rodney Needham [1972] is also relevant here).

A study by Catherine Lutz on the terminology of emotion exemplifies the mapping method. In *Unnatural Emotions* (1988), Lutz structures her portrayal of the social experience of the Ifaluk in Micronesia around an analysis of Ifaluk feelings: how these feelings are defined, how they work, and how they interrelate. Because she is interested in the cultural specificity of emotion, she avoids the traditional method of using short-cut, single-word English translations of emotion terms, their apparent 'equivalents'. Those 'equivalents', after all, work quite differently in the context of English language-culture than the Ifaluk words do in their own context, and even if these differences are later set out in detail, the damage will already have been done: the reader will most likely already have slotted the terms into the patterns of her or his own language-world. Instead, Lutz uses English 'equivalents' only with clear labels of inadequacy such as lists of alternatives: "*fago* (compassion/love/sadness)" (1988:119). The bulk of her analysis works with the transcribed Ifaluk terms directly. In the thirty-page chapter translating *fago*, Lutz describes numerous concrete situations where the term was used by participants, along with Ifaluk explanations of the feeling, what arouses it and what it, in turn, can prompt. In one example among the many situations described, a woman whose brothers had left the atoll explains:

> "When [my brothers] went away to high school, I *fago*. Maybe because I was used to them always coming here to eat. When they left, my *fago* made me unable [to function]. That night, the ship stayed for a while and I could hear the engine and I couldn't get to sleep. I was incapacitated with my *fago*. I sat up, opened the doors, and smoked outside. I just cried and cried. My back hurt so I lay down. ... In the morning, I didn't want to see the house where they slept. Now it [the *fago*] has calmed down a bit because it's been a long time." (ibid:130-31, Lutz's insertions)

The long quotation from Lutz's field notes keeps open a wide horizon on what could be relevant to the emotion, including the physical sensations and behaviour that accompany it in this person's case. Leaving the key term outside target-language grammatical categories of noun and verb ('my *fago*', 'I *fago*') reinforces the demand on the reader to approach the term afresh. Apart from definitions by Ifaluk themselves and narratives that revolve around the term in question, Lutz also uses explicit comparison between source- and target-language terms. She tries to outline the mismatches between the American English 'love', 'compassion' or 'sadness' and *fago*, showing the different boundaries of the emotions and the different roles they play in the emotional worlds of the people who feel them. Setting out to shake up the apparent self-evidence of her own native emotion categories, Lutz uses translation as a force for denaturalization. She calls for patient pacing round the contours of the other category, but assumes enough common human ground to make the journey possible. If we are prepared to take that amount of time and trouble, Lutz implies, other people's emotion categories are not untranslatable, and the test of our translations is whether or not they allow us to communicate with Ifaluk about emotions. According to Feleppa (1988:176), the 'correctness' of translation hypotheses – that is, target-language reformulations – consists in their success in accomplishing coordination between ourselves and our interlocutors. While this limits the number of correct hypotheses to those which work out in practical communication, other plausible interpretations than the one given as our 'translation' could clearly exist. The inclusion of the mass of data if anything emphasizes that fact – certainly more than does the provision of one-word English 'equivalents'.

Todd Jones commends the way Lutz uses one-word translations only to provide a general "ball-park" idea and to warn us against hasty assumptions about Ifaluk terms (Jones 2003:60). The direct discussion of an emotion's interaction with other states and of chains and networks of distinction yields what Jones calls a "syntactical" method of describing beliefs – saying syntactically what beliefs 'do', and not semantically what they 'mean' or 'contain'. Jones's ideal translation would consist of a network of functional interactions between sets of terms in the foreign language without recourse to comparison or introspection. Though an interesting project, this has not been widely pursued, perhaps because of its unwieldiness as a form of description, but perhaps also because of the strongly distancing effect which arises when we abandon the intuitive method of comparing others to ourselves. For over and above the question of 'accuracy' we have been discussing up to now, attitudes to translatability also carry a political dimension. Ethnography has to negotiate its way between two dangers: asserting untranslatability and hence the impossibility of human communication, and asserting total translatability, hence the similarity of everybody to an apparently 'universal' model which in fact is the local product of the West.

Alterity and familiarity in ethnographic translations

Those two poles offer a perspective on the different styles of ethnographic translation – translation here both in the sense of the general approach to explanation and synthesis ('translation of culture') and in the sense of handling actual words or passages translated from the local language. Let's propose for now that the translation style applied in a given ethnography reflects a particular judgement of the commensurability between ways of thinking, and thus a particular position on the question of translatability. Our first case is that of Bronislaw Malinowski (1884-1942), Polish-born, London-based and a key figure in functionalist anthropology.

Asserting distance

Malinowski saw language as a crucial field of study for the anthropologist, and he had a lot to say on how to translate it. In Malinowski's view language is a form of social action, as he explains in the essay on translation that opens Volume 2 of *Coral Gardens and their Magic*, his study of the Trobriand Islands: "The fact is that the main function of language is not to express thought, not to duplicate mental processes, but rather to play an active pragmatic part in human behaviour" (1935, Vol 2:7). As a result, Malinowski argues, word-by-word substitution alone is unlikely to tell us much about the actual 'meaning' of utterances. Since meaning arises out of specific situations, it can only be successfully re-presented through detailed contextualization, through an interpretive reconstruction of the original words' linguistic context, cultural context and immediate setting:

> In the first place, an utterance belongs to a special context of culture, i.e. it refers to a definite subject-matter. […] But side by side with this context of culture or context of reference, as it might also be called, we have another context: the situation in which the words have been uttered. (ibid:51)

Malinowski arranges his contextualizations around passages of transcribed Kiriwinian speech, and *Coral Gardens* is divided into a volume of general description of gardening practices with their associated magic, mainly in English, and a volume containing the "corpus inscriptionum", his extensively annotated selection of 'native' statements collected during fieldwork on the Islands. The use of longish stretches of discourse is a deliberate attack on the then (and still) common practice of discussing isolated lexical items from the local language – something Malinowski refers to as a "mere collectioneering of words" (ibid:67). He admits the transcription plus annotation method is labour-intensive for both writer and reader, but defends it as allowing the material to "stand out, so to speak, stereoscopically" (ibid:3).

The contextualizing style, pointing forward to what would later be called 'thick description' (see Chapter 5), is an explicit rejection of the idea that what the ethnographer saw and heard can simply be 'reproduced' in English. Instead, *Coral Gardens* practically parades the difficulty of comprehension: in order to understand a two-line statement on gardening given by a Trobriand Islander, the English-speaking reader will require many pages of technical exposition by a skilled translator. If that makes the text bulky, repetitive or awkward to follow, then so be it, says Malinowski; it offers the only hope of approaching the meaning of such alien talk.

In other words, heavy contextualization as practised by Malinowski stresses that what these other people say is not self-explanatory, that it is inherently inaccessible to us except with the aid of a specialist mediator. The Trobriand Islanders are just too far from the Western reader – among other things because their culture and language is 'primitive' and thus not well-adapted to the abstraction of the written form (this argument is set out in more detail in an earlier piece by Malinowski, "The Problem of Meaning in Primitive Languages", 1923).

In *Coral Gardens* the transcriptions of passages of Kiriwinian speech, mainly either explanations of gardening procedures or magical chants, are interspersed with lines of 'literal' English translation, formatted to set each English word or phrase below the source-language item it translates. Separately, Malinowski offers a 'free translation'. Here's a three-part line in the 'interlinear' style:

Waga	*bi-la,*	*i-gisay-dasi,*	*boge*	*i-katumatay-da*	*wala.*
canoe	he might go	they see us	already	they kill us	just

were a canoe to sail out, they would see us, they would kill us directly.

(1935, Vol 2:25, 42; Vol 1:163)

We will look at other anthropological proponents of the threefold or interlinear translation method in Chapter 6, and techniques of transcription will be discussed then in more detail. For now, let's focus on the middle line of the interlinear translation, the 'literal' or word-for-word version. Malinowski considers it important in communicating a sense of the particularity of the other language, something that cannot be provided by a free translation. However,

> the literal translation is not sufficient because – as you will convince yourself easily by glancing at any of the ninety or so prose texts and forty-five magical formulae which follow – such a translation simply never makes sense. The wading through the unwieldy jumble of words carries its own reward, but without an additional commentary on the part of the ethnographer, it does not lead to a clear understanding of the text. (Vol 2:10-11)

If 'literal' translation doesn't 'make sense', what does it do? Given the frequency with which ethnographic prefaces tersely call their translation strategy 'as literal as possible', literalism is worth looking at for a moment.

A widely used definition of literal translation is Vinay and Darbelnet's: "the direct transfer of a SL [source language] text into a grammatically and idiomatically appropriate TL [target language] text in which the translators' task is limited to observing the adherence to the linguistic servitudes of the TL", whereby the literal translation "is reversible and complete in itself" (1995/2000:86). In Vinay and Darbelnet's list it is a procedure of first resort which cannot, however, be applied if the result would be "unacceptable" – unacceptable here defined as a message that gives another meaning, has no meaning, is structurally impossible, does not correspond with the experience of the TL or corresponds with a TL expression but not within the same register (ibid:87). In such cases the translator must turn to more 'oblique' methods.

Traditionally, ethnographies do not work with the kinds of closely-related language pair that make reversibility an option. If 'literalism' depends on near-mirroring between the settings of source and target text, then as a large-scale strategy it is doomed on two counts: it could be scarcely less unintelligible than the original text, as Malinowski fears, or it could be misleading due to the incommensurability of categories. Malinowski's contemporary A.R. Radcliffe-Brown warned his readers against taking people's words too 'literally': "when an Andaman Islander says 'hot' he means by the word [not] only what we mean [...but really] a great deal more" (Brown 1922:267). To be sure, the Andaman Islander in question presumably did not say 'hot' but an Andamanese word which Radcliffe-Brown has already pre-interpreted, assigning it to an equivalent slot in English for us. He admits himself that the acquisition of such category matches is not as easy as it looks. "I ask for the word 'arm' and get the Onge for 'you are pinching me'", he complained in his diary in 1906 (cited in Stocking 1983:83). But Radcliffe-Brown can't do without the notion of 'literal', plain or straightforward meaning – 'hot' – if he is going to even begin to explore the non-literal meanings of words. The claim that some English words are at least superficially literal translations of some Andamanese words provides a stable key against which the actual complications can be measured, allowing a contrast between literal and metaphorical or contextualized usages.

In ethnographic translation, especially translations of oral literature, 'literal' translation is often used as a seemingly non-interventionist translation strategy which appears to leave the source text untouched; it is the strategy of the ethnographer-as-collector. The 'free' translation, in contrast, is the business of the ethnographer-as-interpreter, and is presented as the easy, yet also somehow more true, version that offers access to the actual or 'underlying' meaning. In the Malinowski example, the literal line contrasts with the free line as raw versus processed, as unintelligible versus intelligible, and as savage versus civilized. To borrow the term Michel-Rolph Trouillot coined to describe the European category of 'primitiveness' (1991), the literal line here occupies the "savage slot" on the printed page, a necessary complement to the civilized voice of the interpreting European.

The weirdness of the literal line is not pre-determined by the difference in the two language worlds, however. Literalism is not neutral, at least not as long as we agree, as most translators would, that there is no simple token-for-token exchangeability between languages, so that any human translation involves motivated selection between alternative versions. A very interesting analysis by John Sturrock of the excerpt from Malinowski's translation reproduced above makes it clear that the form of the literal translation, far from being non-interventionist, can actively produce strangeness and distance. As Sturrock shows, a kind of 'alienation effect' arises with the literal version's infringement of English grammatical norms (1990:1000). The subject stands without an article and is followed by a subject pronoun ('canoe he might go'), there are no logical connectives or punctuation (though there *is* punctuation in the transcription, where its role is unclear), and the verb which the free translation specifies as 'sail' is here given as the much more general 'go'. Malinowski defends his technique: the grammatical oddities are designed to indicate the difference of Kiriwinian grammar, the semantic oddity to show the breadth of meaning in an individual verb. But the method is duplicitous, since these are particular interpretations by the translator presented in the guise of transparent neutrality. It also creates a pidgin-like effect, as Sturrock points out (ibid:1004), since although they were intelligible and presumably coherent when originally spoken, the Kiriwinian words once transformed into the

English 'crib' become deficient in sophistication and coherence. The excerpt shows that literalism has the potential to "make natives sound as queer as one pleases" (Quine cited ibid:1003; see also Finnegan 1992:188-90).

Evidently, the combination of 'literal' and 'free' translation carries an ideological freight. 'Literal' translations can introduce to recorded words a new aspect of strangeness, distance and in this case 'primitiveness' that belongs to the beliefs of the receiving culture about the source culture, not to the beliefs of the source culture within itself. However, as a general strategy Sturrock approves of interlinearity – by which he means especially the permeation of structures from the source language into the translated version. Its virtue is the way it openly proclaims that translation is not a simple or neutral act and that the other language is in fact other. Malinowski's technique dramatizes the difficulties facing the translator from Kiriwinian into English by including the word-for-word analysis he had to complete in order to reach his free translation. The outsider's sense of the strangeness of another language is represented in this middle line, and while there is obviously a danger that it may come across as an inherent quality of the language rather than an experience of the outsider, at least the interlinear method avoids implying that what other people say is basically just the same as what we say, only dressed in a different set of clothes.

The juxtaposition of strangely literal and soothingly fluent strategies in Malinowski's three-part method recalls the debate on 'foreignizing' versus 'domesticating' translation initiated by Lawrence Venuti. Venuti cites the comments on translation by the German Romantic thinker Friedrich Schleiermacher, who

> allowed the translator to choose between a domesticating method, an ethnocentric reduction of the foreign text to target-language cultural values, bringing the author back home, and a foreignizing method, an ethnodeviant pressure on those values to register the linguistic and cultural difference of the foreign text, sending the reader abroad. (Venuti 1995:20)

Arguing that literary translation in contemporary anglophone culture is highly domesticating, Venuti calls for a more disruptive approach which would shake up home values by confronting them with the foreignness of foreign texts. It's useful to note that the foreignizing approach set out by Venuti is not necessarily based on greater 'accuracy' or 'faithfulness' to the source text. Both the valuation of foreignness and the precise form given to the 'foreign' in fact relate to target-culture requirements and expectations; foreignizing translation attacks the dominant conventions of the target culture as opposed to championing – or even mirroring – those of the source culture. This distinction is important if we apply the Venutian model to Malinowski's translations. He is clearly not aiming for domestication in his Kiriwinian collection, since although the 'third line' is a fluent one, it is overpowered by the other two lines not just in terms of quantity but also by being presented as the least accurate, the least adequate, the least authentic of the three. Instead, Sturrock characterizes the *Coral Gardens* literalism as being made specifically with a view "to exhibiting the non-Englishness of local thought processes" (1990:1000). It stresses difference and opacity – including opacity to the curious ethnographer's eye, as illustrated by a long footnote listing 'doubtful', 'tentative', 'probable' or 'conjectural' translations (Malinowski 1935, Vol 2:220-21). The English text "sets us to puzzling over what occurs in the act of translation" (Sturrock 1990:1008), over how wide the 'bridgehead of understanding' actually is.

Asserting proximity

Venuti's praise for the foregrounding of difference arises from a particular context, namely the dominance of literary translations that deny any divergence from an anglophone norm. But for ethnography, other facets of the foreign-domestic continuum become relevant. As we have seen, the assertion of incommensurability (untranslatability) places narrow limits on communication between source and receiving cultures, and it can end up implying that the difficulty arises from the inherent strangeness of the others, their primitive or inferior existence. Historically, European assertions of 'difference' have gone hand in hand with models of superiority and inferiority, as Abu-Lughod points out (1991), and this has prompted ethnographic approaches which assume a much larger role for what human beings share, a much larger bridgehead of understanding, than Malinowski did.

In the tradition of cultural relativism, anthropologists agree that there are dangers in a very strong focus on shared ground. A claim that we are all, under the skin, more or less the same as each other can too easily become a claim that everyone is, under the skin, more or less the same as myself. In other words, the apparently 'universal' tends to be an extrapolation from the model of humanity held by the Western anthropologist's own, defining culture. In this approach other cultures are not taken on their own terms but scoured for their hidden core of reality, a core which should turn out to be easily translatable because fundamentally harmonious with the reality of European languages and worldviews.

On the other hand, too much focus on incommensurability can become an abdication of communication. The thrust of Gísli Pálsson's introduction to his collection *Beyond Boundaries* is that translations in the Malinowskian style impose a false sense of peculiarity, the anthropological equivalent of 'translationese' (1993:27), which consolidates an idea of radical discontinuity between cultures. Instead of positing separate worlds in the tradition of the 'First World'-'Third World' distinction, says Pálsson, ethnographers should start from an assumption of continuity and only then examine divergence (ibid:12). This may take the form of emphasizing "the inevitable experiential continuity of the human world irrespective of time and place" or of stressing recent change, in view of the fact that "modern means of communication – including transport systems, space technology, and computers – have turned the life-world of humans into a rapidly contracting cultural universe" (ibid:12). The latter line is taken by anthropologists like Appadurai, who are interested in the dissolution and reformation of boundaries in the modern world, and its translation result is likely to be a version of hybrid language, as we will see in subsequent chapters. The former is more personal and individual, and sails close to the danger of false commonality, yet it also echoes the experience of translators in everyday life.

In Pálsson's volume, Unni Wikan (1993) proposes a translation approach based on 'resonance'. She translated the term from a recommendation by her teachers in Bali on how she should translate their words and culture. By 'resonance', Wikan took them to mean the search for those aspects of other people's experience which had hit a nerve, or struck a chord, with her own experience and feelings. Wikan notes that this is in fact what many of us aspire to as a way of communicating with other people in general, and that it is a way of mobilizing the shared experience which is larger than the distinctions in experience between different cultural groups across the globe. Despite the risk of extrapolating from oneself and making hasty attributions, the danger of glossing over the differences in power and privilege that exist across cultures, Wikan concludes that an orientation on shared ground is the way to translate. Her work traces experiential and ideological overlaps and processes of understanding between local people and anthropologist.

Feminist anthropologist Lila Abu-Lughod goes further, arguing that however respectable the egalitarian pedigree of relativism, the power relationships surrounding ethnographic writing mean that emphasizing difference (above all by homogenizing the objects of the ethnography into solid 'cultures') is bound to reinforce a hierarchy of inferior/primitive and superior/civilized. She draws on the experience of women and 'halfie' anthropologists who find themselves "other to a dominant self" in relation to the masculine mainstream (1991:142) and constantly repositioned in a shifting landscape of otherness or sameness. Her goal is to find ways to "write about lives so as to constitute others as less other" (ibid:149), which she intends to do by focusing on the particular, not generalizations, by focusing on shared ground, and by reducing the gap between the language of professional discourse and the language of everyday life (ibid:151). On these counts Abu-Lughod praises some popular ethnographies written by the wives of Real Anthropologists. Criticized as unprofessional and weak-mindedly humanist, but addressing wider audiences and with less to lose by not conforming to disciplinary requirements, these writers are, in Abu-Lughod's view, "more open about their positionality, less assertive of their scientific authority, and more focused on particular individuals and families" (ibid:152). One of them is Marjorie Shostak, whose *Nisa: The Life and Words of a !Kung Woman* (1981) uses extensive interviews and a life-story format to represent !Kung life through the case of an individual woman. Shostak's aim is to find common ground and, as we will see, her translation style reinforces that quest.

At the start of her study, Shostak explicitly sets out her agenda in terms of a search for a universal experience of womanhood:

> Most of all, I was interested in !Kung women's lives. What was it like being a woman in a culture so outwardly different from my own? What were the universals, if any, and how much would I be able to identify with? (1981:5)

There is no pretence here of participation in the supposedly objective gaze of the ideal (male) anthropologist; Shostak has a particular, personal question to ask and, as she explains, it is one that arises from a particular political context:

> My initial field trip took place at a time when traditional values concerning marriage and sexuality were being questioned in my own culture. The Women's Movement had just begun to gain momentum, urging re-examination of the roles Western women had traditionally assumed. I hoped the field trip might help me to clarify some of the issues the Movement had raised. (ibid)

And why should a study of the !Kung, a small and embattled people living on the edge of the Kalahari in Botswana, help her discover this? Because such a study "might reflect what their [women's] lives had been like for generations, possibly even for thousands of years" (ibid:6). This is not just an individual agenda: the !Kung study was part of a Harvard project investigating hunter-gatherer societies that were assumed to be living relics of a stone-age way of life. In these representatives of "our gathering and hunting past" (ibid:16) Shostak hopes to find evidence of an ancient ideal of equality between men and women (ibid:238). Shostak assumes continuity over thousands of years, allowing her to find rich material for universals of human or of women's existence in the lives of her individual interviewees.

The use of the individual life-story as a form of cultural representation will be discussed further in Chapter 5, but one aspect is important here, and that is the centrality of the 'actual words' of the biographical subject. Like Malinowski, Shostak wants the authenticity of quoted speech; however, unlike him she does not use transcription or literal translation. Apart from anything else, this is because language in use is not the focus of her study but is presented, rather, as a medium for the real substance of the encounter between Nisa and herself. Since "much of emotional life is universal" (ibid:7), the complex problems of mapping and category match addressed earlier in this chapter do not arise for Shostak. She learns the language quickly and rather painlessly within the first few pages; here language learning is evidently open to all, not the esoteric preserve of the professional as in Malinowski's account. And when it comes to integrating what Nisa said into the English book, the vision of language as rather transparent and unproblematic continues, as a 'plain' or 'neutral'-sounding English style is used for Nisa's words, with barely a reference to comprehension or translation difficulties. Here's a sample from one of the sections of Nisa's reminiscences:

> This time I cried for many more months. My son had been the only one left. Month after month I cried, until the tears themselves almost killed me. I cried until I was sick, and I was near death myself. My older brother came to me and tried to help. He did medicinal trancing and cured me, laying on hands and working hard, trying to make me better. (ibid:314)

Very occasionally the translator includes a footnote or comment on a translation difficulty, normally the explanation of a !Kung idiom. Early in the text, for example, Shostak describes her encounter with Nisa:

> At last I approached her: "I have some questions I want to ask you. Would you like to work with me?" She broke from her conversation and smiled broadly. Catching my eye, she said "Aiye!" which means, literally, "Mother!" – but this time it also meant "Of course I will, I'd love to." (ibid:30)

In this truncated version of the three-line translation, the free translation "Of course I will, I'd love to" is asserted with confidence and without any reference to the process of reaching such a conclusion. The sense of linguistic ease is reinforced by the naturalness and fluency of the ethnographer's own words, quoted in back-translation from the !Kung she presumably spoke them in.

The inclusion of the three-part process here gives a clue to the scale of adaptation to target-language norms which may have taken place in the rest of Shostak's translation. However, it remains only a clue, and we have no way of judging whether Nisa's feelings really were so universal as to be simply exchangeable one-to-one with idiomatic English or whether Shostak's task was huge. The smooth surface of the end result confirms the feeling of successful communication between the two women across the 'boundaries' of culture. True, this success is cast into doubt by the misunderstandings at the beginning and end of the encounter. The introduction describes the difficulty of finding a suitable interviewee and the tricky negotiations that led up to the interviews, while the concluding section reveals crossed wires when Nisa parts with Marjorie as "my niece", Marjorie with Nisa as her "distant sister" (ibid:371). The style of the translation, however, removes misunderstanding and unintelligibility from the range of possibilities, and leaves us to wonder what further complexities may have surrounded those plain and simple translated words – remembering Malinowski's caution that all utterances are bound up with immense networks of interlocking social actions and beliefs. It offers apparently unmediated access to the words of Nisa, creating the basis for an apparently immediate response to her stories. As a result, 'resonance' is achieved, and the translation brings empathy to the fore; there is an optimistic claim that communication is eminently possible despite the differences in our lives. Shostak importantly sets a feminist sense of solidarity against the Malinowskian all-seeing, all-distancing masculine eye. At the same time, however, her strategy risks deleting what is a historically and politically genuine distance between the two women (see Pratt 1986). By presenting a fluent and easy translation, she downplays the difficulty of the task and thus the extent of her own power to interpret what we read.

The dilemma of difference

The two ethnographies we have considered stand at opposite ends of a spectrum of responses to the question whether the others are very much like us or very much unlike. In the introduction to her work on Ifaluk emotion, Lutz puts the translation problem succinctly:

> The dilemma in cultural description is how to balance the competing demands of these two tendencies such that these other people can be portrayed as recognizably human without 'human-ness' being reduced to the terms of a Western and hence culturally provincial definition. [...] The challenge is to avoid portraying the lives of others as so emotionally different as to be incomprehensible and bizarre or so emotionally unremarkable as to be indistinguishable in their motivational underpinnings from those of our Western contemporaries. (Lutz 1988:11)

The estranging or 'foreignizing' approach avoids that misleading universalization and seems to offer a way to communicate otherness even within the framework of a translation into the European language – the translation being by its very nature a claim of at least some minimal sameness. As Vincent Crapanzano puts it, the ethnographer not only has to communicate the foreign ideas, but like the translator he or she

> must also communicate the very foreignness that his interpretations (the translator's translations) deny, at least in their claim to universality. He must render the foreign familiar and preserve its very foreignness at one and the same time. The translator accomplishes this through style, the ethnographer through the coupling of a presentation that asserts the foreign and an interpretation that makes it all familiar. (1986:52)

We might add that the assertion of the foreign by stylistic means is not in fact the sole preserve of the literary translator, but is part and parcel of ethnographic writing too.

The focus on foreignness can be criticized as a form of exoticization. Pálsson attacks such approaches as a neo-Orientalist mystification of other people which actively inserts difference and stresses the difficulty of reading others to the point of "cultural dyslexia" (1993). How, asks Pálsson, does such translation help us to communicate within our single modern world? For him, an anthropology based on commonality is the only way to achieve that goal. The other extreme in ethnographic translation, the fluent or transparent style, thus has the virtue of enabling communication and solidarity. Yet by over-emphasizing shared ground, this strategy minimizes power differentials between observer and observed, translator and translated. As a 'domesticating' approach in Venuti's sense, it risks effacing the specificity of the other language-world, appropriating it and absorbing it into the dominant language of the translation while leaving that language undisturbed.

We will come back later to many of the issues raised here, looking at ethnographic experiments that try to navigate the troubled waters of the translatability debate. Next, though, I'd like to turn to an aspect of ethnography which has been only touched on in this chapter, the historical settings that condition particular solutions to the problem of ethnographic translation.

4. Historical Perspectives

Investigating translations as part and parcel of their historical context is nothing new to translation studies (despite Niranjana's complaints, 1992:ch.2). Studies in the history of translation, polysystems and other sociological approaches to translation have tried to do just that, and it is these rather than translation quality or cognitive processes orientations which promise to be most useful in the study of colonial-era ethnographies. Since we are looking at what are actually source-less target texts, we don't have the option of making interlingual, comparative analyses – and in the opinion of critic Eric Cheyfitz that kind of analysis is anyway nothing more than a distraction from the heart of the matter: "Our imperialism historically has functioned (and continues to function) by substituting for the difficult politics of translation another politics of translation that represses these difficulties" (1991:xvi). By treating translation as a technical, self-explanatory linguistic process, says Cheyfitz, we 'repress' the actual dynamics of translation and its implication in concrete contexts of domination and power.

This chapter will start from Toury's assumption that translations belong to the culture that hosts them, "are constituted within that same culture and reflect its own constellation" (1995:24), drawing on critical histories of anthropology to try to locate the translations within the webs of ideological and institutional power where they emerged. Rather than looking at the full length and breadth of anthropology in English, I will focus here on British anthropology and its relationship to colonialism, since this is the period of emergence of a style of ethnographic translation which lasted until well into the 1950s and became the target of the wave of textual critiques from the 1960s onwards.

Colonialism and the rise of British anthropology

The moment when ethnographic writing 'began' would be hard to define. After all, we could count as a form of anthropology any curiosity to learn about humankind in its various cultural forms. But it was with the beginnings of European imperialism that this curiosity took on its now familiar European form, and some fascinating studies of translation in that period have been made. Of particular interest are careful examinations of the sixteenth-century encounter between Europeans and Americans (especially Cheyfitz 1991) and Europeans and Tagalogs (Rafael 1988), focusing on ethnographic practices and translation as a mode of imperial knowledge and its subversion. However, only in the later part of the nineteenth century did the by then widespread European and American interest in 'primitive' cultures begin to coalesce into a body of professionalized thinking and doing – a 'discipline'.

The dominant line of anthropological thinking (of course, dominant does not mean exclusive or uncontested) in late nineteenth-century Britain and North America was evolutionism. This framework tried to explain change in human history by assuming that all humans came from a common origin, not a commonsense notion at the time, when it was often argued that different 'races' were separate species. It attempted to trace the process of change over time which led to distinction. In the Spencerian version of evolutionism this meant a process of simplicity evolving towards ever greater complexity, so that societies considered to be 'simple' must be less fully evolved, at an 'earlier' stage in evolutionary time, than industrial societies – and secondarily, within industrial societies the poor must be less fully evolved than the elite. In terms of the study of other peoples this reasoning helped consolidate a category of the 'primitive', defined simultaneously as 'first on the scene' and 'unformed', which could contrast well with the vision of the European elite as a highly wrought example of humanity, polished to a sheen. The contrast itself was vital: as Edward Said (1978) argues, when Europe studied the Islamic world its insistence on polar opposition between archaic or primitive peoples ('them', the Orient) and modern ones ('us', the West) was what made Western-ness possible. Being a modern Westerner was being everything the Orient was not.

In Said's view this dichotomy has survived until the present day, with anthropology as one of its most important proponents. However, the specific claims of evolutionism that 'primitive' societies were minimalist and relatively uncultured affairs did not retain its dominance within the newly forming discipline. With the start of the twentieth century a move to reject evolutionary and openly ethnocentric positions began to gather pace. In the United States it was driven on by the work of Franz Boas and his students, who will be discussed in more detail in Chapter 6. Varieties of cultural relativism arose as the new norm, and insisted that each society (or 'culture') had its own beliefs which made sense from the point of view of the members of that group, and which could not be ranked on a scale of increasing sophistication. While Boasian anthropology focused on language and culture, in Britain the study of society and behaviour came to the fore, with the same credo that exotic beliefs and practices were not irrational but only difficult to fathom – a refutation of the grosser imperialist defamation of subjected peoples as ignorant or incapable of producing meaning. The 'functionalist' interest of British anthropology from approximately the 1920s looked for a rational organization of societies according to sets of behaviour and belief that combined to form regulated, stable systems. The question of historical development and change – the prime interest of evolutionism – was considered outside the reach of scientific certainty and abandoned. This new focus on synchronic description went hand in hand with an important methodological change, 'armchair' speculation giving way to fieldwork as the academically legitimate source of anthropological knowledge.

The fieldwork method was elaborated most influentially by Bronislaw Malinowski and came to dominate anthropology in Britain and later the US. It demanded formalized preparation and time-consuming engagement, validating a practitioner as professional and creating a need for training which would be filled by the profession's emerging institutions. Anthropological learned societies appeared from the mid-nineteenth century in Britain, and later in the century the first academic programmes opened, but it was not until after the Second World War that the discipline was fully established. Its authority was sealed by its practitioners having actually 'been there' and gathered detailed, preferably systematic and generalizable data in a quasi-scientific mode, while the more salacious or dramatic versions of ethnographic writing were banished to the genres of travel writing and adventure tales (Kuklick 1991:10). Theorized fieldwork lent a sense of natural-science empiricism to what had been a more humanistic pursuit, and equally a rather heroic aura to the anthropologists, who risked life and limb to gather authentic information from potentially dangerous elsewheres and bring it back home in a purified, academically usable form.

Clearly, this methodological innovation could not have flourished without the access to 'exotic' peoples that was guaranteed by colonialism. In areas where colonial power was fully implemented, protection from harm and access to information could be enforced through veiled or explicit threats of retribution by the colonial authorities (in the same period, US anthropology was largely concentrated on the similarly 'accessible' Native American population). Thanks to anthropological training, the new 'fieldworker' figure expected to extract most meaningful information in the course of often very short sojourns and without necessarily having more than a skeletal knowledge of the language (see Clifford 1988:30-32). The technique depended on functionalist anthropology's development of grand theoretical frameworks into which pre-categorized data could be slotted. Claims to objectivity and systematic information-gathering characterized the professional, and differentiated him or her sharply from writers of exotic travelogues, nineteenth-century stay-at-home anthropologists, and the colonial administrators and missionaries who were accused of bias and of an unsystematic, hence superficial, approach to understanding 'their natives'.

The kinds of texts produced by 'armchair' anthropologists, missionaries, and the new professionals were very different. The last and most famous exemplar of the 'armchair' method was James Frazer's *The Golden Bough* of 1890, a multi-volume work aiming to synthesize piecemeal information from far across time and space in a demonstration that mankind was gradually evolving from magical to religious thinking and thence to the pinnacle, true science. Frazer aimed for a grand narrative built from thousands of details. In contrast, the work of missionaries and colonial officers often contained large amounts of relatively unsynthesized material, including transcribed passages of the respective source language – the collections were designed primarily as a linguistic resource to help missionaries convert and administrators govern. These texts made no mystery of their practical purpose. *The Masai, Their Language and Folklore*, for example, is prefaced by a reminder that a few hundred pounds spent on teaching government officials the native language and customs "may avert a punitive expedition costing tens of thousands of pounds" (Sir Charles Eliot, in Hollis 1905: xxviii). Hollis offers an extensive grammar and a collection of stories, proverbs and customs, all with transcriptions, translations and explanations of the Maasai originals. Language-based studies like this contrast with the work of the functionalist professionals, which is carefully extracted, concise and synthesized to a fault, unified in voice and becoming more so as the period progressed.

The style of the new British ethnographic writing may, then, be seen as part of a process of professionalization and differentiation from previous generations or competing offers, but equally it was part of the shared historical context of colonial rule. To begin with, the chronological parallel is clear:

> It is not a matter of dispute that social anthropology emerged as a distinctive discipline at the beginning of the colonial era, that it became a flourishing academic profession towards its close, or that throughout this period its efforts were devoted to a description and analysis – carried out by Europeans, for a European audience – of non-European societies dominated by European power. (Asad 1973:14-15)

The circumstances of colonialism were what made anthropological enquiry in the fieldwork mode possible, since colonial relations allowed anthropologists to spend time with their 'objects' without fear of being thrown out or otherwise harmed. The colonial administration's agreement was required, duly sought and often, though not always, obtained for anthropological field-trips. In her social history of British anthropology, Henrika Kuklick (1991, especially ch. 5) traces in detail the reasons why the British government in Africa was interested in anthropological information, albeit on very particular terms. First she notes the technocratic basis of British rule, which predisposed it to anthropology's goal of replacing politics, hence the promise of dangerous conflict, with technical or scientific expertise (ibid:188). Then, in practical terms, knowledge of local customs was essential to the system of indirect rule increasingly established in the period. In indirect rule, centralized structure – the consolidation of small groups into larger units under single local rulers – was to be fostered where it already existed and constructed (or 'reconstructed' from an assumed past) where it did not, easing colonialist intervention via local leaders who were stripped of genuine power. "Subject peoples were expected to obey their chiefs

[...], thinking their power genuine because their customary trappings of sacred authority had been punctiliously preserved" (219-20), and it was the task of anthropologists to discover what those trappings were.

Anthropologists rushed to offer their services, says Kuklick, but though they frequently received funding, they largely failed to deliver the goods, being more than ambivalent towards the colonialist paradigm and much too interested in esoteric matters of little practical value to the administration. Especially with the beginning of institutionalized colonial funding in 1940 and until its cessation in 1960, anthropologists appear to have taken the money but pursued more or less their own agendas, or tried to provide what was wanted only to find their efforts ignored when these did not match the administration's preconceptions or interests (224). In many cases anthropologists criticized the regime – though more indirectly than directly and without permanently jeopardizing their position within the colonial structure. Despite the intimate practical connection of anthropology with government in the period, the discipline was not simply a "handmaiden" of colonialism (Asad 1973:16), but it indisputably played a practical role in colonial administrative strategy.

As importantly, though, anthropology and the written genre of ethnography made less tangible contributions to the colonial project by feeding into colonial economies of knowledge. Said's discussion of Orientalism shows how representations of the 'exotic other', both literary and academic, could become facts that strongly influenced public perceptions and political action. And Tejaswini Niranjana similarly argues that ethnographic translation in colonialism cemented the West's 'knowledge' of the colonial other by seeming to offer self-evident and indisputable representations of colonized peoples:

> In creating coherent and transparent texts and subjects, translation participates [...] in the *fixing* of colonized cultures, making them seem static and unchanging rather than historically constructed. Translation functions as a transparent presentation of something that already exists, although the 'original' is actually brought into being through translation. (Niranjana 1992:3)

In other words, as we saw in Chapter 2, such translation produced its original, as opposed to being produced by it. By representing the 'other' and claiming that the representation was merely a record of reality, the ethnographic text created an entity that was the group in question – and created it as a dominated, a weaker, a 'primitive' entity. By claiming that representation referred to reality, ethnographic translation bolstered a Western epistemology of original and copy, the 'transcendental signified' and the substitutable signifier, something that Niranjana considers to be a founding ideological assumption of Western imperialism. But even without following through her Derridean line of argument, the point still holds, since by making its objects homogeneous and fixed, ethnographic translation could also render them amenable to domination. The cultural units produced by ethnography are capable of being defined and known, thus also of being counted, documented and resettled. By defining them as static and unchanging, they become 'natural' units outside the world of modern civilization. And on a more fundamental level, they are constantly defined as existing in counterpart or contradistinction to 'us', the Western writers and readers of the translation.

Insistence on the distinctiveness of the cultures being studied, then, was a two-edged sword. If the cultural relativist position tried to increase respect for other cultures, it also helped produce the conditions for distance to be upheld and intensified: the relativist translator and the source text are caught in a powerful duality of 'us and them'. We will see shortly how strategies of textual authority helped imbue that 'us' with a scientific and rational character while keeping 'them' outside of scientific discourse in another, more primitive time.

Kuklick notes that the form of early twentieth-century ethnographies also reflects their writers' personal interests inside the receiving culture. For example, their interpretations of 'primitive' social forms were often informed by their class loyalty to political ideals of constitutional monarchy, egalitarianism and meritocratic mobility, and in this respect can be read as critiques of the target culture from the position of upwardly mobile professional men (see Kuklick 1991:ch.2). Whether grand imperialist project or individual self-representation, these translations of culture can clearly not be judged in terms of their 'accuracy' or success in reflecting a pre-existing reality. Niranjana is right to insist on examining the preconditions and the impact of these ethnography-translations: the ways in which they fed into domestic perceptions of empire, in other words their impact on the target audience. What she adds to Toury's perspective is the need to investigate their repercussions on the lives of people living in the source cultures.

Translation practices in 'classical' ethnography

Having looked briefly at the nineteenth- and early twentieth-century political and institutional setting of ethnographic writing in English, how can we align it with the written texts themselves? In other words, what are the textual features, or translation strategies, that illuminate the historical and ideological moment of the texts' writing? To make this kind of investigation depends on understanding ethnographies as written fictions – fictions in the sense of "something made or fashioned" more than, but not to the exclusion of, the sense of "inventing things not actually real" (Clifford 1986:6) – which, as we saw in Chapter 2, underlies the idea that ethnographies are a kind of 'cultural translation'. The critical ethnographies presented in Chapter 5 will show a fuller range of translation dilemmas that arose in the late 1960s out of the literary analysis of ethnographic texts. Here, I will focus only on certain aspects which seem to be helpful in reading one highly influential style of ethnographic translation, the British structural-functionalist anthropology of the first half of the twentieth century.

A small caution: in looking at the history of ethnographic writing in English the category of the translator's 'intention' will not take us any further than it does for other kinds of translating or writing in general (see Davis 2001). Once they hit the world, translations take on their own life and efficacy which can no longer be restricted to what the translator may or may not have wanted. This is an important consideration when we read translations which were to some extent intended as critiques of colonialism, and to some extent also fulfilled that role, yet at the same time were permeated by the assumptions of their time and fed into a system of beliefs they would not dismantle. Bearing this in mind, we can begin with the aspect of ethnographic translation which Niranjana considers the most fundamental and most fundamentally oppressive, its construction of its own source text in the shape of subjugated 'cultures'.

The constitution of unified cultures

The constitution of groups in European terms for the purposes of colonial administration was not invented by anthropology, but it was certainly driven forward and given legitimation by the discipline. First and foremost, the choice of an object of study played its part. As Stephan Feuchtwang notes, British anthropologists in Africa insisted on studying "minute, 'primitive' populations" (1973:78) as opposed to larger conglomerations. They were swimming with the tide of a colonial interest in encouraging, or if necessary inventing, manageable political communities labelled 'tribes' (see Mafeje 1971), as well as enabling the use of their preferred fieldwork method, which is more difficult to apply to large-scale communities. For functionalist theory, 'tribes' had a further benefit: they epitomized the assumption that societies were closely integrated systems of behaviours and beliefs which worked together more or less in everybody's interest. The key role of the 'tribe' in structuring classical ethnographies can be seen in titles like *The Nuer*, *The Andaman Islanders*, *The Azande* and more.

Once the physical boundaries of the presumed community are staked out in works like these, an act usually highlighted early in the text by a series of maps, the impression of its coherence is furthered through microtextual features. The most important of these is probably the use of generalization, assimilating individual events and articulations into generally valid statements of the 'underlying' structure (remember Asad's criticism of 'cultural translation' for assuming the authority to find hidden structures not available to members of the culture themselves). Drawing out general structures from specific details is the key aim of functionalist ethnography, and informs a translation style which elides specific utterances into a synoptic whole. In other words, the individual things that people say and do are fed into a kind of analytical threshing machine which removes chaff and repetition. Generalization sets the accent on regularities or 'rules' of social life, not on conflicts or deviations from the rule, so that a homogeneous body arises from the pages. Named speakers are rare; much more commonly the subject of an action or view is a composite, impersonal figure who represents the 'tribe' as a whole: "the Andaman Islander considers" or "the Nuer believe".

Removing the context-bound specificity of events and statements not only helps produce the 'tribe' as a suitable object for study, but also positions it outside history, since everything its members do and say seems to be part of an endless 'traditional' repetition of received wisdom. Rather than participating in historical change, as the 'modern' Westerner does, the idealized native informant is a natural and timeless being, while the idealized ethnographer is freed from the harsh realities of colonial contact and left in an uncontaminated state of science (I will return to this below).

Ethnographic authority

As mid-century British anthropology uneasily tried to match the status of its big brothers the respectable natural sciences, its hopes lay in the claim to objectivity. Faced with the mass of disorienting subjective experience in the field, an objective-sounding voice in the written record was the guarantor of academic rigour, and of continued loyalty to a Western discourse – of not having 'gone native'. Thus the objective style was important in carving out a disciplinary niche in the target culture of mid-twentieth century Britain. Critical anthropologists have pointed out that the issue of objectivity is difficult in the present day as well: ethnography is an impersonal academic genre that grows out of a very personal history, and the two styles of experience do not easily harmonize in a single text. As Mary Louise Pratt (1986) shows, ethnographic writing often splits them into separate texts. In these cases an academically acceptable ethnography, cleansed of the subjective and intersubjective components of the research situation, is accompanied by a memoir or travel narrative which takes care of the personal side of things.

Ethnographers in the heyday of colonialism and discipline-formation needed to assert a strict personal distance from their objects of study, keeping the observed out of the text by the power of observer-translator's voice. If an ethnography sets out to find the typical in its object, the fundamental structure as opposed to individual and possibly idiosyncratic articulations, then logically enough there will be little space in the text for the *specific*, actual words which people addressed to the anthropologist or said within his or her hearing. And the more confidence the ethnographer has in the power of the summarized abstraction, the less relevant it becomes to include what seems to be the dross of redundant, obscure or personal contributions by the 'natives'. On this scale of confidence Malinowski is slightly less certain of having understood everything, and includes passages of dictation and quotation for potential reassessment in the future, while the more theoretically-minded Evans-Pritchard, as we will see below, eschews quotation almost entirely and sticks to the drawing of conclusions. Minimally less self-assured, but attempting a unified and generalizing style, is the work of the British functionalist A.R. Radcliffe-Brown. This 1922 passage gives his summary of the rules governing a particular kind of incident in the village:

> If a man kills another in a fight between two villages, or in a private quarrel, he leaves his village and goes to live by himself in the jungle, where he must stay for some weeks, or even months. His wife, and one or two of his friends may live with him or visit him and attend to his wants. For some weeks the homicide must observe a rigorous tabu. He must not handle a bow or arrow. He must not feed himself or touch any food with his hands, but must be fed by his wife or a friend. (Brown 1922:133)

Thinking about how the material for this passage will have come into being, it is clear that Radcliffe-Brown was faced with words and meaningful actions, as well as with explanations by the participants of what the words or actions should be taken to mean. This information has been doubly translated, or doubly filtered: it has been transformed from a variety of Andamanese into English (the mechanics of this procedure are treated barely at all, as we will see below), and it has been transformed from a mass of impressions, repetitions, observed actions and interpretations into a smooth synopsis. The credibility of the process depends on the authority of the ethnographer – our reporter and guide in the exotic world he describes.

James Clifford has written in detail on the ways that ethnographic authority is constituted in texts like this one (1988:ch.1). Interesting from the translation point of view are his comments on the issue of free indirect speech (ibid:47). As we see in the passage above, the explanations given by the people being studied are not quoted – not reproduced as parts of specific exchanges between specific participants. Clifford notes that in the process of moving from the immediate 'discourse' to a portable and durable 'text', the "specific authors and actors are severed from their productions". Consequently "a generalized 'author' must be invented" to fill the author slot (ibid:39). Nobody is named in the passage above, and instead Radcliffe-Brown implies that the Andaman Islanders in general always enforce this kind of behaviour and intend this kind of meaning for what they do (conveniently applying, for example, the anthropological category 'tabu'). We have a singular subject, "a man" who represents all Andaman Islanders, and the translator outlines that man on their behalf: 'he must do this', 'he may do that' are injunctions presumably expressed by the Andamanese Radcliffe-Brown talked to, but now their words are depersonalized and incorporated into the translator's voice. Through this use of free indirect speech, the ethnographer reinforces his aura of scientific objectivity by seeming – as a mere translator, not inventor, of culture – to reflect only what was truly said by others and not his own opinion. At the same time, the indirect speech allows the ethnographer's voice to flow on without interruptions from the actual source-language speakers. The only voice to be heard, thus, is that of the ethnographer, unifying the perspective of the text and making the 'natives' into raw material. We will revisit the issue of quotation and polyphony in Chapter 5, but for now let us notice the relative monologism of this passage, which effectively removes the right to speak from the source speakers and transfers it in full to the translator.

Does this mean the translator has overcome a repressive 'invisibility', to use Venuti's (1995) well-known term? Despite the prevalence of indirect speech, an assertive interpreting 'I' appears frequently in *The Andaman Islanders* and although Radcliffe-Brown claims not to have invented but only interpreted his Islanders, his name is given as the author. The ethnographer-translator is visible, but this does not cast doubt on his version or enable alternative readings as a visible translator in Venuti's sense might do. Instead, this translator surrounds himself with the paraphernalia of total authority, not only staking out a position of authorized interpreter but even claiming to have more knowledge of the source text than the source text authors themselves. Putting into English is more than a language-to-language or even culture-to-culture transfer; it transforms what seems to be inchoate non-language into what seems to be exact and irrefutable meaning:

> We may formulate in precise language the beliefs that underlie the ceremonial, remembering always that the Andaman Islanders themselves are quite incapable of expressing these beliefs in words and are probably only vaguely conscious of them. (Brown 1922:305-6)

One could hardly imagine a stronger contrast with the stance of traditional Western literary translation criticism, which sees a highly meaningful original half-helplessly brought across into the target language as a shadow of its former self. Here the original 'author' exists only as a composite being, and a composite being who is outside the language of consciousness; only through the translator does the text attain reality.

So Radcliffe-Brown is a highly visible and assertive translator – but in *The Andaman Islanders* another translator is involved as well, and this one remains unnamed. In the preface to the 1922 edition the anthropologist notes that he benefited from the services as interpreter of an Andaman Islander who "spoke English well and was of considerable intelligence" (ibid:viii). No further detail is given and captions to the two photographs of this man contain no reference to his role as an interpreter. In the photo reproduced in Figure 1, he becomes an illustration of physical stature and weaponry, not of language skill and intercultural mediation. The preface to the second edition lacks even these sparse references to the interpreter; his picture remains but now without any hint of his pivotal role in the writing of the book. The relationship between anthropologist and informant is structured in such a way that *this* translator is almost entirely invisible – so much so that no-one reading the second edition could more than guess at his existence.

Figure 1. "A man of the Akar-Bale tribe", A.R. Radcliffe-Brown, The Andaman Islanders, Cambridge 1922, facing p. 30.

The denial of coevalness

A very influential source in the critique of classical ethnographic writing is Johannes Fabian's *Time and the Other: How Anthropology Makes its Object*. As the subtitle implies, Fabian like Niranjana assumes that the 'studied' of anthropology does not simply pre-exist the study but is constituted by it. In other words, anthropological practices (and especially the writing practices of anthropology) 'make' an other which can be known and described. Fabian considers that concepts of time have been crucial in this process, for example in the nineteenth-century evolutionist paradigm that positions 'us' as being further along a time-line of development than 'them', 'us' as the adults and 'them' as the children and adolescents of human history. This is the key to the concept or category of 'the primitive' – something that is temporally distant from the defining voice or that is even *without* time because it is unchanging. It was the rise of fieldwork as the keystone of anthropology that, Fabian argues, gave rise to one crucial conceptual difficulty: anthropologists in the field obviously share the same time with the people they are studying, but when they get back to their desk in the West, that time is past. Their response is to separate off their own time from the time of the others. The implication that the 'natives' live in a different time from the ethnographer is what Fabian means by the "denial of coevalness" (1983:31 *et passim*). It was an important ideological move for colonialism, which tried to enable the coexistence of colonizers and colonized in one space either by dividing up the space or, more commonly, by dividing up the time so that the colonized were not actually 'present' in the temporal sense (ibid:29). In ethnographic writing, Fabian finds "a persistent and systematic tendency to place the referent(s) of anthropology in a Time other than the present of the producer of anthropological discourse" – producing what Fabian calls "allochronic" discourse (ibid:32).

How does this make itself felt in practice? Firstly, Fabian says, we can look at expressions that signal time difference, such as terms of sequence or duration, or classificatory terms like 'savagery' which are coded as markers of the 'past' of humanity. Secondly, there are syntactical devices which help to temporalize the object of ethnography and create the illusion that the 'facts' of an ethnographic text really do represent a reality in the external world (ibid:78). Two important aspects here are person and tense. Fabian notes the prevalence of the third person in ethnographic writing. Following Benveniste, he explains that the third person is not a 'person' in the sense of being a participant in the dialogue like the first and second persons (ibid:85); the ethnography addresses the academic reader as its 'you' and marks the "other Other" as outside the dialogue, in the third person. Once outside the dialogue, that third person is outside the shared present of first and second person, and occupies a different present, as something viewed from behind glass by the observing I. To keep the distinction sharp, the use of the past tense has to be avoided, since it would draw attention to the specific moment which the observer once shared with the observed. Instead, the simple present tense, an "ethnographic present", is used. It is reminiscent of the discourse of natural history, again reinforcing 'objectivity' as separation between observer and object. Thus, in Fabian's example, the autobiographical experience of the writer 'I never saw them excited' is hidden by the generalizing and apparently objective, present-tense 'They are stolid' (ibid:91), an effect we saw in the passage from Radcliffe-Brown quoted above.

Because of Western conceptions of time as a process of change, this loaded use of the present tense also implies that there is no change in the object, which remains fossilized outside the flux of history. This is where Fabian's argument overlaps with Said's analysis of Orientalist discourse as a means of removing the Eastern 'other' from Western (and universalized) history, to deposit non-Western lives in a stagnant backwater of time. The other side of the coin is that the objective ethnographic tone implies it is itself above history, not influenced by any particular moment in time. As a result of this twofold refutation of history, the actual nature of the relationship of the anthropologist with his audience on the one hand, and with the colonized objects of his study on the other, can be successfully repressed. As Mary Louise Pratt notes, the material relationship of the ethnographer to the group being studied is "one of the great silences in the midst of ethnographic description itself" (1986:42). It's the repression of the relationship of violence that, in Pratt's view, helps to explain why classical ethnography insists on 'traditional' societies, cultures untouched by contact or, if this is not possible, then cultures as they presumably *were* before being touched by contact and in anthropology's real reality, or in their heart of hearts, still *are*.

Fabian, to summarize, is appealing for a more historically situated, dialogue-oriented and reflexive kind of ethnographic writing, which we will consider in Chapter 5. The issue of ahistorical representation will also come to the fore when we discuss museum representations in Chapter 7. First, though, let's try to apply Fabian's diagnosis to an exemplar of colonial-era ethnographic writing.

E. E. Evans-Pritchard's *The Nuer*

The Nuer: A Description of the Modes of Livelihood and Political Institutions of a Nilotic People, published in 1940, is a book-length ethnography by a leading proponent of the British school of functional anthropology, Sir Edward Evan Evans-Pritchard (1902-73). In it he analyzes the political structures of a people of the southern Sudan he studied in the mid-1930s; this monograph was followed up by another two books on the Nuer, covering religion and kinship respectively. The *Nuer* trilogy took on a life of its own, becoming the key text of anthropological research on the Sudanese area and generating numerous later ethnographies which tried to emulate, build on or refute Evans-Pritchard's work.

Looking at *The Nuer* as a translation, we might begin with the conditions of its commissioning and publication. Evans-Pritchard received his brief in the wake of a rebellion by the Nuer against the colonial administration in the late 1920s. The administration hoped that more detailed information about Nuer ways of life would help it to establish the 'settlement' or reorganisation and pacification of this unruly people (see Johnson 1982, who traces in some detail the conflicts between the anthropologist and the Khartoum government in organizing the research trips). Clearly, this act of translation took place in a climate of fiercely pursued interests and counter-interests, a highly ideologized and politicized context. We will see that the text itself has its contradictions, and is by no means a simple piece of propaganda written to support the colonialist cause. However, its very premise as the "description" of "a Nilotic people" brings it into the purview of Niranjana's accusation against colonial-era ethnographies, that by claiming to describe an entity which is self-evidently 'there', unified and indisputable, texts like *The Nuer* help to create that entity as an object of study, simultaneously excluding it from the complexity and change which characterizes the writer's and reader's time and space. With the title itself, the naming and categorization as a "people", the anthropologist supports the colonialist taxonomy of who is who, and who is where, within the colonized region. The title pursues functionalism's interest in "timeless, synchronically presented, self-contained societies" (Niranjana 1992:80), and the rest of the text continues the theme.

One of the most striking aspects of *The Nuer* is its strong and characteristic authorial tone, and especially the way this tone alters between the personal introductory section and the 'scientific' body of the text. This is a division of labour that seems to protect the purity of Evans-Pritchard's data "from the contaminating contexts through which they were extracted" (Rosaldo 1986:88; see also Pratt 1986). It collects all the contextual information Evans-Pritchard wishes to reveal in a hermetically sealed section at the start, leaving the main text almost entirely free of reference to the impact of colonial power on the Nuer and the anthropologist's encounter with them. *The Nuer*'s lengthy introduction outlines the way the ethnographer came to the region and the trials he faced in gathering his information. Evans-Pritchard stakes his claim to knowledge by virtue of having 'been there', elaborated by quite detailed accounts of the tribulations, illnesses and problems with uncooperative 'natives' that earn the intrepid anthropologist the right to be listened to by his peers back in Europe. The author claims the seal of expertise: "I, unlike most readers, know the Nuer", he says boldly (1940:9).

But how did Evans-Pritchard come to this knowledge, enabling him to "describe" and "lay bare" (ibid:7) the underlying truths of Nuer political life? He admits right away that he relied exclusively on direct observation because he was unable to use trained informants, normally an important anthropological source. The reasons given for this inability are revealing, for Evans-Pritchard does not promote a "fable of rapport" with the natives (see Clifford 1988:40-41) or idealize his encounter with them. Instead, in a self-mocking tone he portrays the thorny communication prompted by the arrival of a representative of the British administration – although this is indicated only glancingly in the introduction, Evans-Pritchard's visit was immediately preceded by a British punitive campaign against the Nuer. Under these circumstances, it is hardly surprising that the Nuer he met refused to welcome and honour him; indeed, at one point a fresh bout of British aggression forced him to leave entirely (Johnson 1982:236). This was not only a personal rebuff but a professional problem: the Nuer refused to allow him to define the framework of communication as guiding ethnographer versus guided informant. Evans-Pritchard gives an example of a Nuer man's rejection of his own communicative ideal, commending it with heavy irony as a way for "natives pestered by ethnologists" to drive the latter crazy. Here is the dialogue he recounts:

I: Who are you?
Cuol: A man.
I: What is your name?
Cuol: Do you want to know my *name*?
I: Yes.
Cuol: You want to know *my* name?
I: Yes, you have come to visit me in my tent and I would like to know who you are.
Cuol: All right. I am Cuol. What is your name?
I: My name is Pritchard.
Cuol: What is your father's name?
I: My father's name is also Pritchard.
Cuol: No, that cannot be true. You cannot have the same name as your father.
I: It is the name of my lineage. What is the name of your lineage?
Cuol: Do you want to know the name of my lineage?
I: Yes.
Cuol: What will you do with it if I tell you? Will you take it to your country?

I: I don't want to do anything with it. I just want to know it since I am living at your camp.
Cuol: Oh well, we are Lou.
I: I did not ask you the name of your tribe. I know that. I am asking you the name of your lineage.
Cuol: Why do you want to know the name of my lineage?
I: I don't want to know it.
Cuol: Then why do you ask me for it? Give me some tobacco.
(Evans-Pritchard 1940:12-13)

In the end, writes Evans-Pritchard, the villagers do accept his presence, but just as inconvenient as their initial refusal to respond to the ethnographer's questions is their subsequent extremely garrulous sociability, leaving him barely a moment alone. Worse, he never has the opportunity to control either the setting or the tone and topics of the conversation (ibid:14,19).

The anecdotes in the introduction give an unusual glimpse of the pragmatic difficulties of 'cultural translation' as the Nuer partners refuse to accommodate to the translator's linguistic expectations. Not only do they – understandably – question his self-presentation as a fair-minded and objective visitor, but they overrule his preferred style and content in conversation and reject the categories, such as the terminology of 'lineage' or 'tribe', he is trying to apply. Instead of furnishing pieces of information to fill the boxes pre-designed by the anthropologist, Cuol upturns the conversation in a dizzying attack on Evans-Pritchard's Gricean principles; the assumption of effective communication between the two sides is severely shaken. The dialogue makes it very clear that the difficulties arise at least in part from Evans-Pritchard's status as part of the repressive colonial regime, yet this fact is ignored and the problem reinterpreted as one of perverse obfuscation by the other party. Nor do Nuer objections to the framework of data collection seem to have had an impact on the final version of the translation. By quoting the dialogue with Cuol, Evans-Pritchard admits the difficulty of communication that underlies the translation he offers. Given this acknowledgement we might expect the rest of the text to be beset by doubt about how to interpret what was seen and heard, to wonder or hedge or speculate. But on the contrary, it remains untroubled. It reads as a strictly impersonal 'scientific' account, with the added value of a narrative persona established in the introduction as that of an "honest man" given to "forthright realism", a "detached ironic observer" (Rosaldo 1986:92, 93). After the tantalizing hints of the introduction, Evans-Pritchard's ethnography rolls out in a magisterial tone of absolute conviction, an effect impressively analyzed by Clifford Geertz in a set of essays that could almost be read as translation criticism, *Works and Lives*. Discussing Evans-Pritchard's work on Africa, Geertz finds an "easy certitude of perception" (1988:57-8), a sense that what the ethnographer has seen is indisputably thus, contains no insuperable obscurities, and can be successfully analyzed by the skilled observer. The certainty is expressed in Evans-Pritchard's distinctive style, says Geertz: "Everything that is said is clearly said, confidently and without fuss. Verbally, at any rate, there are no blanks to fill in or dots to join" (ibid:61). The verbal clarity is achieved by the insistent use of simple declarative sentences – a striking feature of *The Nuer* – and summary lists are important as well ("The main characteristics of Nuerland are: 1. …", Evans-Pritchard 1940:55), imparting a sense of comprehensive finality in the ethnographer's explanation. The page reproduced in Figure 2 is an example of *The Nuer*'s frequent use of graphics, especially line drawings, diagrams and charts with all their edges sharply defined. The emphasis on the visual aspect supports the author's reliance on 'observed' data in priority over spoken information.

THE LINEAGE SYSTEM 201

the depth of a lineage (the vertical line of ascent) is always in proportion to its width (the base line representing living lineage groups in the clan system).

A Nuer clan, therefore, is a system of lineages, the relationship of each lineage to every other lineage being marked in its structure by a point of reference in ascent. The distance to this

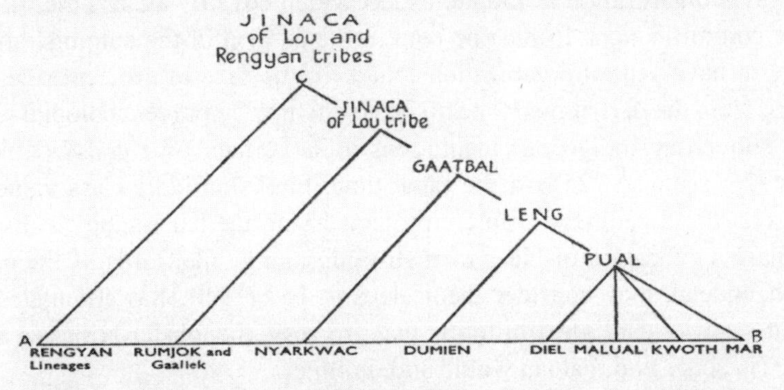

point is what we call the time depth of a lineage. In theory the genealogical relationship between any two clansmen can be traced through this point, and Nuer can actually trace it if they take the trouble. However, they do not consider it necessary to know the exact genealogical relationship between persons who are known to be distantly related by membership of their respective lineages. Thus it is sufficient for a man of the GAATBAL lineage to know that another man is of the GAALIEK lineage without his having to know the man's exact descent, for these two lineages stand to one another in a certain structural relationship, and therefore the two men stand to one another at that distance. Nuer are conversant up to a point—generally up to the founders of their minimal and minor lineages—with the full range of their genealogical relationships. Beyond this point they reckon kinship in terms of lineages. It is necessary

Figure 2. E.E. Evans-Pritchard, The Nuer, Oxford 1940, p. 201

These devices contribute to the sense offered by the whole text that details of behaviour (and to a lesser extent beliefs and values) can all be elucidated if one applies the correct analytical framework. Thus the use of diagrams and the measured tone are not just translation tricks for the reader's convenience. They give expression to Evans-Pritchard's confidence in the potential clarity and comprehensibility of his material: Geertz finds that Evans-Pritchard's equanimous and matter-of-fact authorial voice serves to convince readers that the alien reality, though perhaps strange at first, is actually quite compatible with – explicable by – their own domestic categories. On the one hand, says Geertz, this project complies with imperialist claims by attributing universal validity to British categories of explanation; on the other, it undermines imperialism's assumption that Africans are radically different from those who are entitled to human and democratic rights. In fact, in *The Nuer* this dual point is made rather explicitly in a section on Nuer antipathy to commands and to domination. The Europeans are themselves to blame for the trouble with the Nuer, the anthropologist implies, because they act in ignorance (1940:134) of the admirable character of these "hard", "egalitarian", and "deeply democratic" people (ibid:181).

Evans-Pritchard's insistence that Nuer society shows no centralized or state-style organization is another aspect which covertly attacks the translation's commissioners. It must be read in the context of the administration's desire to have central organization found for the sake of efficient rule, and seems, from the determined tone, to be an attempt "to prevent colonial rulers from subverting indigenous institutions to serve their own ends" (Kuklick 1991:275; see also 225). At the same time, English middle-class values of democracy and egalitarianism are projected onto the Nuer subjects. Evans-Pritchard's evocation of Nuer men strutting along "like lords of the earth, which, indeed, they consider themselves to be" (1940:183) articulates the author's own social ideal in terms that are rosy, though far removed from home (in space and, Fabian would add, in time).

We see here the ambivalent position of the anthropologist employed by the colonial government and with a particular task to fulfil that did not fully match his own plans, engendering the series of conflicts and compromises traced by Douglas Johnson (1982). To be sure, Evans-Pritchard contributed to colonialist 'knowledge' of the Nuer, setting out a terminology to describe their political structures that drew the parameters of description for its time and far beyond (ibid:240). The strictly ahistorical approach of *The Nuer* masks the realities of colonial violence, thus helping to perpetuate such violence as well as positioning the Nuer outside history and agency – for as Niranjana remarks, when history is repressed, timeless 'nature' remains as the defining characteristic (1992:75). But Evans-Pritchard's experience of colonial power at work and of the life of the Nuer also prompted him to advocate a more distanced stance towards the administrators (Johnson 1982:241). Among other things, the colonial administration was interested in a 'translation' of Nuer life that voiced only political – not, for example, religious or aesthetic – dimensions: a translation was required which would present Nuer political structures in such a way that British rule could be mapped onto them both as ideological justification and as a practical means of control. In *The Nuer* Evans-Pritchard refused to deliver the required grid, insisting that Nuer had no powerful individual chiefs who could be co-opted into the colonial system of rule. His anthropological contribution did not attack colonialism directly or in principle – in fact Kuklick notes that his interpretation of Nuers' own colonizing policies implicitly praises a pattern of domination and willing self-subjugation (Kuklick 1991:276) – but it did withhold from his employers the particular type of translation that they desired. Accordingly lukewarm was the enthusiasm of the British government in Sudan for their anthropologist's work.

As regards the rightfulness of the colonialist cause, then, there is a certain ambivalence in the conclusions that Evans-Pritchard draws from his studies. But the style of translation is very much the voice of dominance. *The Nuer* adopts an irrefutable 'it is so' authorial voice and quarantines off the elements of dialogue – or failed dialogue – with the others which threaten to undermine the translator's singular authority. Thus although the difficulties of attaining knowledge emerge in the introduction, they are almost fully repressed in the body of the text, and the words of Nuer people themselves have virtually no presence. This begins with the naming of the people as "Nuer", which as Evans-Pritchard concedes is "sanctioned by a century of use" by Europeans but does not coincide with the self-naming as *Nath* (1940:3), and it is carried through in an almost consistent absence of quotation (the dialogue with Cuol remains an exception). Individual native words are used and explained as a means to elucidate particular aspects of Nuer life, in some cases at length and with comments on the difficulty of translating them (for example pp. 135-6 on the term *cieng*). Occasionally legends are paraphrased, and once or twice another person's opinion than Evans-Pritchard's is voiced, but otherwise the visual quality which Geertz noted takes shape in a strongly observational, third-person style of writing. The distance between observer and observed is strictly retained and the physical encounter in shared time is downplayed. As Fabian noted, the denial of coevalness has its two mutually confirming aspects: if the illusion of objective purity and separation is to be upheld, then the ethnographer's involvement and, with it, the whole encounter between Africans and Europeans must be silenced, and if the inequality of this encounter is to be upheld, then there must be no doubts cast on the objective purity of colonial 'knowledge'.

Looked at this way, the absence of direct speech in Evans-Pritchard's translation style is a way of denying the concrete situation of dialogue in which he found himself as a rather troubled participant. Additionally, we can situate it in Evans-Pritchard's professional situation and his moment of disciplinary history. Kuklick's study (1991) shows that British anthropologists in the first half of the twentieth century were working at building their disciplinary identity and needed to differentiate themselves from the competition: colonial administrators and missionaries. Both these amateur groups normally had much longer-lasting contact with 'their' peoples and thus in many cases much more extensive knowledge of the local languages. Hence, perhaps, the rather anxious tone of Evans-Pritchard's defence of the shortness of his sojourn with the Nuer. He insists that scientific method, the domain of the new structural-functionalists, can achieve what "haphazard" information-gathering cannot (1940:261). The dig is probably directed at Malinowski, but non-professional gatherers of information were at least as haphazard, being satisfied to collect primary material without analysis. The colonial administrator R.S. Rattray, for example, collected Asante proverbs and stories and published them with transcription, translation and linguistic commentary (1916). He was making a contribution to the colonial effort in terms of both language learning and ethnological information, and even a contribution to literary art – but not a contribution to the pursuit of theory or anthropological science. Where Rattray's work is organized around Asante self-portrayals and includes long passages of Asante language, Evans-Pritchard's insists on the authority of his own professional discourse as (with some very small exceptions) the sole language of his text.

We have seen, then, a classic British ethnography, written in a context of colonialist power and in the aftermath of the violent suppression of a rebellion, asserting authoritative status for its 'translation' of an East African people. In premise and tone it underpins the British claim to 'understand' the dominated people in a way that can never be reciprocated. 'Simple', 'primitive' and knowable by observation alone, the Nuer are worlds away from the British reader. However, it would be a mistake to assume that the its historical environment monolithically determines the text. Evans-Pritchard praises the Nuer at many points, finding them rational and admirable in their adaptation to the ecological constraints of their inferior land (see, for example, 1940:51). Secondly, even in this most controlled and controlling of texts, the traces remain of a less controllable encounter in the form of the "Nuerosis" which Evans-Pritchard says he suffered at the hands of his recalcitrant informants (ibid:13). Not only does the introduction cast great doubt on the ethnography's claim to realism, since the sources of information are exposed as the unreliable products of tricky negotiations. Phrases of uncertainty like "I do not know how often" (ibid:78) creep in, and the ethnographer records moments of discomfiture like the time he was told a pack of nonsense and everyone "roared with laughter" at him for having believed it (ibid:183).

Also, the apparently consistent use of the distancing third person is, every now and again, disrupted by a slip into a kind of identification with the people described by using a potentially inclusive 'one': "One does not fornicate with girls of one's own village" (ibid:167, rapidly replaced by the more usual 'he' in the next sentence). In rare moments like this, the authorial voice seems to lose its separation from the objects of description. Despite his battery of charts and graphs, declarative statements and implied 'of course's, Evans-Pritchard can't quite keep hold of a fully confident sense of knowledge-dominance over the people he has come to visit. The experience of personal culture-shock and confusion manages to assert itself between the lines of even this translation, albeit without seriously weakening the confidence of political power that is articulated and bolstered by the text.

In this chapter I have treated as one period a long time span which covers massive differences in historical experiences of colonial rule, resistance and liberation struggles or even extinction – and collapses hundreds of different source languages by taking the perspective of a more or less unified target language. We can do this in line with Toury's injunction to treat translations as "facts of the target culture" (1995:23) and there is much to be gained by it, since otherwise we would have no possibility of investigating the practice of ethnographic translation as an institutional and historical object of study. However, in this context it becomes painfully clear that ignoring the realities of the source culture, and in particular ignoring the impact of the target text on its source culture, is unsatisfactory. Even if the workings of the translation in the target culture were to be studied in detail, an account of the translation's impact on the source culture and that culture's responses to it is still required. This is the kind of work pioneered by Vicente Rafael (1988) and hopefully to be continued at length by other scholars.

To be sure, Toury's admonishment in 1995 was aiming less to eliminate the source culture from translation studies than to shift attention away from the long-standing obsession with fidelity or the truth-value of relationships between source and target text. 'Is the translation faithful?' is the question Toury would like us to set aside when studying literary translation. In the case of ethnographic translation that question has to be posed completely differently, since the ethnographic translation traditionally claims to represent reality itself and not another text. But it is this very claim that has been experiencing serious tremors (whether from postcolonial critiques or from the destabilization of the notion of truth) along with the rest of the social sciences, culminating in the 'crisis of representation' to which we will now turn.

5. Critical Innovations in Ethnography

In his short and accessible book, John Van Maanen (1988) classifies traditional and more recent styles of ethnographic writing as various kinds of narrative – as realist tales, confessional tales, impressionist tales and so on. This kind of definition of social science texts in literary terms emerges from the work of scholars like Hayden White (1973), who analyzed the narrative conventions and fictionality of historiographical texts, and it parallels developments in translation theory away from the search for accurate reproduction of identifiable, fixed meanings and towards a view of translation as interested, partial, mutable and polysemic. The same trend underlies the 'textualist' turn set out in the 1986 collection *Writing Culture*, which starts from the assumption that 'scientific' texts as much as any others need to be read as cultural artefacts drawing on particular sets of poetic resources and conventions, and not as the objective mirrors of reality they sometimes claim to be. For translation studies, this text-oriented approach is of great interest, bringing both practical and political issues of translation to the fore. In particular, the experiments in ethnography since the late 1960s, in the throes of what has been called the ethnographic 'crisis of representation', seem to offer much food for thought to scholars of translation.

The mode of ethnography we looked at in the last chapter, exemplified by Evans-Pritchard's *The Nuer*, is one that Van Maanen calls the 'realist tale'. In realist ethnography – the dominant mode in the Anglo-American tradition from the 1920s to the 1980s, according to Marcus and Cushman (1982) – the ethnographer takes a confident stance that recalls the omniscient narrator of realist fiction. His narrative authority is backed up by personal credentials (in the case of Evans-Pritchard, the heroic, cool and analytically superior persona presented in his introduction) and enables an "interpretive omnipotence" unchallenged by other voices in the text (Van Maanen 1988:51). Just as the realist novel deploys concrete detail to create a feeling of vivid totality, realist ethnographies focus on the minutiae of everyday life, generalized as 'typical' within a theoretical framework that seems to represent a culture in its totality. Messy or unrecuperable data are excluded to avoid muddying the pool. It is the voice of the author which holds together the details and reassures the reader that reality is something stable and knowable; hence the importance of our faith in the ethnographer's authority and the "redundant demonstrations that the writer shared and experienced" the world he describes (Marcus & Cushman 1982:29).

Realist representation insists that through the offices of this *fidus interpres*, we as readers can ultimately come to know the precise contours of someone else's existence, and it is this insistence which the 'postmodern' critics of ethnography since the mid-1980s have been trying to undermine. As we will see, they have taken many different lines of attack on the realist mode, especially by questioning the absolute power of the author-translator. This route is hinted at in what Van Maanen calls the 'confessional' mode of ethnography.

Confession and the translator's preface

The confessional tale in Van Maanen's sense is a full-length memoir of the fieldworker's experience, published as a personal account and not as a 'translation of culture'. Not all 'confessional' writing is so extensive, however. In fact, a smaller confessional component has long been an expected accompaniment to texts that remain largely realist overall. In this case it consists of a first-person account of the constraints faced by the fieldworker, typically referring to both practical obstacles and the experience of culture shock, and often setting out the personal relationship – for example a role as the apprentice or student of a respected teacher-informant – which yielded the ethnographic data presented. This kind of account 'humanizes' the ethnographer, asks for the reader's identification and forbearance, and partly demystifies the fieldwork which formed the basis of the finished book. At the same time, by highlighting the personal limitations of ethnographers it ought to cast doubt on their authority to speak for and about 'the natives'. When we move on to reflexive and dialogical ethnographies, we will see that effect taken up and pursued to the point of serious narrative self-doubt, but in realist ethnographies the confessional component is likely to remain "upbeat" in tone and clearly separated from the 'actual' material (Van Maanen 1988:79). The distinction is most often effected by means of an introduction or preface. In *The Nuer* we saw the author's confession of his limitations in the introduction, and many similar, though less extensive, versions can be found in traditional ethnographies. The arrangement serves less to question the project's plausibility than to remind the reader of the authority of empirical experience: 'I was there and I know what I saw'. In this form, the confessional dimension acts as a seal of authenticity and establishes the author's credentials, whereas the body of the text retains its stance as an objective record of the 'native point of view', hiding the ethnographer's personal participation. Prefaces like these do little to open up the role of the ethnographer-translator in the production of the text.

The division of labour between confessional preface and realist text has been described in gendered terms. Barbara Tedlock (1995) shows that when the confessional 'preface' is an entire book, it is often one written by 'the ethnographer's wife' as the human face of her husband's 'serious work'. The wifely analogy may be relevant again if we compare the ethnographic confession to the genre of the translator's preface. There, the translator offers at least a shadowy image of her- or himself as a writing subject, an impression that immediately fades when the translation proper begins and the translator steps back behind the screen. The preface itself typically bemoans the difficulty of the task and the translator's own shortcomings, without, however, really retracting his or her authority to have made the translation. It is noticeable that ethnographers' prefaces tend to be significantly longer and much more personal than the prefaces of literary translators into English, yet the general principle is a similar one. In both cases the writer's interests and objectives briefly materialize, to disappear shortly afterwards into the bustle of the 'real world' being portrayed.

In view of the difficulty of language and representation shared by literary translators and ethnographers, it is striking how little the confessional ethnographic preface tends to say about language as an issue in the ethnographer's practice. It has been suggested that the reluctance to discuss the details of the ethnographer's linguistic knowledge is a virtual conspiracy of silence, masking a frequent lack of deep and thorough familiarity with the language (see Keesing 1989). In the case of Vincent Crapanzano's *Tuhami*, which we will return to later, no claim is made to profound knowledge of Arabic, the language of the fieldwork interviews, but the mechanics of language mediation in the data-gathering process are minimized. Much space is devoted in the confessional sections to the psychological role of Crapanzano's Arabic-French interpreter Lhacen, yet Lhacen's interlingual interpretation is barely mentioned. The implication is that linguistically the ethnographer had 'direct' access to Tuhami's words, considerably obscuring the complexity of the translation in the work.

Other prefatory comments mention translation as a technical matter of recording people's words 'faithfully' or 'unchanged'. This is the line taken by Shostak in *Nisa*, a book based largely on translated interviews:

> These interviews [...] produced close to thirty hours of tape in the !Kung language and hundreds of pages of typewritten, literal transcriptions. These were written mostly in English, with many !Kung expressions retained so that the final translation could reflect nuances unique to !Kung. The chronological sequence in which the narrative is presented does not necessarily reflect the order in which the stories appear in the interviews. [...] Other changes come from the deletion of clarifying remarks and the modification or elimination of a word and phrase repetitions – a dramatic device for emphasis in !Kung but distracting in English, which accomplishes the same purpose with adjectives. Apart from these changes, the narrative is faithful to the interviews. (Shostak 1981:42-3)

'Faithfulness' is easily achieved by Kevin Dwyer, too, since like Shostak he accommodates interlingual translation in the list of general 'changes':

> I translated all the interviews from Moroccan Arabic. Otherwise, I edited them only by excising several sections in order to remain as faithful to the Faqir's expressed wishes as I could (these deletions are indicated by ellipses inside parentheses), by changing some names and eliminating others where I thought it appropriate, and by substituting names for pronouns in a number of places for the purposes of clarity. Pauses are indicated by a series of dots; interruptions are shown by speech beginning at midline. Aside from these changes, the dialogues are transcribed here just as they were recorded. (Dwyer 1982:xxi)

Both Shostak and Dwyer give the reader detailed insights into the ways their personal experience of the fieldwork impacted on their data and interpretations, yet the specific issue of language difference is sidelined almost completely in their versions of the translator's preface. We have already seen that Shostak works with a notion of meaning as universal, so her approach to interlingual translation is rather consistent, but Dwyer is less confident about intercultural communication, which makes his silence on interlingual difference more striking. It recalls the way that handbooks of anthropology relegate translation to the role of a rather minor technicality; the sceptical line taken by Quine or, in his very different way, Malinowski finds no favour in these texts.

In short, although the confessional opening *qua* translator's preface makes the ethnographic translator highly visible (if only for a moment), it does not do the same for the translatedness of the words behind the text. Even so, the attention given by confessional ethnographers to their personal experience of the fieldwork conversations is interesting from a translation point of view: it implicitly destabilizes the authority of the ethnographer-translators and de-essentializes the knowledge presented in their 'translations' of culture. Indirectly, at least, the apparent transparency of the translation is challenged by their attention to who spoke to whom about what, when, where and why.

Dialogical ethnography

The confessional preface or memoir can partially erode the illusion of the ethnographer as a mere objectivity-machine, faithfully recording reality from the field. But as long as it remains separated from the body of the text, its potential to transform the translation is limited. Proponents of a 'dialogical' style of ethnographic writing aim to bring the specifics of the ethnographic encounter into the text itself, attacking transparency much more radically by highlighting the shared construction of the 'data' that enters the ethnography.

Dennis Tedlock, in his seminal study of the problems of transforming spoken exchange into writing, criticizes the traditional "analogical ethnography" in which the voices of the other speakers are overlaid by the anthropologist's monologue (1983:ch.16). In this mode, even if individual native words are included, the natives never utter complete sentences; that privilege is reserved for the ethnographer-translator, whose discourse fully replaces the original conversation. At the other end of the spectrum, texts based on ethnolinguistic collections in the Boasian tradition, as we will see in Chapter 6, also use the monologue form, this time recording the 'native informant' alone, with apparently not a single word contributed by the interviewer. In Tedlock's view, the analogical style confirms an illusion that content exists independently of the specific situation of speaking and can be recorded in isolation from it – and, in turn, that such content can be transmitted unscathed into a different linguistic setting. He proposes instead a 'dialogic' mode of writing which emphasizes "betweenness" (ibid:323).

The idea of betweenness is elaborated in a later work co-edited by Tedlock, the collection *The Dialogic Emergence of Culture*. In their introduction, Tedlock and Bruce Mannheim argue that the culture recorded by the ethnographer is the "joint construction" of asker and teller (Mannheim & Tedlock 1995:13), so that removing one of them from the record will automatically falsify the account. They draw here on Mikhail Bakhtin's concept of the dialogical nature of utterances. For Bakhtin, what people say never starts from zero but is always part of an ongoing discussion:

> the living utterance, having taken meaning and shape at a particular historical moment in a socially specific environment, cannot fail to brush up against thousands of living dialogic threads, woven by socio-ideological consciousness around the given object of an utterance; it cannot fail to become an active participant in social dialogue. (1981:276)

The word, as a "living rejoinder", depends on previous and parallel words, and it also anticipates a response (ibid:279-80); each utterance is inextricably bound up in a larger network of other utterances. Thus, language "lies on the borderline between oneself and the other. The word in language is half somebody else's" (ibid:293). It is this understanding of speech which informs Mannheim and Tedlock's argument that the knowledge arising out of conversations is neither fully in the hands of the ethnographer, nor fully out of his or her hands. Fieldwork conversations are moulded by both parties, and this must be addressed in the ethnographic record. As for a dialogic translation based on this model, such a translation could not be a transcript of settled reality but must trace the unresolved *negotiations* about reality between the translator and the translated, and likewise between the languages of the translator and the translated.

What, though, does dialogical ethnography look like in practice? After all, as Fabian (1990) argues, the very act of writing may be structurally a betrayal or negation of the dialogical nature of experience 'in the field', since it establishes distance (between the past of the experience and the present of the writing) and imposes the power of dominant literate culture onto the world of orality. Certainly the dialogue that takes place during research is not replicated – or even represented – in writing simply by arranging text in a dramatic or ostensibly 'dialogue' form. As Mannheim and Tedlock (paraphrasing Bakhtin) point out, text could be arranged like this and yet still concentrate all the power of definition on one side; conversely, running prose can be dialogical if "multiple voices and multiple cultural logics contend with each other" within it (1995:4; see also Clifford 1988:44). Nor is the mere addition of 'context' to the record of particular utterances enough, because this would suppose that content exists prior to and independently of the conversation (1995:12). Rather, the dialogical ethnography should turn the spotlight onto the conversation itself and the reciprocal impact of the dialogue partners on each other's words and worlds.

To a certain extent, this is attempted by Kevin Dwyer in *Moroccan Dialogues* (1982). Dwyer's study takes the conversation between the ethnographer and a single interlocutor as its focus. The book is arranged around a set of discussions with a Moroccan dignitary known as the Faqir, and makes the encounter between the two men a springboard for reflections on the nature of anthropological dialogue in general. The bulk of the book consists of the translated interviews with the Faqir, surrounded by a methodological preface, a "prologue" and two closing theoretical chapters. In each 'dialogue' chapter an episode of fieldwork experience is described, methodological questions are set out, and then the related conversation presented.

In the conversations, Dwyer records his own questions as well as the Faqir's responses, using different typefaces to distinguish between his preplanned questions and the ones that arise in the flow of the discussion. His aim here is to make physically visible the unpredictable contributions of the ethnographer to the conversation, which are made as a human being rather than as the scientific monitoring device that is Evans-Pritchard in full flow. And the Faqir's explanations, rather than being a reliable recital of the Facts of the Matter, show up as a set of responses to specific guiding prompts in the ethnographer's questioning. To this extent, the two-person form begins to debunk the illusion of depersonalized, neutral and objective factuality as the outcome of ethnographic translation. Dwyer goes further in his claim: he attaches importance to the ways in which the Faqir himself steers the conversation, contributes to the setting of the agenda and responds to the ignorance of his interlocutor, for example by using 'empathetic' cultural comparison to get his point across (thus, the Faqir carefully explains an insult: it's "as if I said to you, 'Ah, you American traitor!'"; 1982:78). Dwyer's point is that an ethnography of dialogue can reveal the interdependence of self and other in conversation, and specifically their mutual vulnerability: "In the confrontation between anthropologist and informant, each changes and develops while interacting with the other; during their actual encounter and in response to the other, each creates himself in part as a reaction to the other" (ibid:xviii). This sounds like a translation practice where the translator is personally affected by the process of translation, as much written-on as writing.

In practice Dwyer, like other 'reflexive' ethnographers, finds it difficult to put into linguistic form the mutuality of meaning he experiences during the conversations. Although the Faqir's words are recorded, giving him a very strong presence in *Moroccan Dialogues* compared to the largely silent Nuer in Evans-Pritchard's study, the book as a whole is clearly the outcome of a strong editing hand. Most striking is Dwyer's decision to structure the ethnography in a dramatic form with a "cast of characters", a "prologue" and vignette-style chapters ("The Mad Migrant", or "The Bicycle Theft"). Dwyer does address the difficulties of the ethnographic genre and the authority which it gives him as the editor; in an interesting discussion, he notes that not only are the questions which guide the interviews dictated by his own cultural assumptions, but his organizing principle of event plus interview, too, depends on his own editing work in distilling particular 'events' "out of my own concerns and out of the tissue of the Faqir's life" (ibid:138). This does not deter him from using his 'events' as the framework of the ethnography; Dwyer retains his own editorial control and quarantines off the reflexive co-text in preliminary sections, outside the 'primary', apparently untouched material of the dialogues. At points where he feels the Faqir is too unrepresentative or even wrong in his account, he intervenes by means of an academic footnote to clarify the real situation. And his own contributions to the conversation, if we are to believe the 'transcription' (ibid:xxi), are always terse, almost always cogent and coherent, rarely personal in their tone. To this extent we could complain that the form is not so much dialogue as interview, albeit an interview with a degree of self-questioning comment and contemplation.

To work as a 'dialogic translation' of the conversations between Dwyer and the Faqir, the text would, among other things, need to pay more attention to the language difference between the two men. Considering how much soul-searching goes into the question of interview technique and the construction of coherence, Dwyer is surprisingly reticent about the language move from Arabic to English, as we saw above in his cursory note on translation. The clash of discursive perspectives is hinted at, however, for Dwyer does not delete his interlocutor's strict judgement on the framework of the 'dialogue':

> As for me, I know that I'm not concerned with a single one of your questions. I know that these questions serve your purposes, not mine. I think about the questions, whether they are small questions or large

> ones, and I think about them because they serve your purposes, not mine. (ibid:225-6)

The anthropologist could ask about snakes, turtles or anything else, says the Faqir, it wouldn't matter to him. This passage seems to contradict the use of the word 'dialogue' in the sense of reciprocity, since the Faqir's own evaluation of what might be worth saying is overruled by the partner in the conversation who has the power to fix the written record. A related point is picked up by ethnographer Vincent Crapanzano: in real dialogue the speakers do not simply take turns, saying their own thing in an alternating rhythm or even working towards consensus. Their words collide in the space between the speakers, and bend or buckle under the pressure (1992:193). To represent this aspect of ethnographic dialogue, an interview format may be insufficient, and other ethnographies interested in dialogue take a more far-reaching reflexive approach.

Reflexivity

Reflexive ethnography specifically sets out to destroy the illusion of pure or indisputable facts, to "shock the anthropologist and the reader of anthropology from [their] complacency" (Crapanzano 1980:xii). It does so by shifting the focus of the study to the conditions under which the research was carried out, and especially to the role of the ethnographer as a knower and as an arranger of the knowledge that he or she has gained. The writer of a reflexive ethnography therefore features in the text as an individual, but the cultural constraints are stressed, including (to varying degrees) the political constraints of the unequal relations between representer and represented. As a result, reflexive ethnographies are about the culture of the target language and the discipline itself as well as about the culture of the source language. Like the confessional mode, the reflexive ethnography presents the writer as a fallible mortal, but it tends to be more interested in epistemological issues than in the personal or autobiographical aspect.

The first of three ethnographies of Morocco that set the agenda for reflexive or dialogically oriented approaches during the early 1980s (the others being Crapanzano 1980 and Dwyer 1982), Paul Rabinow's *Reflections on Fieldwork in Morocco* argues that ethnographic writing cannot aim for a natural-science neutrality but is bound to be an interpretive undertaking. He cites Ricoeur's definition of interpretation as "the comprehension of the self by the detour of the comprehension of the other" (Rabinow 1977:5) – not a psychological quest but one to explore "the culturally mediated and historically situated self which finds itself in a continuously changing world of meaning" (ibid:6). It is through the attempt to understand someone foreign to us that we learn about ourselves, and in practice this means that *Reflections on Fieldwork* is written almost consistently from a first-person perspective, noting the feelings, reactions and failures of the ethnographic narrator and tying ethnographic observations to individual, personal encounters of the American anthropologist with the Moroccans he visits. In particular, Rabinow experiences uncertainty and a destabilizing of his own cultural and professional identity. Rabinow's model thus does not emphasize clear dividing lines between source and target culture. Instead of a two-character exchange, he sees fieldwork as an alarming but productive conversation that triggers change in every direction, both between and within the participants, in a "process of intersubjective construction of liminal modes of communication" (ibid:155).

We might describe this 'liminal mode of communication' itself as the translation process, as shifting talk on the boundaries of self and other that recalls the idea of the 'third space' as a space of translation, discussed in Chapter 2. It also features strongly in Crapanzano's *Tuhami* (1980), where interviews with a Moroccan tile-maker are the basis for an unconventional life-story format that mixes quotation with ethnographic commentary, direct and indirect speech, factual and dream or mythical sequences, biographical details and generalized accounts.

Starting from a psychoanalytical framework, Crapanzano assumes that the dialogue (actually a trialogue, since the interpreter Lhacen is always present) will have to work with ambiguities, mutual projections and unresolved questions. It will entail a lack of consensus between translator and translated: as Crapanzano puts it in a later work, "dialogue has a transformational as well as an oppositional dimension – an agonistic one. It is a relationship of considerable tension" (1992:197). A concrete example is his account of the terms on which the conversation took place. Crapanzano writes, "I was primarily interested in information, Tuhami in evocation. We did listen to each other, though, and soon our discourses began to vacillate between the informative and the evocative" (1980:14). That this really was a vacillation and not a resolution on the terms of the target discourse of anthropological generalization is shown by the structure of the book, which does not claim to be either Crapanzano's more accurate version of Tuhami's life or a measured compromise between Crapanzano's and Tuhami's versions. Instead, the text abruptly juxtaposes passages of quoted dialogue or narrative with background information and Crapanzano's own interpretations of Tuhami's comments. None of these three strands takes a clearly privileged position; the interpretations are left to stand as interpretations and do not become definitive explanations of the quoted material. This example is taken from a section in which Tuhami relates how he stayed at a saint's tomb:

- How did you eat?
- Eating was not important.

> – Why did you leave?
> – They let me leave. I went back to the Moroccan's factory in Meknes.I was never sick again.
>
> The identity of the "they" who let Tuhami leave is not at all clear. Saint? *Jinn*? Tuhami was of course sick again: "Sometimes I still think about going back there." (ibid:67)

The ethnographer's comments highlight his uncertainty (although not about whether Tuhami was or was not ever sick again: "of course" he was). The layout of the quotations, some introduced by a dash and some in quotation marks, visually indicates the mixing of versions. Although the dialogue continues after the interruption by the ethnographer's voice, the insertion of the differently marked quotation shows that the account is not intended to be a 'literal' or chronological report of the conversation. Likewise, the story of Tuhami's infancy is told in the third person with an air of confidence quickly dented by the author's parenthetical admission:

> He slept on a little straw mattress next to [his mother] and Driss. She gave him her breast whenever he cried (I am reconstructing here from traditional Moroccan child-rearing practices) – that is, until he was about two. (ibid:48)

Thus, in *Tuhami* the translation, far from being a record in English of Real Reality, bears the 'tool-marks' (Tedlock 1983:331) of its construction and a feeling of disorientation, not reaching a single clear-cut reading of Tuhami's life. It is the unfinished outcome of a process of negotiation, in the manner proposed by Bachmann-Medick (forthcoming). *Tuhami* is a case where the style of the translated words themselves is almost consistently fluent and colloquial, but the structure of the book and its theoretical assumptions are 'foreignizing': they disrupt assumptions of full intelligibility between individuals, let alone between individuals from different language-cultures.

The potential of the dialogical mode

The dialogic approach has not been without its critics. If it potentially opens up the stage for conflict and disagreements on interpretation, it can also go the other way and bolster the 'fable of rapport' – the fiction of a speech situation where communication difficulties are "overcome or transcended, so that the recipient of the speech is also authenticated" (Murray 1991:126). The dialogue format in Dwyer's *Moroccan Dialogues*, for example, risks underplaying the conflict or misunderstanding between the dialogue partners with what Mannheim and Tedlock refer to as an "illusory leveling effect" (1995:19). At the very least, to claim a book is dialogical in the sense of being jointly produced is in the vast majority of cases an exaggeration. As Graham Watson complains about Dwyer's study, "It is an attempt to play chess with oneself, making the moves for both black and white pieces" (1991:85). In a more material sense, the writing and selling of the books is still the province of the translator, so that ultimately the division of labour persists – natives speak, ethnographers write (Van Maanen 1988:137) and the academic peace remains undisturbed by opposing voices. The examples of dialogism we've examined so far address the question of people's rights to be heard, but do not translate that concern into the material modalities of publishing the research.

Marcus and Cushman make the interesting point that reflexive and dialogical ethnography may in fact contribute to an assimilative effect. The reflexive ethnographer's account of the difficulties of his or her encounter with the strange prepares the ground for the reader's own experience, so that readers "slide into a receptivity for descriptions that could otherwise appear implausible to them" (1982:48). The reflexive style is subtler in this respect than early travel accounts, which explicitly warned the reader to be ready for some surprises, but the effect of carving out a space for the weird is similar. In this pessimistic account, reflexivity risks becoming a harmless standard requirement, restricted to comments on the conditions of the research and autobiographical components of the study and a token insertion of passages of first-person comment with highly edited 'other' voices. This kind of reflexivity risks deflecting the ethnography away from the power relations that bred the text and towards the primarily technical challenges of writing to postmodern specifications.

Yet the potential as a translation strategy is there. Reflexive approaches can turn attention to the processes of cross-cultural communication and of translation itself, and if interlingual translation has been much neglected in the genre, that doesn't mean it could not be brought into view. A reflexive translation practice might offer a route out of the relativist dilemmas of estranging or appropriating that were discussed in Chapter 3: instead of focusing on the other's degree of distance from the writer's own location, a reflexive translation could examine that location itself and the implications of the act of writing from it. Reflexivity accepts the perspectival nature of knowledge and that knowledge is therefore bound to change in transit between languages. To be sure, once we apply the concept of reflexivity to a context of literary translation, its major downside soon becomes apparent: such a translation may end up casting plenty of light on the translator but rather little on the translated, thus ultimately eliminating its own raison d'être. Accordingly, the criticism that reflexive ethnographies fail to engage with other cultures is the one most frequently and strongly made ("But enough about you," said the anthropologist's informant, "now let's talk about me"). Said, for example, accuses reflexive ethnography's textual orientation and epistemological ponderings of helping anthropology to "block out the clamor of voices on the outside asking for their claims about empire and domination to be considered" (1989:219).

Even so, within the terms of the discipline the dialogic and reflexive approach as an experimental form of representation has much to recommend it. It offers to disperse the translator's authority, lessening the concentration of power in the translator's hands. It emphasizes what Fabian (1983) calls coevalness, where both sides of the conversation are present and contribute to the experience (though, as Fabian later pointed out [1990], the fact of face-to-face dialogue is not necessarily reflected by 'dialogical' forms of writing). And it places the contingent aspect of conversations – governed by the practical, personal and political context of the moment – above typifying generalizations or scientistic certainties. As a result, translation and conversation no longer appear as a process of information being channelled from one person to the other, as "an objective act that in no way influenced the object's true significance, a significance that existed prior to the act of observing it" (Dwyer 1982:257). They move onto much more shifting ground, as a process of mutual constitution and alteration. This puts the metaphor of 'translation of culture' in a new light, since the dialogic account cannot hope to present 'a culture' as a firmly boundaried thing. In theory it could begin to draw out the competing interpretations, the ambiguities and disagreements, and the mutual attributions that make up the encounter between 'cultures' as represented by the ethnographer.

Quotation

Dialogical or not, all ethnographies depend on the words of other people, and Mannheim and Tedlock argue that the voices of those people, in the form of texts and transcripts gathered in the field, "should remain in play rather than being pushed into a silenced past" (1995:3). The ethnographies we have considered so far remained almost exclusively within the target language, but if the 'translation of culture' is approached in radically new ways, how does this affect the 'translation of language'? This section moves on to the translation issues raised by the use of quoted speech.

The representation of the 'native point of view' as the material of ethnography has been an anthropological article of faith since the early twentieth century. At first sight such a task could best be fulfilled by asking the 'native' to speak from his or her own 'point of view' and quoting the resulting words. That quotation may be more or less extensive, more or less source-language oriented, and more or less clearly bracketed off from the ethnographer's voice.

Quotations translated into the dominant language of the ethnography – in our case, academic Anthropo-English – inevitably ripple its monological surface to some extent. Unlike paraphrase, they highlight the fact that individual words were spoken in real time by real people, and they diffuse the power of definition by offering different versions in different speaking voices. This practice can challenge the illusion of perfect transparency, of facts unrolling before the observer, so that the visual mode (see Geertz 1988) is partly replaced by a more auditory one: we 'listen to' the native's point of view rather than having it shown to us. However, there are several problems associated with the translation of passages of speech in this way, as we will see.

Souvenirs

A self-respecting ethnography can hardly do without at least a handful of 'native words': individual lexical items that seem to be 'untranslatable' and offer the basis for sometimes quite extensive anthropological interpretation. Often they are listed in a glossary at the end of the book. Dennis Tedlock has described those native terms in the English text as souvenirs of the original encounter, giving evidence, "just as souvenirs do, that the person who now occupies the armchair was once in the field, talking to actual people in an actual far-off place" (Tedlock 1983:324). In Tedlock's view the inclusion of such words does not make their speakers present in the text but, on the contrary, only stresses the distance between the 'then' of conversation and the 'now' of writing – underpinning the 'denial of coevalness' in Fabian's sense. Marcus and Cushman, too, are sceptical. They argue that native terms are put to work in realist ethnographies as a balance to academic jargon, helping to bridge the theoretical gap between abstract generalization and the particularity of the culture under study. Temporarily abandoning jargon in favour of native terms and their explication "gives such writing a superficially even more realistic tone" (1982:35) since the analysis seems to be rooted firmly in the genuine words of the observed. This truncated form of quotation actually bolsters the illusion of immediacy under attack by the Writing Culture critics.

From this point of view, native terms play a mainly emblematic role in the translation, as a seal of authenticity and exoticism. But can source-language terms do anything more helpful in ethnographic representation? For one thing, they can call into question the adequacy of the target language to represent everything of the source language's reality; they stress the difficulty of the translation process. Writing about transliteration (the transfer of written notation into another writing system) and transcription (rendering stretches of spoken discourse in written form), Brinkley Messick notes the disruptive aspect of untranslated words:

> Compared with the total transformation wrought by translation across languages, the movements carried out by transcription and transliteration appear stalled or interrupted. The resulting fragments are betwixt and between, in a halfway stage of language, having neither completely departed from the reported language nor completely arrived in the reporting language. (Messick 2003:180)

Such snatches of the source language thus signal the translation's existence as a space of often conflictual encounter between languages (see Wolf 2002), preventing complacency about the ease of comprehension. This is in part how Lutz uses source-language terms in the study discussed in Chapter 3. She also relies on transferring terms with long contextualization as a way of achieving greater 'accuracy' in her translation, a method with a long history. It is used, among others, by Evans-Pritchard in *The Nuer*. He tells us that the word *cieng* cannot be translated with the single word 'home', because its meaning is as a relative concept (i.e., home always in relation to some larger, less-home, entity than the place the person happens to be at that moment; Evans-Pritchard explains the permutations at length). The variability of the word *cieng*, says Evans-Pritchard, is "not due to the inconsistencies of language, but to the relativity of the group-values to which it refers" (1940:136). Here, the translation problem is secondary to the value of the untranslatable term in illustrating the ethnographer's theoretical claim about the "structural relativity" (ibid:135) of terms.

In Lutz's ethnography, the source-language terms take centre stage, as if they were to be introduced into the target discourse – indeed, entry into the receiving language is one function that transferred terms can fulfil in general, perhaps especially journalistic, translation. More common, though, is a supporting role for native terms, given an explanation at their first occurrence in a footnote or at best in the text body, then left to fend for themselves. Such non-English terms are usually set off in italics to remind us that they are qualitatively different from the language of the narrating ethnographer, which subsumes into paraphrase most of what was said.

Paraphrase versus quotation

In a paraphrase style like Evans-Pritchard's, what was originally said in Dinka or French or Nahuatl is absorbed into the flow of English without any indication of who said what and to whom, under what circumstances; the referential content and the translator's interpretation are important, not the precise texture of the speech. Mannheim and Tedlock put it more strongly, noting that the British functionalist tradition "tended to treat the utterances of natives as falsehoods and illusions concealing truths that could be revealed only by anthropologists" (1995:5). The privileging of the target discourse by absorbing all words into it is what Dwyer tries to defy when he makes such extensive use of translated quotation – we will see later in this chapter that Ruth Behar (1993) takes a similar line though in a different form. By quoting their interviewees, dialogically minded anthropologists try to draw into the text the fact that the other person was *speaking* – as opposed to simply 'being' – and also that she or he was speaking *to*. Quotation is thus an automatic insertion of dialogism in the sense that Mannheim and Tedlock propound, although it by no means automatically represents the reciprocal nature of meaning-making in conversation, especially if it is set out as a formalized interview in a fiction of coherence and chronology. But the personal aspect of named quotation is important: according to Trouillot (1991:40) a focus on the first-person voice is preferable to the use of anonymous or generalized composite speakers who in classical ethnography were required to fill the "savage slot", a category produced in advance by the receiving culture to contain discourse by (or better still, about) the other. In theory, once the other is situated historically as a named speaking voice, the self, too, should lose some of its aura of timeless neutrality.

Quoting in English thus breaks up the synthesized, objectifying voice, but paradoxically it also creates a new synthesis by merging the original conversation – held in the source language or, just as likely, in a mixture of languages with the help of one or more interpreters – into a single target language. The shape of the language used for such quotation has already been discussed in Chapter 3, along with the dilemma of how far to domesticate the words of the other speaker. The translator of quoted language can present an exoticized picture or might choose to follow Dryden's lead, having the informant speak "such English as he would himself have spoken, if he had been born in England, and in this present age" (1697/1997:174) – as Van Maanen puts it, making the natives sound "like quite ordinary well-spoken chaps" (1988:70). But aside from the foreignizing/domesticating spectrum, there is another aspect of translating quoted material which overlaps with the concerns of literary translation: the representation of mixed language or 'heteroglossia' in translated discourse.

Heteroglossia

Bakhtin's notion of heteroglossia (*raznorečie*), formulated in the context of fictional narrative, starts from the basis that there is no such thing as 'a' language. Rather, 'national languages' are made up of constantly changing and conflictual strata, re-constellated in every utterance according to the specific social, historical and individual situation of the speakers at that moment. Bakhtin sketches the internal stratification of languages as including "social dialects, characteristic group behavior, professional jargons, generic languages, languages of generations and age groups, tendentious languages, languages of the authorities, of various circles and of passing fashions, languages that serve the specific sociopolitical purposes of the day, even of the hour" as well as traces of different national languages (1981:263). The list is, of course, not exhaustive. If a translation were to aim for 'accurate' representation, it would have to attempt to distinguish all these speech styles (along with the layers of voice which I will come to in a moment) – clearly a tall order, and especially so for ethnographic translators, who in many cases are language learners of only a few years' standing. Yet if there is no indication at all of any plurality of language in translated quotations, the reader will be left with a one-dimensional view of the words which were spoken.

The dilemma already arises in literary texts which present themselves as monolingual and non-translated. Writers trying to represent the speech of marginalized characters confront the twin risks of assimilating them into the dominant variety or creating stereotyped, even insulting versions (see Toolan 1992). These may involve 'eye dialect', the difference-flag that uses non-standard orthography as an emblem of non-standard language even if, once sounded out, the word proves phonetically identical to the dominant variety – spellings like 'woz' for 'was', for instance. Eye dialect is a form of translationese without translation, but in the case of interlingual transfer the difficulty of representing heteroglossia is intensified, since differences are all too easily flattened out in the receiving language, or else swallowed up by 'equivalent' distinctions within the receiving discourse (something that Antoine Berman, for example, decries: "An exoticization that turns the foreign from abroad into the foreign at home winds up merely ridiculing the original"; 2000:294).

If there is a plurality of styles and languages within each stretch of quoted speech (and Bakhtin argues that far more of speech is 'quoted' than we like to pretend), then an ethnography is a miniature world of plural voices. We saw in Chapter 4 that the 'classical' ethnographic style repressed this plurality as much as possible – in other words, not entirely – by the use of a highly authoritative narrating voice which overruled the text's other participants. Experimental ethnographies have tried to re-introduce plurality precisely through quotation – a device which seems to give the other a direct voice and achieve 'polyphony', a co-existence of different voices competing in the text. Clifford, although sceptical about the reach of quotation in achieving polyphony, cites with approval a series of texts that re-trace the steps of collection, discussion, editing and translation behind a famous ethnography by James Walker, *The Sun Dance* (1917; see Walker 1980). The four volumes edited by DeMallie and Jahner "in effect reopen the textual homogeneity" of Walker's monograph by presenting the words of other authorities, Walker's private notes, the writings of his interpreter Thomas Tyon and many other sources. Clifford calls the result a "polyphonic exposition" (1988:53) which undermines the monophonic fluency of the classical ethnographic style.

More subtle and difficult to pin down is the extent to which the words of source-language speakers seep into those of the translator – whether as forms of indirect speech (often veiled, like Radcliffe-Brown's) or as traces of the other language ('interference' or calque) – and create a language of translation 'worked on' by the source (Pannwitz, cited in Benjamin 2000). The norm of fluent or inconspicuous translation attempts to disguise the extra languages that translation adds to the heteroglossic mix. This duplicity is what moves Sturrock to argue for styles that highlight translatedness itself. He quotes a passage from a Hemingway novel which uses grammatical calque to characterize the dialogue as having been translated from Spanish:

> "To me, now, the most important is that we be not disturbed here," Pablo said. "To me, now, my duty is to those who are with me and to myself." – "Thyself. Yes." Anselmo said. (*For Whom the Bell Tolls*, cited by Sturrock 1990:1013)

Through his extreme "translationese", miming a literal or through-translation of Spanish into English, Hemingway insists that the fictional dialogue he gives in English was 'actually' held in Spanish. The resulting hybrid of Spanish and English is presented as a mere convenience to eavesdropping on the real thing; a somewhat similar, though much less dramatic, version of this device is used by Ruth Behar in the ethnography we will look at later in this chapter.

Finally, translation complicates the issue of ethnographic quotation because of its own vacillating position between speaking in its own and someone else's name. A translator's voice can be regarded as a form of indirect discourse, 'reporting' what someone else has said rather than being the unambiguous subject of the words:

> the translator, in re-enacting another utterance, does not speak in his or her name only, which results in translations possessing a hybrid discursive subject, somewhat like direct or indirect quotation. (Hermans 1999:142)

As Deborah Tannen (1995) points out in a study of fictitious or highly adapted 'direct speech' in everyday conversation, the reporting of speech reinforces the absence of the person said to have said the reported words. In her example, a criticism of you by your mother, reported to you by your sister, can only happen on the basis that your mother isn't present at the scene of the reporting (and on the basis that you weren't present at the original scene, if there was one, of the criticism). As the words travel into different conversational constellations, not only their form but their meaning and impact may change almost beyond recognition.

From this perspective, it is difficult to claim that translated quotation in an ethnography can remain sealed off from the 'quoted-ness' of the rest of the text. There cannot really be a watertight distinction between authorial comment and authentic quotation, for each of the levels is hybrid and the distinction between them porous. It is this dissolving effect of translation which partly informs Bachmann-Medick's call for the concept of translation to be instated as a replacement for traditional notions of individual, bordered and impermeable 'cultures' (forthcoming; see also Bhabha 1994).

Bilingual quotation

So far we have discussed only quotation in English, perhaps fortified with individual source-language terms. Another option is to quote in the source language, with the English translation normally in parallel format, in an interlinear two-line or three-line pattern, or separately before or after the source-language material. In all formats, practical problems of transcription immediately arise.

In Chapter 2 we saw that the 'translation of cultures' in the wider sense has to produce its source 'text' before it can translate, but it would be a mistake to think that this problem does not apply to work with recorded interviews or other verbalized material. True, such material is expressed in sequences of words, unlike the infinitely more complicated and probably non-existent 'culture-as-text' – but those words are spoken and not written, so that they have to undergo serious transformation before becoming a source for interlingual translation. The problem is addressed in detail by Dennis Tedlock in *The Spoken Word and the Work of Interpretation* (1983). We will consider his recommendations for transcribing verbal art in the next chapter, but some key issues apply to transcription in general, such as the importance of pauses, amplitude, different voices, gestures and signals of assent or disapproval by other participants in the conversation.

As Tedlock notes, changing technology – in particular the advent of the tape recorder – has altered the conditions of translating from the spoken word to the page. Now not 'only' the words but also their delivery can be recorded, "freeing the ear" (1983:3) for the music of the language and improving both the written transcription's accuracy (it can now be refined at leisure) and its accountability (because a far fuller version of the source text is now available to other listeners at other times, enabling later re-interpretation). The risky one-off nature of the moment of hearing has been overcome and, though not transparent, the aural record of people's words seems significantly less limited than the exclusively written one, since it can cope with hesitations, interruptions and other components of real-life conversation. Video recording adds a further layer of sociolinguistic information to the record. However, none of these recording techniques in fact offers objective or transparent information, if only because speech takes place in almost incalculably dynamic, non-replicable contexts. The presence of recording equipment of any kind – and the presence of the ethnographer her- or himself – will, for example, always affect the process of a conversation. Tedlock recounts his experiences with different versions of stories told with and without a tape recorder. The machine brought in a whole history of contact and mutual image-making which the storyteller tried to take into account as he spoke (ibid:292). Clearly, audio recordings are an advance on dictation, but important elements of a communicative event, including the visual and tangible, do not lend themselves to audio recording and require careful notation.

Aside from strictly linguistic (or ethnography-of-speaking) approaches, ethnographic transcription in its published form is often far from fulfilling all the technical strictures set out by fieldwork handbooks. Van Maanen worries that experts in conversational analysis would throw up their hands in horror at the highly edited, "sanitized" records used in much dialogical anthropology (1988:70). Even setting aside the interlingual movement, the version of quotation presented by Dwyer or Crapanzano is evidently extremely stylized. The conversations that form the core of their books include virtually no hesitation, repetition, or stumbling, and very little reference to paralinguistic components such as changes in pitch or facial expressions. They are coherent and accessible, and arranged in the formats set out by the translators before (Dwyer) or after (Crapanzano) the fact. This is not an accusation of bad faith; after all, a complete transcription of such long and involved conversations would be readable only by the most highly trained and dogged of sociolinguists. However, it is important to remember that transcribed quotation is not of itself transparent or 'faithful' in its translation of oral to written discourse.

Additionally, the use of transcribed material alongside English translations often falls foul of material and disciplinary constraints. It involves elaborate typography and lots of space – space which might be considered wasted in view of the small number of readers who will actually read the transcribed material. When Billie Jean Isbell proposed long passages of Quechua and English parallel dialogue, including her own questions in the native language, the publisher warned her that for her book to qualify as a readable and academically acceptable ethnography, the bilingual text would have to be cut down to almost nothing (cited in Tedlock 1983:336).

These constraints help explain why bilingual is so much less common than monolingual quotation in ethnography. Nevertheless, there are enormous benefits to the parallel text approach. The inclusion of source-language passages makes accessible a further layer of content; it opens up the implied audience; it dilutes the translator's power by enabling different translations to be proposed; and it points out translatedness, making visible the presence of other languages in the fieldwork conversations.

In English-language literary translation traditions, the retention of the source text alongside the translation is a venerable method of presenting classical works, particularly those from Ancient Greek or Latin and particularly those in verse. Here, the presentation technique bows to the cultural value of the source texts, which are too sacred to be replaced by the translation and can only be supplemented. It establishes a hierarchy by making the English translation a reading assistance or 'crib' to the Actual Text, and as such it borders on ethnographic translation's claim to be interested less in the beauty of the English translation than in the authenticity of the source-language words. Apart from anything else, the parallel text allows the translation to pass back some of the responsibility for fullness of meaning onto the source text: you may not be able to read the heteroglossia, or the puns, or the rhyme in English, it seems to say, but have a look at the transcription and you'll see them undamaged, waiting to be discovered.

I will now look briefly at two examples of bilingual quotation in ethnographic texts, one a narration by a single speaker and one the record of part of an interview. In the first example, Jane Hill (1995) presents not a dialogue in the superficial, two-character sense of the word but a stretch of Mexicano narrative that includes embedded dialogue. Telling Hill about the death of his son, Don Gabriel incorporates multiple voices. Hill identifies thirteen different 'characters' whose speech is reported and five "self-laminations of Don Gabriel" (ibid:117), such as 'neutral narrator', 'evaluator' or 'father'. She adds two "intonational shadows" which colour the voices they appear with, and two languages, Spanish and Mexicano, which bring additional ideological dimensions to the speech. This is a sample of how Hill indicates the rich heterophony of Don Gabriel's narration (1995:103):

Episode 4.B

>Ōnictlahtla'nīto in īcu'ñado]$_{112\ O}$	When I went to ask his brother-
>ye 'nōn ōcatca	in-law,$_{112}$ the one who had been
presi'dente,]$_{113\ O}$ >in	president,]$_{113}$ his brother-in-
īcu'ñado.]$_{114\ O}$ (spits) que lo	law,]$_{114}$ it was the
'mismo quil a´yāmo huītz.]$_{115\ P,H}$	same, that he "hadn't come."]$_{115}$
Toz neh ōnicmalpen'sarōh	Then I didn't like him since]$_{116}$
como]$_{116\ N,P}$ ō'catca 'fuerte in ..	their uh .. politics used
in política den yeh-huān.]$_{117\ N,P}$	to be fierce.]$_{117}$
Niquihtoa "A lo 'mejor <xāmo	I say, "Most likely maybe
ōquinmā'gaqueh.]$_{118\ N,R}$ <īpan 'yoal	they beat him up.]$_{118}$ At night
ōquimispia'rōqueh.]$_{119\ R}$ A ´ver	they spied on him.]$_{119}$ Let's see
^{h}\tlen sudērihui.]$_{120\ R}$ ^{h}\Āquin	what happens.]$_{120}$ Who
nictlahtlanīz?"$_{121\ R}$	will I ask?"]$_{121}$

The numbers divide the text into clauses for reference, and the letters indicate the different narrative voices: of the twenty used in the ten-page, seventeen-minute passage, our excerpt contains the voice of the son's brother-in-law (H) and Don Gabriel speaking as N 'neutral narrator', O 'involved narrator', P 'evaluator' and R 'strategist' (his own 'inner voice'). The notation also indicates aspects of intonation and pitch (ibid:139-41). Hill's rich and detailed analysis of the narrative shows how Don Gabriel's uses of voice, along with his sophisticated combinations of Spanish and Mexicano, allow him to set his own moral position in the Mexicano-speaking community against the Spanish ideology of the marketplace (ibid:116). Though demanding to read, this transcription-translation shows its colours as an interpretation of the speaker's words and rhetorical strategies. It throws into relief the sheer density of potentially translatable information which faces anthropologists using transcribed and translated quotation.

Don Kulick's study of Brazilian transgendered prostitutes, or *travestis*, is another of the rather rare ethnographies which use extensive parallel quotation. Whereas Hill is interested in the use of language itself, as a human art and an articulation of criss-crossing ideological forces, Kulick focuses on members of a particular social group and the ways they view themselves and their lives. For him, the virtue of quotation is that it allows the actual words of the speakers to stand. This alters the balance of power, since the dominant mode of representing travestis in writing is a distanced and often contemptuous 'writing *about*'. Bilingual quotation also enables careful mining for the precise content and wording used by the speakers to identify themselves. In this excerpt, grammar as eroticized gendering is key to the conversation. Travesti Keila is explaining to the ethnographer her distaste for gay-identified male clients (*mariconas*):

> Keila spelled out the problem in detail. When the travesti is penetrating a client,

Keila: Eles dizem "Ah eu sou gostosa! Diga que eu sou gostosa. […]	**K**: They say, "Ah, I'm *gostosa* ["delicious and sexy" with the feminine grammatical ending *-a*]! Say I'm *gostosa*. […]
Don: Mais elas … as mariconas mesmo falam/	**D**: But they… the mariconas themselves say/
Keila: "Gostosa."	**K**: "Gostosa."
Don: "Gostosa"?	**D**: "Gostosa"?
Keila: Falam, falam.	**K**: They say it, they say it.
Don: "Gostoso" não.	**D**: Not "gostoso" ["delicious and sexy" with the masculine grammatical ending *-o*].
Keila: Não. "Gostosa." É "gostosa." Ela tá se sentindo mulher enquanto eu tou comendo ela. Então, ela tem que se sentir mulher, ela tem que usar o termo feminino. Elas dizem.	**K**: No. "Gostosa." It's "gostosa." She [the client] is feeling like a woman when I'm penetrating her. So she's feeling like a woman and so she's using the feminine term. They say that.

(Kulick 1998:162-3; Kulick's brackets). The use of grammatical gender is an important part of Kulick's argument that for the travestis, gender is changeable and takes shape through sexual practices. If he had reduced the interview to English only, we would have seen his interpretation, with its strong highlight on the adjective use, but not the way that Keila switches gender with confidence (from *eles*, masculine plural, to *elas*, feminine plural) or the conversational flow of what she says. And for an ethnographer not interested in gender, the use of adjective endings in this way might have disappeared entirely in English translation. Because the source-language form is given, alternative interpretations by the reader are not ruled out, and the same goes for Hill's work with its interest in narrative: the bilingual solution allows the material to be read through different prisms, of which the translation offered is only one.

The retention of the transcribed material alongside its translation thus involves a significant change in the balance of power between the translator, the source-language speaker, and the target-language reader. In the classic synthesizing approach, all discourse flowed through the translator's unifying voice, with the speakers reduced to a faraway, anonymized data source and the readers forced to take the translator's interpretations more or less as given – in Clifford's terms, an unbroken "ethnographic authority" (1988). By including untranslated material, Kulick and Hill in their different ways reduce that authority: they enable different readers to read from different perspectives and try to preserve the specific voice of the other speaker in the conversation. In Kulick's case, this means making visible the two-way nature of such discussions by including his own contributions, an important aspect of 'dialogic anthropology'. The format highlights translatedness, confronting the reader with the fact that the ethnographer is an active mediator as opposed to solely a representative of the receiving culture; he is not based fully in the target language but has 'gone over to the other side' for the purposes of the conversation. The quoted dialogue gives visible shape to the ambivalent identification of the ethnographer-translator instead of hiding it in the folds of the target language. Bilingual quotation thus cracks open the monological façade of the ethnography far more effectively than can an English-only representation like Dwyer's.

If the use of transcribed quotation makes the process of translation visible, it also heightens the visibility of the source text. Rather than replacing the source-language words, Anthropological English here supplements them in the form of a guide to reading, not of an adequate interpretation. This lends the source texts an aura of sacredness or authority which we have seen in the European tradition for the most canonized classical texts. It is also a method widely used since the nineteenth century by Americanist ethnography, as we will see in Chapter 6.

The translator as orchestrator

So far, so positive for the use of quotation. It brings in other voices and reduces the absolutist power of traditional ethnographic authority, and seems to promise a high degree of authenticity. However, Tedlock insists that quotation is in fact just as artificial as the synthesizing style:

> A paraphrase [...] is one kind of artifact, and a re-created quotation is another, but I don't see that the one kind of "material" is more highly processed than the other. What I do see is a misplaced concreteness, a concreteness that has its roots in the mechanical reproduction of discourse by means of printing. In effect, ethnographers approach the quotation of spoken words as if they were citing a written source – or, better, as if they were citing a native who was citing a written source. (Tedlock 1995:279)

In other words, quotation may be used as if it were a fixed accredited source waiting to be opened by the ethnographer; in fact, quoted discourse is unfixable because spoken in a specific, fleeting moment, and it is artificial because it draws its meaning in the text from the translator's decisions in editing, selecting, translating and framing the words. Nor, evidently, can there be a single most representative selection from the vast amounts of data which flow around the listening ethnographer, captured or not on tape and in notes. To be sure, it is not only the ethnographer who determines the selection process: Mannheim and Tedlock note that the observed are not powerless dupes but contribute their own notions of what is important or otherwise suitable for the ethnographer to know (1995:14). Picking one, or a few, voices to quote may clash with representations desired by other participants in the language community concerned, and the outcome of such conflicts is not always visible in the finished translation.

When quotation is used merely to illustrate the arguments made by the dominant ethnographic voice, it may act as authentification for the realist mode by seeming to contribute hard evidence from outside the text – more convincing than the exclusively paraphrasing style, yet not disrupting the logic of the univocal text. Even when quotation is used extensively and centrally, the passages for quotation are always chosen, condensed and arranged by the ethnographer in pursuit of a particular narrative or interpretive purpose. Dwyer, too, despite his claim to present 'unabridged' quotation, is clearly arranging his material into a particular dramatic structure. Come to that, he cannot avoid producing particular interpretations by the way he frames the quotations. As Bakhtin argues, quoted speech is inevitably changed by its framing in a new context:

> Another's discourse, when introduced into a speech context, enters the speech that frames it not in a mechanical bond but in a chemical union (on the semantic and emotionally expressive level); the degree of dialogized influence, one on the other, can be enormous. (1981:340)

It should be added that Bakhtin's implication of a two-way influence does not take account of the material circumstances of editing ethnographic quotation. In all our examples so far, it has been only, or at least very largely, one partner in the dialogue who holds the reins regarding deletion, footnotes, caveats, organization and interpretations (see Marcus & Cushman 1982:44).

Authorship and copyright

Because translation always involves selection at some stage, perhaps all translation could be seen as an editing of other people's realities into the terms of the receiving culture. In the case of ethnographic translation the use of quotation is subject to particularly severe constraints, since the finished text aims to find a place inside a discipline where the voice of the 'native' needs to be subordinated to that of the academic. After all, the task of interpretation is the ethnographer's claim to her place in the profession, and ceding it to the other speaker entails the danger of losing authorship.

This raises an important question: if Thomas Mann is the author of a novel in an English that's written by Helen Lowe Porter, then who is the author of *Nisa*? Ioan Lewis calls ethnographers "plagiarists, *bricoleurs*, living parasitically upon our ethnographic sources" (1973:11) and dependent for legitimacy on the 'evidence' of what other people do and say. Yet the other people appear only secondarily in even the most careful of critical ethnographies, and certainly have no statutory right to royalties on their contribution to the finished text.

There is a clash here between critical ethnography's wish to break up objectifying representation and the insistent claims of the academic institution. Whereas the interpreter in Radcliffe-Brown's *The Andaman Islanders* was entirely anonymous (see Figure 1), speakers in the 'experimental' works of the 1970s and beyond are more likely to be personalized and named, but pseudonymized for reasons of confidentiality. The prefaces of oral-literature-based ethnographies like those described in Chapter 6 list the performers and, more rarely, the translators and co-translators who put their words into English. And in texts like Shostak (1981), Crapanzano (1980) or Behar (1993), the speaker's name (or pseudonym) takes a place in the title of the translation of their words. However, those speakers do not therefore become the 'authors' of their own life stories. Instead, it is the American anthropologist in each case who claims both authorship and copyright. Dwyer notes that his partner in dialogue and the joint author of the book "himself was illiterate and never would read it" (1982:177), and Ruth Behar discusses a similar problem, as we will see later in this chapter. Compare this situation with the distribution of power and money between translator and author when the sending and receiving cultures stand in more symmetrical relations of power: then, as Lori Chamberlain (1988/2000) has shown, the translator appears as the feminized servant of the original. Here, in contrast, the translator of Nisa's words is also her author.

Plural or collaborative authorship is the "utopia" proposed by Clifford (1988:51), but he concludes that it remains a dream because in practice the project will be initiated and the authoritative version closed by the ethnographer. In fact, "the very idea of plural authorship challenges a deep Western identification of any text's order with the intention of a single author", a real constraint which, however, he considers to be under threat: "anthropologists will increasingly have to share their texts, and sometimes their title pages, with those indigenous collaborators for whom the term informants is no longer adequate, if it ever was" (ibid). This is an aspect of ethnographic translation taken up in the area of oral literature, as we will see in the following chapter, and it will also prove relevant for the case of museum representations.

Quotation, to conclude, is not as innocent as it may first appear. It doesn't offer a non-interventionist role for the ethnographer-translator – if only because, translation scholars might say, non-interventionist roles for translators simply don't exist.

Thick translation

To be a form of ethnographic translation, as opposed to transcription alone, quotation requires commentary and contextualization. It is the translator who has to decide on the amount of background information needed to 'make sense' of quoted language. How much cultural context must the ethnographer add to the words of the other person – how 'thick', in other words, does ethnographic translation have to be?

'Thick translation' is Kwame Anthony Appiah's (1993) adaptation of the term 'thick description' propounded by Clifford Geertz in the opening essay of *The Interpretation of Cultures* (1973). Geertz assumes that each detail of a person's thought and action is embedded in hugely complex realms of cultural meaning; each detail is worth studying, and each detail is important in order to understand other details and the contextual whole. If such complexity is difficult to interpret, it is also difficult to convey in the linear and skimpy medium of the written word. Appiah's 'thick translation' is a response to this difficulty as it affects the translation of African oral literature. He calls for literary translation to address head-on the extreme compaction of meaning in literary and cultural texts, by using extensive annotations and glosses "to locate the text in a rich cultural and linguistic context" (1993:817). Appiah aims to promote less reductive readings of non-Western literature by calling attention to the different sets of conventions and intentions which produced the source-language words. Ibrahim Muhawi, in a thought-provoking application of Geertzian approaches to the translation of literary performance, points out that Appiah's thick translation differs from Geertz's thick description in being compelled to separate out the annotation and interpretive extras from the text itself, because "in translating, we are not speaking in our own but in a 'borrowed' voice which is ours and someone else's at the same time" (2006:370). This makes it necessary to distinguish the translator's contribution from the first speaker's, whereas the Geertzian 'translator of culture' offers a package combining context and text, without sharply distinguishing between the words of the 'natives' and those of the interpreter. Thick description thus synthesizes the participants into a single voice, and Tedlock complains that by eliminating quotation from the multiplicity of information, Geertz tries "to construct an exhaustive argument while hiding the previous discourses on which that argument is based" (1983:337). In this respect Appiah's separation of text and context is useful in making proper acknowledgement of the differences between the voices contributing to the translation – though it is important to remember that the written-down 'source texts' are not untouched originals but themselves the products of textualizers following particular methods and agendas.

Appiah talks about literary translation for use in teaching, but the notion of 'thick translation' seems productive for other areas of writing too. At the very least it reveals the overlap between ethnographic writing and some forms of literary translation. Thus, Geertz's and Appiah's examinations of the amount of shared knowledge underlying communicative exchanges bring to mind Maria Tymoczko's comments on the metonymics of translation (1999). Because texts depend on hinterlands of shared meaning (what Appiah calls "mutual knowledge") too large to be reconstructed, translators have to privilege some aspects over others. As a result, "certain aspects or attributes of the source text come to represent the entire source text in translation. By definition, therefore, translation is metonymic: it is a form of representation in which parts or aspects of the source text come to stand for the whole" (1999:55). The new version, in turn, is metonymic of the new cultural location, and takes on a subsequent life or lives of its own.

It is worth looking briefly at the overlap between literary and ethnographic translation in this respect. Geertz complains that whereas a literary critic can assume shared knowledge with her or his readers, "this is usually not the case for the anthropologist, who is faced with the unattractive choice of boring his audience with a great deal of exotic information or attempting to make his argument in an empirical vacuum" (1983:36). The amount of 'background information' needed for thick translation is potentially vast, and ethnographers are forced to set borders to the meaning-hinterland where none present themselves 'naturally'. Taken to its logical conclusion, thick description would demand a never-ending chain of explanation back and back until some human universals are finally reached where no further comment is required or else the paper runs out. But concision has virtues other than the obvious environmental ones. When used as an aesthetic device, it causes notorious headaches for literary translators. Discussing the difficulty of translating a highly compressed Irish poem, Tymoczko echoes Geertz: "to explain the cultural material is to destroy the genre, but to preserve the genre is to leave the audience ignorant about the cultural specifics" (1999:52). In ethnographic translation the generic constraint may seem less pressing, yet many non-literary speech genres also depend on concision; bulky, rambling paraphrases lead the reader far, far away from the experience of the original listeners to the words. As a result, contextualized ethnographic writing can offer a plethora of insights but not the source listener's vantage point, the "native's point of view" (see Geertz 1983). For the original participant in a conversation or performance, things may have been relatively immediate and obvious, or they may have been valuable precisely in their lack of straightforwardness, asking not to be explained. The common experience of trying to explain a joke in another language hints at the kind of problem at stake here, one which redoubles in force when ethnographers study explicitly aesthetic production, as Chapter 6 will show.

There are, then, practical restrictions on contextualization. Moreover, to contextualize means to lose the impact and immediacy of the speech being represented, and with it one of the key functions of direct speech in conversation, its dramatic force (see Tannen 1995). Inseparable from these problems is a more fundamental issue relating to the notion of 'context' itself and taken up in detail by both anthropologists and linguists: context is not a given, something that can be reified as existing independently from text. As linguists Duranti and Goodwin note in the introduction to their 1992 collection, recent work has shown that context is not "a set of variables that statically surround strips of talk"; instead, "context and talk are now argued to stand in a mutually reflexive relationship to each other, with talk, and the interpretive work it generates, shaping context as much as context shapes talk" (1992:31). Quotation and contextualization are thus fully interdependent, like the dialogical relationship between the interpreter and the interpreted as defined by Tedlock and Mannheim (1995) and Fabian (1990).

Contextualization is part and parcel of anthropology's anti-universalizing stance, which insists that different sets of meanings are possible and are valid from within the perspective of their users (Dilley 1999:25). It is no coincidence that Malinowski's early and very influential exposition of 'context' as an ethnographic principle took the form of a meditation on the difficulties of translation. Translation is made more difficult by relativism, and contexts are the stuff of relativist understandings: "contexts are sets of connections construed as relevant to someone, to something or to a particular problem, and this process yields an explanation, a sense, an interpretation for the object so connected" (Dilley 1999:2). When he defines contexts as specific sets of connections, Dilley stresses that to determine relevant connections is also to determine which of the potential connections around an object are irrelevant, unconnected, non-context. Contexts are thus patterns of exclusion, ways of ordering knowledge – not, positivistically, existing objects which can themselves be known. As a result, asking how much context to include is really a theoretical question on what is to count as relevant in a particular case, and contextualization is itself interpretation. At the same time, Dilley points out that not only is there no limit to the potential construals of context, but the process of contextualization is limitless, since each definition of context can itself be contextualized within a new context (a reflexive commentary on the context of interpretation, for example, or a confrontation of the anthropologist's contextualizations with those of the people being studied). The process "is open to infinite regression" (ibid:22).

Adding context in 'thick translation' is therefore very much a theorizing or interpretative – a translating – move. In order to make that move more accountable, Dilley argues that anthropological 'translations' must include an awareness of the theorizer's own frames of reference, acknowledgement of the power relations that inform contextualization as a social practice, and entry into dialogue with native frames of reference (ibid:37-9). These latter requirements suggest that if contextualization is part of the fabrication by the writer and arises out of talk, then thick translation ought to include specific attention to such talk – conversation with the people being described and also conversation in a wider sense with the institutions and genres that informed the translator's work.

Translation as exegesis

I want now to look at two examples of ethnographic 'thick translations', the first of which uses an exegetical style of description focusing on the layered nature of interpretation in an oral genre. Karin Barber's *I Could Speak Until Tomorrow* examines Yoruba *oriki* in the Nigerian town of Okuku. Oriki are "a genre of Yoruba oral poetry that could be described as attributions or appellations: collections of epithets, pithy or elaborated, which are addressed to a subject" (1991:1). Barber chooses this literary genre as a means of studying the town of Okuku because the poems both influence the town's life and reflect upon it (ibid:2-3). 'Condensations' of the experience of the townspeople and their forebears, the oriki that Barber listened to generated long commentaries by their performers. Oriki call out for completion by the listener's contextual knowledge: as S.A. Babalola puts it, they "are full of 'half-words'; words that you say to a sensible or knowledgeable person, and when they get inside him or her, they become whole" (cited in Barber 1991:19). For the translator, the exegesis of the oriki is an attempt to produce some echo of this wholeness in the mind of the un-knowledgeable target-language reader. In this undertaking, Barber takes her cue from interpretative practices of the Okuku townswomen. They 'translated' their poems for Barber using techniques of "etymology, etiology, personal memory, and something like riddling" (ibid:4), a procedure applied by Barber in a book-length analysis which, although it does not necessarily avoid anthropological categories, closely follows the paths dictated by the texts (presented in Yoruba and English) and their detailed exposition by Okuku women. Thus the book is not divided into text and context, but is organized throughout as networks of explanation of particular oriki, a term which itself can be used in Yoruba to translate the English word 'definition' (ibid:12). In this respect, *I Could Talk Until Tomorrow* resembles Lutz's exploration of Ifaluk emotion terminology, but Barber's focus on a finely wrought literary genre and indigenous traditions of literary interpretation moves the strategy further onto the ground of translation practices in the source-language tradition.

As a translation of Yoruba oriki, Barber's study seems to follow closely Appiah's notion of thick translation. There is a snag, though: the *genre* of Barber's work, identifying itself as ethnographic and not literary translation, in practice relegates the aesthetic dimension to the background, even while the *content* of the study makes it central. Institutionally, in other words, *I Could Talk Until Tomorrow* does not function as a literary translation – the very effect which Appiah is after when he deliberately lines up his proposed source texts with canonized or 'classic' literature in the university curriculum.

My second example makes no claims to literariness and thus falls outside Appiah's scope. It is interesting, though, in its technical innovation as a new form of heavily annotated textual translation. Discussing textual commentary as a genre of ethnographic description, Johannes Fabian argues for a form evoking medieval European translation methods, which accompanied close translation of a sacred original by extensive notes. By this means the original was left relatively untouched, while the contemporary potential could be drawn out and interpreted by bold translators (2002:777; see also Ellis 1989).

In Fabian's commentary approach, layers of interpretation are added to a source text using the technology of Web-based archives. His translation of a history entitled "Vocabulaire de ville de Elisabethville", available online in the Archive of Popular Swahili at www2.fmg.uva.nl/lpca, includes a facsimile of a 1966 typescript by André Yav and the transcription of a spoken-aloud version in Shaba Swahili (the 'reoralized' version, as Fabian calls it) accompanied by Fabian's English translation in parallel text with footnotes. Another layer transcribes and translates the conversations with Fabian's co-translator, Kalundi

Mango. The sample below, the beginning of the first conversation between the two translators, shows how this method keeps visible the interaction between them as well as the heterogeneity of their speech:

F: sawa uliisha kusome hii vocabulaire: wa: mawazo yako unaona namna gani? ni document ya namna gani? mbele: luga: donc: kinywa: Swahili/ hii Swahili: ni Swahili ya hapa? **K:** ii Swahili: iko ya hapa: mais iko Swahili ya kiLamba/ **F:** ya kiLamba? **L:** oui parce que banamêlermêler ovyo: haina Swahili kabisa/ **F:** mm/ **K:** haina Swahili kama ya waSwahili/ **F:** eeh/ **K:** voilà/ eko bisSwahili: c'est une langue véhiculaire/ **F:** véhic: d'accord/ **K:** oui/ **F:** d'accord/ na tena nili: niliona kama mara ingine ulikuwa na magumo ya kusoma/ juu ya nini? **K:** ni pale nalikuwa kusoma: parce-que: iko kiSwahili mubaya/ **F:** mm/... **K:** ...?... **F:** mubaya namna gani? kwa mufano/ **K:** kwa mufano: ni kiSwahili: haina kiSwahili kabisa/ mi niko muntu wa Tanganyika/ **F:** mm/ **K:** niko na kiSwahili ya ule mule yangu ingine/	**F:** Now that you have read the Vocabulaire aloud, what do you think about it and how do you see it? What kind of document is it? To begin with the language, Swahili. This sort of Swahili is this the Swahili [spoken] here? **K:** This Swahili is the local kind, but it is a Swahili [that comes] from the Lamba language. **F:** From Lamba? **K:** Yes, because they just mix [languages]; this is not really Swahili. **F:** Mm-hmm. **K:** It is not the Swahili of the Swahili people. **F:** I see. **K:** You see, there are different kinds of Swahili; this one is a vehicular language. **F:** Vehicular, right. **K:** Yes. **F:** Also, I noticed that sometimes you had problems with the reading. How come? **K:** That happened when I read [aloud]. [It is] because this is bad Swahili. **F:** Mm-hmm. **K:** ...?... **F:** Bad in what way? For instance? **K:** For instance – this is a kind of Swahili that is not really Swahili. I come from [Lake] Tanganyika. **F:** Mm-hmm. **K:** My Swahili comes from there and it is different.

(www2.fmg.uva.nl/lpca/aps/index.html)

Along with the commentary on the co-translator's comments, this record goes some way to uncovering the nuts and bolts of ethnographic knowledge-gathering and writing (Fabian 2002:779). It highlights the medium of the source text, historically and socially situated forms of Swahili with traces of French, and the presence of those fractures in the source language as both medium and topic of the experts' readings. The presence of the co-translator Kalundi is asserted, as a reminder of the dialogical nature of the ethnographic work and a detailed acknowledgement of the way the English "Vocabulaire" came into being. As for the transcription, it is itself both an item in the linguistic archive and a document of the translation processes – the processes that had to happen before the Swahili conversation arrived in its relatively smooth, neat and accessible English version. The parallel text also seems to appeal for contestation and new interpretations along the same or perhaps quite different lines of inquiry.

By suggesting the multiplicity of participants in the making of the translation, this strategy counters the essentialization of texts and cultures that was criticized in the Writing Culture debate. Fabian warns of a danger that his medieval-style commentary approach could succumb to the "textual fundamentalism" (ibid:779) which in language-oriented ethnography contrasts fallible commentator with infallible, immovably original text. The texts that anthropology uses as source material are, Fabian reminds us, not simply 'there'; they have to be produced for consumption before they can gain their authority. However, he hopes that the medium of the Internet can offset the risk of textual essentialism by drawing explicit attention to the tasks that have to be carried out before the 'text' reaches its readers – virtual or otherwise.

A potentially useful aspect of the layering translation proposed by Fabian is its capacity to represent the instability of context, where figure and ground can switch places so that context becomes object and object context (see Dilley 1999:28), text becomes commentary and commentary text. It's still limited and selected, to be sure, but provides more transparency than if we read the English "Vocabulaire" alone, or even than if we read the English version of the expert's interpretations without their source text. Layering draws attention to the specificity of the commentator, in Fabian's case by counterpointing different perspectives on the source and attitudes to the task of translating it. In this respect the layered, thick translation is reflexive and comments on itself as well as on the translated text – the act of translation is not repressed and the agency of speaker, translator and their sponsoring communities come to the fore. Rather than searching for polyphonic techniques within one version of the translated text, this form of 'thick translation' offers juxtaposition as its key device to resist assimilatory effects.

Both Barber and Fabian work with written texts as opposed to cultures-as-texts in their commentary-style translations, and we will look at further experiments in this vein later on. The question remains open whether similar methods can be applied to cultural description on a larger scale, or whether the notion of exegetical, 'thick' translation inevitably denounces synthesis and generalization in favour of small-scale studies and modest knowledge-claims. For now, however, I would like to turn to a different issue. If quotation replaces synthesizing translation-of-culture as the ethnographer's task, the distance between observer and observed will shrink. In the next section we see what happens when that distance and its collapse are brought to the centre of attention, in 'ethnography at home'.

Ethnography at home

The growth of close-to-home ethnography in the West is a relatively new development, disturbing the conventional distinction between 'anthropology' (object: exotic other societies) and 'sociology' (object: our own society) and pushed forward in the 1960s by Chicago School sociologists studying urban American life. Many such studies have described 'domestic others' – ethnic minorities, poor communities, youngsters – and American anthropology has been accused of ethnicizing these groups, treating them "as so many isolated and exotic tribes" (Ortner 1991:166), but work is also being done, if hesitantly, on Western anthropology's own academic 'tribes'. At the same time, 'ethnography at home' covers the work being done by indigenous scholars in the regions once the preferred hunting grounds of European and American anthropology.

At first sight, ethnography at home seems to avoid the dilemmas of translation in two respects. For one thing, there is no language gap and thus no need for interlingual translation. Secondly, when an anthropologist belongs to the society being studied, there is no fundamental mismatch between the natives' own conceptual models of their lives and the analytical framework through which the ethnographer filters them to produce the final text. Marilyn Strathern presents the example of English villagers studied by English anthropologists: both sides share fundamental notions of 'relationships', 'roles' or 'community', and the anthropologist may appear to be "simply using these ideas in specialist ways" as opposed to rendering them into an exogenous language of explanation (1987:26).

No translation there, it seems. A second glance, though, reveals that the issues of translation we have discussed so far are not actually eliminated when the anthropologist speaks 'the same' language as the people being studied. All the complexities of transferring oral to written discourse apply when the transfer occurs within the same language, and if a visible distinction is made between the narrating authorial voice and the specimens of the other's speech then, on the page, the oral-written translation may look little different from an interlingual translation. Furthermore, Strathern's subtle essay goes on to greatly complicate her point about shared conceptual frameworks, noting that anthropology is a highly specific "genre of knowing" (1987:31) and produces accounts that will not be continuous with native accounts except within its own, very narrowest, originating context. There is, though, a still more pressing question: what do we mean by 'the same' language? Defining the edges of 'languages' is a notoriously tricky business, and differences of class or personal biography can mean researchers encountering an unexpected language gap. For example, a bicultural anthropologist who has previously spent only temporary spells in the place she wants to study might find that the linguistic competence acquired in childhood is insufficient to deal with adult interactions over a longer period. Or a strong sense of ethnic and political solidarity might not coincide with a shared language, so that the anthropologist has to speak to other members of her community in a language which either for her or for them is a second language or lingua franca.

This is the case in Barbara Myerhoff's absorbing study of elderly Jews at a cultural centre in Venice Beach, California (1978). The last of the first-generation immigrants from Eastern Europe, their mother tongue is Yiddish and it is Yiddish which largely defines their sense of home or belonging. Myerhoff belongs to their grandchildren's generation, and can only communicate with them in English. In most cases this is the medium of her data, spoken in the interviewees' second (at least) language and with quotations or narratives translated by them from Yiddish. Yet beyond the English–Yiddish difference there is a sense in which Myerhoff shares a language with the elderly people. She fits (though not always painlessly) into the categories of her informants' lives and their ways of thinking, and she identifies fully and explicitly with them, noting that she herself "will be a little old Jewish lady one day" (1978:19). The strong feeling of empathy that drives this ethnography gives rise to a moment of quite audacious ethnographic translation when Myerhoff puts words into the mouth of Shmuel, a man she feels particularly close to:

> I missed Shmuel often, never more than in the days after Jacob's death. There was so much I wanted to ask him. In my imagination, we conversed and argued, as was our custom after important Center occasions.
>
> "Shmuel, I can't help but feel somewhat sad that your death was so little noticed while Jacob's was given so much attention. You deserved more honor and gratitude."
>
> "Now you are talking like one of the bobbes," he answered. "Haven't you learned from me that one thing has nothing to do with the other? 'Az ikh vel zayn vi er, ver vet zayn vi ikh?' [If I would be like him, who would be like me?]." (ibid:227-8; Myerhoff's brackets)

This early example of a reflexive ethnography draws out the feeling of closeness that arose between 'self' and 'other'; the imaginary dialogue highlights the degree of inventedness of all quotation but also the personal identification which translation can involve.

In Myerhoff's case, social and ethnic identification with the studied does not imply identical language, so that translation still has to take place both in the ethnographic encounters and on the printed page. But the identification she describes is itself not without translated aspects, as Kirin Narayan makes clear in her discussion of what it means to be an 'insider' ethnographer or 'native anthropologist'. Narayan attacks the well-established "dichotomy between outsider/insider or observer/observed" among anthropologists:

> The loci along which we are aligned with or set apart from those whom we study are multiple and in flux. Factors such as education, gender, sexual orientation, class, race, or sheer duration of contacts may at different times outweigh the cultural identity we associate with insider or outsider status. (1997:23)

Narayan herself, with one Indian and one German-American parent, moves between categories in her daily life. However, in Narayan's analysis it is not just what Abu-Lughod (1991) calls 'halfie' anthropologists but all anthropologists who face the confusion of identity, since they belong both to their home communities and to the academic discipline – just as, we might add, translators are bound to belong to more than one language-culture at once. The collection *Women Writing Culture* shows how women anthropologists in the West have always been simultaneously an observer-'self' in the field and an 'other' of the male anthropological establishment (Behar & Gordon 1995:19; see also Wolf's comments on otherness within the self, 2002:181). Furthermore, the Western anthropologist is not really separate from the lives of the 'others' but intimately implicated in them within the world of political relations and global flows (Narayan 1997:29). Because every one of us is 'native' to at least one community, Narayan proposes abandoning the term 'native anthropologist' and focusing instead on the specific and multiple ways that each person is "situated in relation to the people we study" (ibid:31). Doing ethnography means "enacting hybridity" (33). In this way, the vacillations and conflicts of cultural identity that 'native anthropologists' report can act as a critique of the fixing and fossilization of 'culture-units' by traditional Western ethnography (see Niranjana 1992:3).

This kind of attack on the dichotomy of 'self' and 'other' offers a useful corrective to perceptions of translation as a transfer between sharply defined language-entities – perceptions which exclude the person of the translator as a mediating agency and site of mixing and, in the case of ethnographic translation, serve to deny common ground and produce 'essential' difference. However, such anti-positivist paeans to hybridity have not gone unchallenged. In their detailed critique of the politics of Writing Culture, Balmurli Natrajan and Radhika Parameswaran, for example, argue that by insisting on the death of the subject, Western experimentalism has upheld the exclusion of 'Third World' people's agency. Non-Western writings are virtually absent from the

Writing Culture debate, and disempowered groups are located not as subjects of knowledge production but at most as readers for "emerging anthropological works produced exclusively in the First World" (1997:41). Natrajan and Parameswaran call for a much more politically oriented ethnography which tries to "counter hegemonic knowledge" not by dissolving distinctions but by critically highlighting the difference between 'native' and 'non-native' (ibid:53), and not by inserting multivocality into writing styles but by seeking out counter-hegemonic practices in social reality (48).

A similar perspective is put forward by contributors to the collection *Black Feminist Anthropology* (McClaurin 2001b). Subjecthood in Irma McClaurin's view is necessary in order to wrest 'ethnographic authority' from the academic establishment, re-valorizing denigrated cultures and opening up the field for previously silenced voices to speak. She points out that the Western academy has imposed a double bind on 'native anthropologists', whereby their authority is denied if they are considered too fully integrated through their Western training (and thus no longer fully culturally other) and again if they are considered too little integrated (and thus subjective, emotionally involved, unreliable witnesses; McClaurin 2001a:57-8). McClaurin calls for 'autoethnographies' in the terms outlined by Mary Louise Pratt in *Imperial Eyes*, namely as texts in which

> colonized subjects undertake to represent themselves in ways that *engage with* the colonizer's own terms. If ethnographic texts are a means by which Europeans represent to themselves their (usually subjugated) others, autoethnographic texts are those the others construct in response to or in dialogue with those metropolitan representations. (Pratt 1992:7)

Such self-descriptions make use of Western literary and conceptual conventions in order to attack Western political structures, not reproducing but "transculturating" Western discourses (ibid:102). This form of anthropology translates "the speaker's/writer's subjective discourse" into the colonizer's language as a "dialogical" or dialectical movement aiming to attack dominant representations (McClaurin 2001a:65).

Natrajan and Parameswaran's vision of the translator's role is not so different. They extend their call to all ethnographers, including the 'First World' mainstream: researchers must "define their roles as agents who should help create the conditions of possibility for self-definition of the subjects of research" (1997:44). In this view, whether or not the anthropologist is a 'native' identified with the people being studied, the task of ethnography as translation should be to offer itself as a medium for those people to speak, and not as a product, the prime property of the Western academy. This claim for 'representation' in the political sense explicitly contradicts Spivak's (1988) view that *Vertretung* cannot genuinely allow 'others' to speak. Natrajan and Parameswaran are concerned that Writing Culture's focus on textual experimentation – the form of translation or translation style, in our terms – fatefully distracts from the far more important question of the content and political goals of ethnography. Thus, whereas Spivak implies that within the discourses of Western science about the 'Third World' there is no voice for the Third World writer, Natrajan and Parameswaran zestfully take up the challenge to produce "alternative knowledge" that subverts the colonizers' traditions. Their interest is not in defamiliarizing or 'foreignizing' textual strategies but in oppositional content, such as a study of rural North Indian women's songs and proverbs or of the anti-patriarchal critique expressed by Lucknow courtesans (1997:48). By putting the erstwhile objects of anthropology into the subject slot, they hope to undermine the idiom of Western ethnography from within.

When they read what we write

Once the distance between ethnographer and ethnographized begins to shrink, ethnographers are forced to participate personally in disagreements among the studied as to who is who and what is right and proper. Anthropologist and museologist Sharon Macdonald recounts how, when making an ethnographic study of a museum team, she felt in painful detail the ways that participants attempted to make use of her presence. "As a scribe in their midst, I was there to be won over" (1997:163); competing factions did all they could to influence what she discovered and how she wrote about it. Despite the ethnographer's insider status, misunderstandings were rife. Macdonald describes them apropos of a punctuation dispute. Her draft contained many quotation marks to indicate terms "which, were it not the case that my subjects share the same mother-tongue as myself, would be in a foreign language" (ibid:170). She was applying the conventions of 'native word' distancing, so that the word 'management', for example, was recorded as an untranslatable term specific to the 'native point of view' and not to be absorbed into the ethnographer's narrative. However, the inverted commas were read by some participants as conveying ironic or pejorative intent – "'management'" was taken to mean "'so-called management'" (ibid). The shared native language turned out to be full of fractures and gaps, into which rushed currents of material interest relating to disciplinary factions, funding patterns and museum policy.

Although it seems obvious that different coalitions have different versions of their 'culture' to propound, in traditional ethnography this fact was frequently obscured by the belief in tribes as homogeneous units. Thus, a nineteenth-century anthropologist was perplexed when Two Crows disagreed with the statements made with such a definitive air by other Omaha informants (Brightman 1995:518): how could people 'governed by tradition' differ so vehemently on what that tradition was? But when the spotlight is turned onto cultures the readers know rather well, the notion that no-one could disagree about habits or beliefs becomes absurd. This suggests that generalized 'authenticity' and 'truth' in cultural description are impossible goals even for insider accounts, and that far more provisional-sounding translations are required. As Macdonald's example shows, the insider translation also has to cope with the comeback of the described in a way that colonial-era writers could avoid: "subjects of the ethnography expect to read what is written about them and they are likely to be forthcoming in voicing their views about it" (1997:171). This dimension of ethnography – accountability to readerships, or 'reading back' – becomes more central with the spread of literacy and the growth in ethnography at home; it is explored in Caroline B. Brettell's 1993 collection *When They Read What We Write.*

Genre-blurring

McClaurin's paper on Black feminist anthropology makes a strong connection between situated ethnography and autobiography. Taking up this point, I'd like to touch briefly on the use of "blurred genres" (Geertz 1983) crossing between ethnography and other literary forms. If ethnographic translation is a creative and ordering task that uses fictional devices, literary translation does not simply transfer individual words but mediates larger cultural contexts to readers in the receiving language. In fact, primarily 'literary' translations may be used or may market themselves in a quasi-ethnographic framework. For example, Richard Jacquemond (1992) makes an interesting argument that the acceptance of Arabic works in French depends to a large degree on their perceived ability to provide representations of Arab culture and society – representations that need to fit as closely as possible to existing French traditions of 'knowledge' about the Orient. This is a situation (anything but rare, and perhaps even typical of translation relations between politically unequal regions) where translated fiction takes on an ethnographic role in the receiving culture's literary market. It is 'ethnographized' fiction, which may stress its exotic provenance through cover design and marketing, or may, as in Jacquemond's example, stress difficulty and distance by means of copious learned footnotes (ibid:149). The footnoting style interpellates "a totally ignorant reader, confronted with a totally new world, unable to come to grips with it unless he is guided step by step by the steady and authoritative hand of the omniscient Orientalist-translator, trained to decipher the otherwise unfathomable mysteries of the Orient" (150).

Mystery is the literary twin of ethnographic distance, and it is a key value mined from ethnography by Ezra Pound in his translations of Chinese poetry. As Yunte Huang argues in *Transpacific Displacement*, a rich study of intertextual relationships in American translations of Chinese literature, Pound's Imagism "constitutes a modern ethnography that reinvents an 'image' of Oriental linguistic culture" (2002:23). Translated poetry in this scheme not only drew on and if necessary "reorientalized" (ibid:68) ethnographic texts, but also fed into American culture's intertextual web of knowledge about China. Huang shows that literary translation is inextricably bound up with ethnographic writing, and can have partially ethnographic intent and effects within the receiving cultures.

Yet there is an important difference in the perceived mission of self-declared literary and ethnographic representation, as art and science. As Sherry Ortner points out, we may agree that ethnography is a 'fictional' form, "but if the question is meant to imply that in most ethnographies any resemblance to cultures living or dead is purely coincidental, then the answer [...] is certainly no" (1991:179) – ethnographers may use literary genres, but in pursuit of non-'literary' aims. In Gloria Anzaldúa's uncategorizable *Borderlands/La Frontera* (1987), for example, poetry, autobiography and history are interlaced to form an autoethnographic manifesto for 'the new mestiza'. Anzaldúa makes language itself the focal point of her text, and her form of translation casts an interesting light on the debate around Narayan's paper as described above. She celebrates and actively employs hybridity and borderland existence – not, however, as a postmodern virtue in itself, but as a political appeal for subjectivity and agency both within and against a dominant US culture:

> Living on borders and in margins, keeping intact one's shifting and multiple identity and integrity, is like trying to swim in a new element, an 'alien' element. There is an exhilaration in being a participant in the further evolution of humankind, in being 'worked' on [...] And yes, the 'alien' element has become familiar – never comfortable, not with society's clamor to uphold the old, to rejoin the flock, to go with the herd. No, not comfortable but home. (1987:Preface)

If this identity sounds like a 'translated' one in Rushdie's sense (see Bachmann-Medick 2006), Anzaldúa describes her use of language as a *refusal* to translate, a withholding of translation into the dominant idiom. Her combination of English, different forms of Spanish, Tex-Mex, Nahuatl and "a mixture of all these", as the new language of the Borderlands, is a rejection of linguistic homogeneity and of the requirement placed on marginalized speakers to re-express themselves in 'pure' English. Instead, "Today we ask to be met halfway. This book is our invitation to you – from the new mestizas" (ibid). The following short excerpt shows how markedly Anzaldúa's language differs from conventional ethnographic styles like the English paraphrase, the 'sprinkling of native words', or the parallel text:

> "Drought hit South Texas," my mother tells me. "*La tierra se puso bien seca y los animales comenzaron a morrirse de se'. Mi papá se murío de un* heart attack *dejando a mamá* pregnant *y con ocho huercos*, with eight kids and one on the way. *Yo fuí la mayor, tenía diez años*. The next year the drought continued *y el ganado* got hoof and mouth. *Se calleron* in droves *en las pastas y el* brushland, *pansas blancas* ballooning to the skies." (ibid:8)

Intensifying the blurring of genre through its blurring of language boundaries, Anzaldúa's text goes beyond the tradition of the ethnographizing frame used as a mark of exoticism and brings the ramifications of translatedness into both content and form.

Ruth Behar's *Translated Woman*

I will close this chapter by looking at a feminist reflexive ethnography that explicitly foregrounds translation. *Translated Woman: Crossing the Border with Esperanza's Story*, by Ruth Behar (1993), presents the life story of a sixty-year-old Mexican woman by the pseudonym of Esperanza, as told to Behar over a period of several years in the 1980s. Esperanza makes a living by selling garden produce from door to door, and as a single mother and peddler she occupies "the lowest rung of the town social ladder", considered sharp-tongued, loose-living and even dangerous by her neighbours (ibid:3). The central chapters of the book consist almost entirely of Esperanza's narrative, in English translation edited by Behar and consistently set in quotation marks. Short italicized introductions to each chapter relate the setting of the conversation and the part played by the ethnographer. As the book goes on Behar's own contributions to the conversation are increasingly included, and she is the speaker in the framing chapters: the introduction and 'Reflejos/Reflections', three chapters closing the book which include an autobiographical piece.

Translated Woman, true to its title, presents itself as both a translation from spoken Spanish into written English of Esperanza's life story and a contemplation of translation across the Mexican-US, Spanish-English border. Behar's concept of translation draws on Chicana writing about the borderlands where cultures meet, as exemplified by Anzaldúa's work. The 'translated woman' of the title is thus not only Esperanza in her "second life" (or Benjaminian 'after-life') in English (ibid:16), but also Behar herself as a Cuban Jewish woman in the US, living in different worlds and languages and constantly renegotiating her own identity. The double reference of "translated woman" is built right into the text, which takes as its focus the play of likeness and distinction between the two women. Although Behar's study does not use a dialogue form as proposed by the ethnographers of speaking contributing to *The Dialogic*

Emergence of Culture, it is 'dialogic' in the sense that it tries to make both sides of the ethnographic conversation visible rather than hiding away one partner. As Mannheim and Tedlock point out, Behar does not have to draw information out by wiles and ruses, for Esperanza "has already narratized her life, to her children and neighbors, and articulates her discussions with Behar as a kind of confession in which her life will be carried across the border to the United States" (1995:14). In marked contrast to the classic 'translation of cultures' approach where the expert ethnographer divined truths inaccessible to the natives, Esperanza herself has thus already determined on the shape of her story and asks Behar to record and disseminate it – though not in Mexico, where she feels it will not be understood, but only on 'el otro lado'.

Such, anyway, is the image of the translation process that Behar offers. She represents herself as the more passive partner in the conversation by stressing that Esperanza sought her out (1993:4), made her feel foolish (ibid:28), gradually won her loyalty in town politics (ibid:109), made her change her ethnographic project (ibid:127), told her the correct attitude from which to speak (ibid:263). Agency and personal power in the translation is attributed to Esperanza in episodes like this, and the organization of the translation, too, aims to sustain the agency of the translated. To start with, the book is constructed as an ethnographic life story. Behar's decision to write a life story rather than a generalized ethnography resulted partly from a wish to counteract synoptic forms that swallow individual lives, individual speaking voices and particular ways of making sense (ibid:269-70). The ethnographic life story as a genre is not necessarily so particularist: remember Shostak's *Nisa*, which reached out for generalized conclusions and locked 'Nisa' to her status as 'A !Kung Woman'. In fact, Behar explicitly relates her work to Shostak's, noting that *Nisa* presents a heterosexual utopia downplaying male violence, which *Translated Woman* brings to the fore as a kind of intertextual complement or counter-translation (1995:79-80). Like Shostak, Behar is following a feminist agenda, and like her (though in a much more detailed form) she positions herself as worked-upon by a strong woman subject, but Behar follows her biographical subject's own narrative directions in a way that Shostak, with her ethnographically ordered and commentated chapters, does not.

Esperanza's voice comes across in Behar's translation as that of a formidable story-teller. She uses a dramatic dialogue form with differently voiced characters contributing their parts. In this short sample from a much longer narrative, Esperanza is a child, her mother has finally left her violent father, and her paternal grandmother has just taken her in. 'Comadre' is how Esperanza addresses Behar, referring to her role as a godparent or 'co-mother':

> "*¡Híjole!* Now what's to come. Mine is a very long life, a very long historia, comadre!

> "So, she took me with her, leading my cattle through the path with her cattle. And then I suffered a black life with her.
>
> "She gave me food to eat, but then it was, 'Come on, hija, to the hills. Bring me firewood. Now bring me water. *Andale*, wash the dish. *Andale*. Grind the nixtamal. *Andale*.'
>
> "She taught me where to go with the cattle. 'You'll come back through the hills. This field is mine. Look, hija, I have a lot of fields for you to inherit. If you lean on me, when your papa returns you can get together with him, and you will become the owner of all these fields. Look, I've got land, your papa's got land. Now that your sister and your mama don't want to be here – well, help yourself. Stay put here.'
>
> "Yes, she egged me on, however she could. Those months passed.
>
> (Behar 1993:43)

Esperanza employs quotation to give voice to her wicked grandmother, reporting both harsh words and honeyed ones, which she then evaluates (as unscrupulous 'egging on'). The grandmother's part is translated into Esperanza's own narrative for her own purposes, using the techniques of constructed direct speech outlined by Tannen (1995). Behar points out that Esperanza's dialogic narrative allows us to glimpse the viewpoint of other people in her life, even those who the narrator clearly condemns (1993:285). These sections of *Translated Woman* are onion-layered: Esperanza frames the characters in her story and Behar frames Esperanza, marking her contributions carefully with quotation marks (the first-person sections in *Nisa* are not marked in this way, a choice which helps naturalize them as true accounts). Behar further tries to reproduce Esperanza's personal style by using spoken-language contractions and colloquial phrasing, such as "then it was", and she includes Spanish words sometimes italicized, sometimes not. This produces a bilingual mix that was not present in the original all-Spanish conversation – a deliberate move, says Behar: "I will patch together a new tongue for her, an odd tongue that is neither English nor Spanish, but the language of a translated woman. Esperanza will talk in this book in a way she never talked before" (ibid:19). She adds that the very form of the telling is a transgressive translation, dealing in public with matters that the norms of Mexican rural society prefer to see kept private (ibid:20).

While the Spanish words embedded in the English speak to plurilingual readers, thus making a statement about audience, they also have an emblematic effect. The mixing which the translator adds to the source text is there to signify translatedness, the "odd tongue". However, although not normally glossed (or sometimes glossed much later in the text), they are not unintelligible. Looking for a "strategy for provoking translation", Carol Maier (1995:31) notes that the inclusion of source-language words can "trigger" monolingual readers to try to make sense of them, their context and the implications of the juxtaposition.

Using such words communicates not only their 'meaning' but also their very presence, the existence of an other language-world buried under the weight of English in the text. The non-Spanish-speaking reader of *Translated Woman* has to be ready to switch codes and guess at meanings, drawn herself into a border experience.

Although Behar comments in her framing chapters on the task of carrying Esperanza's words into a different cultural setting, within Esperanza's sections the use of 'native terms' is the main indication of the translator's verbally mediating presence. Moments of linguistic confusion are rarely noted, and disagreements only very occasionally, for example when Behar persists, against Esperanza's resistance, in trying to get the answer she expects (ibid:178), or when, unusually, she adds an evaluative adjective: "Esperanza replies, unabashed" (ibid:161). In the latter example, the translator is indirectly remarking that Esperanza ought naturally to feel abashed when admitting she has whipped her daughter many times. In general, though, the translation upholds a markedly neutral stance – hiding the darts and seams where Behar 'snipped and snipped' and sewed at Esperanza's words to fit them into the constraints of a book (ibid:19). The ambivalence of the would-be faithful interpreter comes to a head when Behar tells Esperanza that the book "will be in your words, based on what you've told me" (ibid:233). Whose words, in that case, are we reading?

The power of the translator is a constant worry for Behar. More than her power to voice the words of Esperanza's story, as a feminist she struggles with her position in the unequal relationship between literate American professor and illiterate Mexican peddler. Although the 'borderland' where Ruth and Esperanza meet is fertile and to some extent enables an unsettling of cultural identities, the book does not evade the more intractable aspects of the political and economic context. Behar points out that the two women's 'comadre' relationship, initiated by Esperanza, conventionally links one more and one less economically and socially powerful woman in friendship and fictive kinship (ibid:7), but as a 'gringa' Behar is an unusual comadre. In the background is always the material divide. Behar remarks that Esperanza's life story "can cross the border with me, but she herself cannot make the crossing except as an undocumented domestic servant". Esperanza makes the crossing "vicariously" through the translation, while Behar can cross and recross, in person, as often as she wishes (ibid:241). Thus the translation becomes an export commodity:

> Just as rural Mexican laborers export their bodies for labor on American soil, Esperanza has given me her story for export only. Her story, she realizes, is a kind of commodity that will have a value on the other side that it doesn't have at home – why else would I be 'using up' my life to

> write about her life? She has chosen to be a literary wetback, and I am to act as her literary broker, the border-crosser who will take her story to the other side and make it be heard in translation. (ibid:234)

Esperanza herself cannot read the book she has co-written. Like other ethnographers, Behar is both metaphorically and materially a cultural broker: it is Esperanza's story that she carries to a wider audience, but she is the one to reap the material benefits, despite her gifts to Esperanza and later royalties (see Behar 1995).

Behar clearly pays an unusual amount of attention to the dilemmas of ethnographic translation, caught between mediation and appropriation, but it is this very attention which has prompted criticisms of the book as being too self-concerned. Maya Socolovsky (1998), for example, finds that Behar fails to tolerate the contradictions of the borderland that she describes, its ambiguity and painful separations, in the way a writer like Anzaldúa does. Instead, the guilty ethnographer tries to write her power out of the world by claiming identity with her subject. The idea of the two women as mirrors of each other runs through the text (for example, Behar 1993:302). Both are 'translated women', and in Socolovsky's view they are made to fit as two halves of a whole along a classic self/other divide (1998:78). Certainly, when Behar describes herself as a wetback like Esperanza, a "literary wetback in the world of academic letters" (1993:340), she makes a fair point about the position of Latina women in white academia, but a stretched one about the parallels between her own life and Esperanza's. To this extent the ethnographer's identification with her subject can be read as an abdication of responsibility.

Yet if Behar's choice of title hints at a mirror-like relationship between the book's two protagonists, it also stresses the process of translation. In contrast, the first-person title of another Latin American life-story, *Me llamo Rigoberta Menchú*, as Dingwaney and Maier (1995a) argue, reveals ethnographer Elisabeth Burgos-Debray 'displacing' the difficulties of communication – and the inequities from which they arise – by "appropriating Menchú's identity, her world, her cause, even her voice itself" (ibid:305). From this perspective Behar's reflexive approach at least gains by trying to leave the speaker be and thematize the space between translating and translated woman. However, Dingwaney and Maier go on to ask whether Burgos-Debray's suppression of the ethnographer's visibility might not be a tactical move designed to keep Menchú at centre stage (ibid:307). They point to the danger that extremely reflexive work can edge the translated to the margin while the translator herself engages in a form of "self-aggrandizement" (ibid:316). Here lies the potential downfall of the reflexive ethnographic approach, in which a focus on the processes of translation may actually grab the narrative space that should have been occupied by the other person's account.

Discussing *Rigoberta Menchú* as a Spanish translation and in English, Dingwaney and Maier conclude that 'cross-cultural texts' need to move constantly between simulating "an unmediated narrative in order to engage the reader" and "insisting on the very fact of mediation" by demonstrating the translator's intervention (ibid:312). They stress even more strongly the role of the reader in keeping in mind those multiple perspectives of immediacy and mediatedness as she reads a translation. Even if Behar fails to achieve this kind of balance, her *Translated Woman* does at least enable such multiple readings by offering an array of perspectives on the story she recounts – the story of Esperanza's life and the story of its being told and retold.

6. Ethnographic Translations of Verbal Art

This chapter will look at the debates on translation in one area of cultural anthropology, the study of Native American oral literature by linguistically oriented anthropologists in Canada, the United States and Latin America. This is a field of work where an unusual amount has been written on the technical and political aspects of translation practice as an ethnographic practice; key collections are Swann and Krupat (1987), Swann (1992) and Sammons and Sherzer (2000). This is not to suggest that no similar work has been done in other parts of the world, but Americanist anthropology has taken a particularly consistent interest in the recording and translation of oral literature.

The translation of oral literature with ethnographic intent casts light on many of the issues discussed in the previous chapter. Among other things, we will be looking at some experiments in thick translation, heteroglossic translation, the unpicking of different dimensions of meaning (Tymoczko's 'metonymics' of translation), and the contested boundary between 'art' and 'science' in ethnographic translations of literature. This latter point needs addressing as a terminological issue right away. The content of the Americanist studies we will be looking at in the following pages is orally transmitted knowledge studied as an anthropological resource, but it is framed in artistic terms, performed under aesthetic constraints, and in many cases occupies a position in the source-language setting that is comparable to 'literature' in literacy-based settings. The question of category match arises, and is not resolved by any of the labels anthropologists have given to this type of cultural production, whether 'oral literature' (with reference to, and stressing equality of value with, written literature), 'oral tradition', 'folklore', 'orature' or 'verbal art'. As we will see, the remit of translation into English in such cases has to include the task of defining the roles which the source-language talk actually plays in its source setting, while the translation's presentation and interpretation will locate its niche in the target-language system.

The concept of 'verbal art' that I will use (though not exclusively) in this chapter has particular currency among ethnographers of speaking like Dell Hymes and Joel Sherzer. It implicitly rejects the primacy of the written word and indicates a desire to include within one spectrum both formalized and spontaneous forms of the aesthetic use of words, communal-anonymous and individual-authored art along with all the stages in between. The term covers playful, ritual or aesthetically ordered speech in any shape, though in this chapter we will be looking mainly at more long-lived, 'passed-down' forms of narrative and poetry. This kind of speech may be interpreted as an artistic event open to aesthetic analyses, or as an expression of ethnographically relevant symbolic meanings – or, as the ethnographers of speaking have it, as a social practice that is prime material for anthropological analysis. The status of the 'text' as text is disputed here. Tedlock, for example, criticizes a tendency he sees among ethnologists since Boas to try to reconstruct a true authentic text which then serves as a sacred original, whose interpretations and retellings are mere weak echoes or ghosts (1983:237). Instead, he says, oral literature in use does not know the dilemma of original and non-original, since in speech traditions texts exist and survive as permanent rewritings. There is no reason not to re-tell, and if the text 'changes' in the process that is no indictment; as Tymoczko shows, songs and tales in the oral tradition change from one telling to the next while also recapitulating "established patterns that the teller or singer inherits and in turn passes on" to later generations (1999:41). In this balance of constancy and mutability, there is no such thing as a sacred original which could give birth to the perfect translation – which does not stop us evaluating different translations in terms of their ideological assumptions, the degree of their accountability and their political effects.

Clearly, if literary translation is a difficult task and so is ethnographic representation, it's no wonder that Americanist ethnographers translating verbal art have quarrelled at times. Disagreement can arise not only on what aspect to emphasize, but also on quite practical difficulties of reworking a multi-medial event into a written medium. In the classic (and most studied) case, story-telling, the translator faces not 'simply' a verbal text – with all the technical and epistemological traps that beset its transfer into written form, as discussed in Chapter 5 – but also a moment of performance replete with meaningful aspects that go 'beyond words'. The influential folklorist Alan Dundes has distinguished here between textural features (such as rhyme and pitch), text (the version being told) and context (the specific social moment of telling), all of which need to be included in the folklorist's record (Dundes 1980:22-3). Sammons and Sherzer further specify the difficulties in translating verbal art from the spoken to the written form and from one language to another. They list transcription (deciding whether and how to represent lines and episodes, gestures, voice modulation, and other paralinguistic elements); grammatical markers (especially where grammatical variations are used as a stylistic element); speakers' manipulation of register and figurative language; symbols and personal or intertextual allusions; language play and humour; and presupposed contextual knowledge (2000:xiv-xv).

Ruth Finnegan (1992:191-2) adds elements specific to spoken performance which are not susceptible to written expression, such as atmosphere and onomatopoeia, and Tymoczko's work on early Irish literature (1999) outlines the richness of generic, intertextual and cultural reference that additionally awaits the translator of oral literature. Some experiments in gathering these types of information will be described below. Yet despite the intricacy of such translation, North American anthropologists and poets have been attempting it in many variations for well over a century. As Arnold Krupat argues in his brief history of 'ethnopoetic' translation, there has been a division of labour here, with the anthropologists and linguists "in charge of that which is *unlike*", while poets and critics have taken responsibility for "that which is *like*" what we know as literature (1992a:4; see also Krupat 1992b). We'll follow that disciplinary distinction here, though as Krupat points out it is in dialectical interactions of likeness and unlikeness that some of the most interesting translation experiments have been made.

Early twentieth-century collectors

American oral traditions were intermittently collected and published in translation as early as the eighteenth century (see Krupat 1992a, Swann 1992). However, it was in the late nineteenth and early twentieth century that artistically oriented efforts were complemented and outstripped by 'scientific' collection on an ambitious scale. The work of Franz Boas, in particular, was influential. Boas (1858-1942) was a German-Jewish anthropologist who settled in America in 1886, taught at Columbia University and worked with the Bureau of American Ethnology based at the Smithsonian Institution. He trained his students and co-workers (including such famous names as Edward Sapir, Zora Neale Hurston, Ruth Benedict, Margaret Mead and many others) to consider language as the prime source of anthropological data and linguistic records as the anthropologist's main tool. Rather than behaviour and artefacts speaking for themselves, it was the words – the cultural texts – surrounding these which made them meaningful and which were thus the proper object of cultural anthropology's attention. The Bureau of American Ethnology investigators were to take dictation from Native American 'informants' on traditional knowledge, especially in the form of stories, myths and poems presumed to go beyond the individual knowledge of the particular speaker. These texts were transcribed in special phonetic systems and published in volumes that ideally included the transcriptions, an interlinear or parallel English translation, a grammar of the language, a vocabulary or dictionary, and sometimes explanatory anthropological notes.

Boasian faith in the collected text rested on a conviction that words are the treasures and key possessions of human culture, capable of being amassed in permanent form. Describing the speaker of the Kathlamet texts, Boas notes that "Charles Cultee (or more properly Q¡Eltē) has proved a veritable storehouse of information" (1901:5), apparently ready to be siphoned from him onto the page. The plan of the Bureau of American Ethnology, founded in 1879 by John Wesley Powell and issuing bulletins from 1881 to 1932, was to harvest linguistic data, then collate them into a complete map of the continent's languages, culminating in a huge *Handbook of American Indian Languages* under the aegis of Boas (published 1911-1941). Boas stressed the diversity of languages, opposing the eighteenth-century theory of a single origin for all the North American languages (Darnell 2001:10). Importantly, he also rejected the prevailing view that the languages of aboriginal North America were inferior to the truly civilized European languages. Instead, each language was equally capable of expressing all that humanity needed, and each was of equal intrinsic worth. Later anthropologists in the Boasian network, most famously Sapir and Whorf, followed this line into a far-reaching theory of linguistic relativity, as discussed in Chapter 3, but more generally the value placed on indigenous languages became mainstream in Americanist anthropology, and as we will see the Boasian method re-emerged in the later twentieth century in new, experimental forms.

At the time when the Bureau was recording oral traditions, it was very obvious that the languages and cultures being studied were under immediate threat of extinction. Thus, Boas notes in his preface to *Kathlamet Texts* (1901:5) that when he was collecting the texts, in the early 1890s, only three speakers of Kathlamet remained, and Regna Darnell (2001:16) cites an estimate that the 209 North American languages still spoken in 1995 represented less than half the number in use when the Europeans arrived; of those 209 only a fifth were still spoken by children, in other words as fully living languages. Faced by the imminent, more or less violent, death of so many American languages, the Boasians practised a 'salvage' anthropology that aimed to preserve traces of the dying cultures for analysis by future generations of anthropologists.

'Salvage' necessitated careful textual work as the core of the anthropological record. The Boasian collections thus included dictated and transcribed texts (often stories or myths), an interlinear or parallel English translation or both, and accompanying linguistic and ethnographic material. Figure 3 is a sample page from the collections dictated to Franz Boas in the 1890s by one of those three remaining speakers of Kathlamet and published as Bulletin 26 of the Bureau of American Ethnology in 1901. The format is three-part: a prose translation above and then, taking up around two thirds of the page, the Kathlamet transcription with interlinear translation. The prose translation makes virtually no comment on the performance of the story, apart from the isolated stage direction "[indicating]", and neither does it attempt to adapt the style to English expectations of literary narrative. In fact, it comes rather close to being a transposition of the interlinear translation into a different layout, as opposed to the polished 'literary versions' which we will see in later versions of the same principle. Conversely, the interlinear translation is itself reasonably accessible, certainly more so than some later versions of the format, which intersperse large amounts of grammatical information in the English words (see below, the passage from Parks 1991). Boas's rather minimalist application of the morphologically 'literal' component reduces the

MYTH OF NIKCIAMTCĀ'C (TOLD 1890)

There was a maiden. The Panther was the chief of one town. Now Blue-jay said to the maiden: "Go and look for the Panther; he is an elk hunter." One day she went. She went a long distance and came to a house. She entered. Now the house was all painted. She stayed at the bed of the Beaver. She stayed there. In the evening the Mink came home and carried trout. Then the Otter came; he carried steel-head salmon. Then the Raccoon came; he carried crawfish. Then the Muskrat came; he carried flags. The Lynx came; he carried ducks. The Mouse came home; she carried camass-roots. All came home. Only their eldest brother was not there. "Maybe our elder brother fell down." The woman thought: "Oh, maybe he is a canoe builder." In the evening a man came groaning. He came home. His belly was that large [indicating]. After some time he went near

NIKCIAMTCĀ'C ITCĀ'K¡ANĒ

NIKCIAMTCĀ'C HER MYTH

1 LXelā'etîX aēXā't aLā'hat¡au, awā'wa. Ik¡oa'yawa iLā'Xak¡Emana
There was one maiden, it is said. The panther their chief

2 La-îtci ēXt giLā'lXam. Aqa itcō'lXam iqē'sqēs aLā'hat¡au, inā'xLam
those one people of a town. Then he said to her blue-jay the maiden: "Search for

3 ik¡oa'yawa, imō'lEkumax iā'k¡etēnax. Igō'n ē'kua aqa igō'ya.
the panther, elks hunter." One day then she went.

4 Igō'ya, kElā'îX igō'ya. Igogoā'qoam tqu'Lē. Igā'ckupq. Aqa
She went, far she went. She arrived at a house. She entered. Then

5 ka'nauwē itā'kēmatck taXi tqu'Lē. Aqa iqā'nuq iā'lXemitk igō'La-it.
all painted that house. Then beaver his bed she stayed.

6 Igō'La-it. Tsō'yustîX igiXatk¡oā'mam kō'sa-it. Itcā'Lam ā'q¡EXEnē.
She stayed. In the evening he came home the mink. He brought a trout.

7 Igitē'mam ē'nanaks. Itcî'Lam iq¡oanē'X. IgiXatk¡oā'mam iLatā't.
He came the otter. He brought a steel-head salmon. He came home the raccoon.

8 ItcLî'tam LqaLxā'la. IgiXatk¡oā'mam its¡Enē'sts¡Enēs. ItctE'Lam
He brought crabs. He came home the muskrat. He brought

9 tElkoā'tē. IgiXatk¡oā'mam ipu'koa. ItctE'Lam tguēXguē'Xukc.
flags. He came home the lynx. He brought ducks.

10 IgaXatk¡oā'mam ā'cō. IktE'Lam tE'lalX. Ka'nauwē iguXoatk¡oā'mam.
She came home the mouse. She brought camass. All came home.

11 Aqa k¡ā'ya ē'LalXt. "LXuan igēXgē'itcomē ē'lxalXt." IgaxLō'Xa-ît
Then none their elder brother. "Perhaps he fell upon his own body, our elder brother." She thought

12 aqagē'lak: "IkEnī'm Lqa Laxōtck¡ē'na." Xā'pîX aLXilqā'yax LgoaLē'lX
the woman: "Canoe I think a builder." At dark he groaned a person

13 Ltēt. Aqa iLî'tpqam LgoaLē'lX. Ē'4wa iā'qa-iL iLā'wan. Lä2, aqa
coming. Then he entered the person. Thus large his belly. Long, then

20

Figure 3. Franz Boas, Kathlamet Texts, Washington, DC: Government Printing Office/Smithsonian Institution 1901, p. 20

amount of linguistic information stored in the 'inter'-line, though he includes a separate grammar and vocabulary to fill the gap. At any rate, the resulting text seems rather matter-of-fact and remarkably un-strange; equally, it makes little concession to aesthetic facets. It seems to aim for as close as possible a reproduction of the original weighting and as little explication as possible. Not all the texts in the Bulletin series follow exactly this format – they may, for example, set the transcription on the left-hand page and the English on the right – but the relative recuperability of the dictated text is a common feature of the linguistic approach. As we will see below, the record of the source text has proved an essential resource for later generations with very diverse interests in the stories.

Boas's focus on the particular and specific in the language-cultures of North America meant that the exact wording of what people said was of paramount importance – a more useful source of knowledge than what people did or what they made, and a more reliable indicator of what they thought than any other method. The same material could be translated in a very different mode, as we find in the structuralist interpretations made by Claude Lévi-Strauss in his four-volume *Mythologiques*. There, myths collected mainly by the Boasian-trained ethnologists are analyzed, categorized, commentated and sorted into sets of principal themes. While Lévi-Strauss pays extremely close attention to the specificity of each story, his project is clearly to gain a total overview and discover unifying patterns, in contrast to the particularist, unaggregated approach of the Bureau of American Ethnology publications. As contemporaries famously complained, Boas's 'five-foot shelf' of Kwakiutl texts was all very well but quite unreadable and unintelligible; Lévi-Strauss, in contrast, gives us pared-down translations into a scheme of mythological structure. Here is a translation of the translation of a Coyote myth collected by Melville Jacobs (Lévi-Strauss 1981:265):

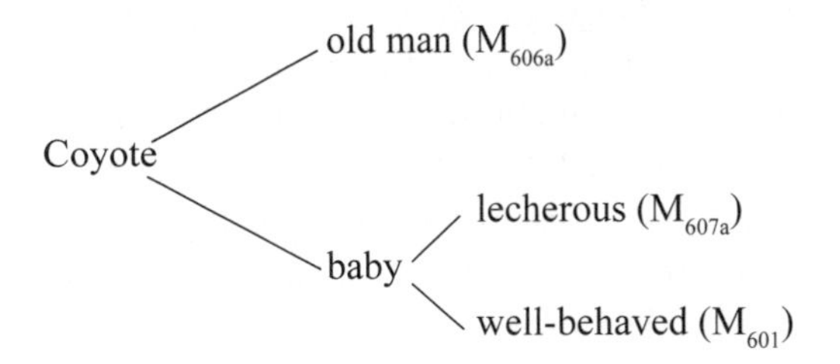

The numbers refer to myth components listed in an ambitious cross-cultural survey. Lévi-Strauss's structuralist approach attempts to move from superficial detail to shared underlying structures in a kind of extremist translation: the 'essential' fundament is extracted from the chaotic surface and presented in an almost mathematical form. The specific source language is no longer important and a rarefied target discourse remains alone, accessible to only a very narrow target-language readership. In contrast, the heirs to the Boasian method have worked out much more strongly source-text oriented translation techniques. The tendency is to thicken Boasian dictation in a range of ways, of which we will look first at attempts to reinstitute at least some elements of the physical presence of the spoken texts: things which distinguish verbal art from talking in general, and oral literature from its written counterpart.

The performance dimension

Americanist folklore and oral literature studies over the course of the twentieth century attached increasing importance to the performance dimensions of texts and the ways that these can be accounted for in the transcription, translation and analysis of Native American literature (phases in this process are usefully outlined in Fine's study of the folklore text, 1984, especially chapter 2). Particularly from the 1960s, oral literature was considered more and more to be inseparable from its moment of speaking, and its transcription and translation to be in need of far more sophisticated systems. Of the various experiments in this direction, including recent ones making full use of technological innovations (see Fine 1984), we shall look here at some important attempts by translator-ethnographers to add a sense of the performance to primarily written versions.

In a 1965 essay, Dell Hymes sparked renewed interest in the complex questions of transcribing, translating and evaluating Native American oral literature by criticizing the lack of a solid philological and linguistic foundation in the translations of North Pacific Coast poems. Though praising Boas and some of his students for their careful records of tales and poems, Hymes complains that the Boasian 'literal' prose versions fell far short of genuine accuracy because they eliminated the narrative sophistication and literary density of the texts they collected. The danger of the 'plain-language' style, says Hymes, is that it can confirm an image of Native American culture as simple and 'primitive'; at the other extreme, literary versions made without solid linguistic study of the original texts are irresponsible. We will see below that Hymes responded to the deficit with an interpretive transcription system highlighting complexity in what, based on other ethnographic evidence, he considers culturally significant rhetorical patterns in Native American literature.

A similar concern about the representation of indigenous cultures inspired the work another anthropologist and linguist, Dennis Tedlock. In *The Spoken Word and the Work of Interpretation*, discussed in Chapter 5, Tedlock accuses previous translators of Native American literature of having neglected the "art of translation" (1983:40) by over-valuing content at the expense of style, or else, like Boas, assuming that style is bound to disintegrate in translation and might therefore just as well be abandoned from the start. Tedlock's credo, in contrast, is the translatability of style. He puts forward various methods of reproducing the stylistic aspects of Zuni stories from New Mexico in a way that will rescue them from the taint of being merely 'primitive' and draw out their poetry, which can hold its own against the European canon (ibid:51). His key device – key because in Tedlock's view it is fundamental to spoken narrative across languages – is the pause. He transcribes the pauses in narrative as line breaks, using special typographical markers for longer ones. This versification, in contrast to Hymes's, is based on spoken records by tellers and re-tellers. Tedlock uses the oscillograph's record of how the teller actually paused as he spoke, and includes other information on the acoustic aspects of his texts. His aim is that the translation should be capable of reconstruction as a performance, of being re-told by another speaker in English.

A short example will give a better idea of how Tedlock translates. This is the beginning of the story "Coyote and Junco" from Tedlock's influential translations of Zuni stories, *Finding the Center* (1978:77). It is translated on the right-hand page with the transcription of the Zuni on the left, both following the same typographical system (the other stories are in English only, without transcriptions).

SON'AHCHI.
LO——NG A
SONTI GO
•

AT STANDING ARROWS
OLD LADY JUNCO HAD HER HOME
and COYOTE
Coyote was there at Sitting Rock with his children.
He was with his children
and Old Lady Junco
was winnowing.
Pigweed
and tumbleweed, she was winnowing these.
With her basket
She winnowed these by tossing them in the air.
She was tossing them in the air
while Coyote
Coyote
was going around hunting, going around hunting for his
children there
when he came to where Junco was winnowing.

The guide to reading aloud (ibid:xxxiii) explains the format, designed to enable a reconstruction of the stress and hence narrative structure provided by the speaker: the dot indicates a pause of at least two seconds, a soft voice is to be used for the smaller font and a loud one for capital letters, vowels with dashes ("LO——NG") should be held and split lines chanted. Zuni repetitions are reproduced rather than being tidied away, and some source-language items are retained, especially the conventional story-opening formulas. The anthropological apparatus is kept outside the text body, in endnotes and parts of the introduction. It is a division that allows the willing reader to follow the translation with reasonable ease (though not everyone agrees – Muhawi [2006:374], for instance, finds Tedlock's system "unworkable" in this respect).

Although Tedlock's transcriptions may seem bizarre at first, on closer reading – or rather, on reading aloud – we realize that he is working with existing resources of spoken English, such as extended vowels, repetition, long sentences, or cliff-hangers (see Tedlock 1983:42). The wording of Tedlock's 'scores' is also deliberately unexotic. He insists on natural-sounding phrasing, and is willing to bend his own rules on pauses to get it: where sticking to the source-language pauses would produce an un-English structure like "Her clothes / she bundled", he uses transposition to avoid it (ibid:50). In the introduction to *Finding the Center* he defends his conscious avoidance of inversions, aiming to indicate something that "sounds like ordinary Zuni" by means of something that "sounds like ordinary English" (1978:xxi). The inversions that remain are there to mark Zuni inversions. The emphasis on neutrality of wording serves an ideal of reversibility, so that the translations should enable a spoken reconstruction in English of the original performed poem, and should be capable of immediate back-translation into Zuni. Proudly Tedlock reports that his English translation was read aloud straight into Zuni by a Zuni performer (ibid:xi). As for the retention of Zuni formulaic phrases, they are there not as an exoticizing flag of alterity but because Tedlock's Zuni consultants considered the phrases to be untranslatable framing devices rather than actual words (xxviii). He tells us he has translated names wherever possible and retained in English the more or less standard Zuni metaphors (for example, where the word for 'road' is intended in a metaphorical sense as 'life', Tedlock retains 'road' for us to interpret as we will, xxviii). But although he proposes as close as possible a translation, Tedlock contrasts himself to earlier proponents of 'literal' translations from Zuni. Boasian literal translations, by removing apparently extraneous 'style', made the source texts seem unsophisticated, playing into surrounding conceptions of Native Americans as primitive. Tedlock cites an excerpt from Ruth Benedict's work, where the choppy effect fails to reflect the cohesion of the Zuni narratives. The problem arose, he says, because the translator eliminated (perhaps as pointless 'repetition') the Zuni device of parallelism to tie clauses together:

> Her eyes were almost shut. She was skin and bones. She was too weak to sit up and she scratched herself all the time. He jumped up. He ran to the house of Pekwin's son. His wife was just as old. (1935, cited in Tedlock 1983:38)

A different form of literalism is exemplified by Elsie Clew Parsons, who in Tedlock's view gave too much credence to the word order of her Zuni interpreter: "The straps the man carried wood with, in the other room he would hang up" (1930, cited in Tedlock 1983:37). The unfamiliar syntax here seems designed as a badge of authenticity, a device taken to extremes by ethnographer Frank Hamilton Cushing in the 1880s. Cushing's translations from Zuni include flourishes of his own which add an exotic touch: similes or picturesque oaths – "By the bones of the dead!" – never used, says Tedlock, by Zuni storytellers themselves (ibid:35). What Tedlock is after is not exoticism or literalism but a translation that is closely correlated with the source text's organisation of information while adapting the devices of English oral narrative to reproduce the Zuni poetics. In this respect, his translation comes close to Venuti's ideal of a foreignizing translation. It takes a devalued domain of target-language discourse, in this case oral narrative, and uses it to reconjure the power of the source text.

At times Tedlock's translator's notes read as a statement of personal taste, and in a detailed critique of both Tedlock and Hymes, Anthony Mattina (1987) accuses the two translators of hugely over-generalizing from their own preferences instead of focusing on the context and content of individual texts. But Tedlock explicitly stakes out his right to his own interpretation:

> there is no single, 'correct' picture of a given story even from one Zuni to another. What makes a narrative work for anyone other than the narrator himself is this very openness, and I think that some of the present narratives are open enough to permit the reader to do some picturing of his own. (1978:xxxi)

Any telling of a story is bound to summon up new images and it is the prerogative of the new recipient to create her or his own idea of what happens in the tale. In other words, this translation collection is closer to the literary motivation for translation than the anthropological one, yet it is undertaken from a clearly anthropological position and knowledge base.

Tedlock admits that other crucial aspects of the performances he translates, especially sounds and movements, are lost in his version. The audience's responses, for example, could not be included, nor could their laughter (ibid: xxv). Given the physical limits of the printed page, this is partly a technical problem – but ultimately it is the familiar dilemma of the literary translator who has to decide which aspects of a text's potentially endless meanings to elaborate, which to renounce. If Tedlock chooses to highlight the sound-poetry, Hymes the rhetorical complexity of Native American verbal art, other linguistically oriented ethnographers have translated with a focus on the interactions within which verbal art takes place, and draw the boundaries of such art wider, to include conversation and playful language as well as formalized, relatively stable works of 'oral literature'. The collection *Translating Native Latin American Verbal Art*, edited by ethnographers of speaking Kay Sammons and Joel Sherzer (2000), is of special interest here. Seventeen short essays each give a stretch of translation preceded by a commentary on the translation process and the difficulties that the translator-ethnographer faced. Sammons and Sherzer set out their approach as a discourse-centred one most interested in the "context" of verbal artistry. For these ethnographers of speaking, 'context' has two aspects:

> Context signifies, on one hand, the social and cultural backdrop, the assumptions, beliefs, and symbolic associations that are necessary for an understanding of the texts presented. These include aspects of the local ecology, such as plant and animal life; the nature of politics, curing, and other rituals; figurative and allusive uses of language; history; and humor. Context also signifies, on the other hand, the immediate location and situation in which a particular performance occurred and was recorded, including the relations and interactions among those present; recent, relevant local, national, and natural happenings; and the specific goals and meanings of words and actions. (2000:xii)

As we saw in Chapter 5, even this lengthy shopping list is anything but exhaustive, instead selecting and excluding from potentially infinite 'relevant connections' (Dilley 1999). But it is already an ambitious supplement for the translations, demanding very concrete attention to both the communal ('cultural') and the one-off ('individual') aspects of a literary act, both the anthropological and the poetic dimension. Neither the story's location inside a larger cultural network nor its specific provenance in a momentary constellation of individuals need be sidelined. When Sammons and Sherzer insist on the need to keep the translator's work visible within the translations (2000: xiii), they are adding a third, important dimension of context which is often neglected in the English presentations of Native American oral literature.

In practice, the essays in the collection achieve their contextualization by means of extensive commentaries on all three aspects. The translations themselves take a range of different lines; some are harder to read than others but the general approach is not to domesticate. The translations are designed as a provocation: "they challenge readers, indeed force them, to enter into the worlds of indigenous Latin America in and on their own terms, rather than in easily digested and packaged forms" (ibid:xiv). True, readers can hardly be 'forced' to do anything, and this excellent collection is unlikely to make the bestseller lists. Still, the results are of great interest to translators. Let's look at one example, Laura Martin's analysis of a recording of a Mocho conversation about volcanoes.

Martin's translation, made up of text and commentary, aims to bring out the richness of the exchange in terms of rhetorical artistry. She focuses on the uses of formalized language, especially stylized forms of repetition and parallelism by both the narrator and his co-conversationalists, to achieve proximity to the ritualized language appropriate to a serious subject. Accepting that no account of a conversation can offer anything like a comprehensive or definitive version, she sets out her reasons for targeting her translation at "the change of quality that characterizes the ritualized sections and distinguishes them from the more ordinary passages" (2000:110). Martin's threefold contextualization addresses the general cultural background that gives rise to the conversation, an analysis of the conversation in relation to its individual participants, and an acknowledgment of the translation's limited aims. One excerpt from the middle of the conversation is presented in a version of the Boasian three-line method, with transcription, a morphologically marked-up 'literal' middle line, and a 'free' version with punctuation and grammatical interpretation added. A is Ambrosio, V is Victoria (Martin 2000:116):

46. A *hi'ma'lo'h,*
exist perhaps ash
Maybe there's ash,
47. *hi'ma'tz'e'ka',*
exist perhaps hot water
maybe there's hot water,
48. *hi'ab asúfre aabii*
exist rep sulfur rep
they say there's sulfur, is what they say.
49. V *huu'y*
Oh, yeah.
50. A *hi'ma'asúfre,*
exist perhaps sulfur
Maybe there's sulfur,
51. *asúfre x-pokw-i baatanh*
sulfur 3E-explode-iv first
sulfur will explode first.
52. *tehe'ni ch-'ak-i we'tz'e'ka'*
there already 3A-come-iv def boiling water
After that comes the hot water.

53. *tehe'ni ch-'ak-i we'si'k'*
there already 3A-come-iv def cold
After that comes the cold.
54. *poch'-bal huune'tíra winaq*
kill-nom one time man
Everybody is killed off all at once.
55. *ha'n we'witz muu qa-sup-u si'k'saqla'h*
foc def mountain neg ɪp-stand-tv cold early
It is because of that mountain that we cannot stand the morning cold.

In Martin's analysis, lines 46-53 show Ambrosio's use of a "familiar Mocho rhetorical figure, a kind of chiastic structure in which a series of parallel elements are presented again in reverse order" – ash, sulfur, hot liquid, cold liquid. Ambrosio varies his use of the Mocho particles that indicate hearsay, a fact which would be veiled in a smoother translation since English doesn't offer a lexical equivalent that would show up; his motivation seems to be to move his phrase closer generically to folktale and myth, where "hearsay particles are ubiquitous" (ibid). Encouraged by Victoria, on line 50 Ambrosio restates 48 but using the exact structure from 46 and 47, creating a powerful triplet, and Martin goes on to elucidate other forms which tie the segment back to earlier parts of the conversation. The clinching line 54 stands out in sharp focus and closes a circle from the very beginning. Martin's use of this form of translation, the traditional linguistically oriented three-line version plus literary analysis with a social dimension, allows her to indicate the density and artistry of the conversation and embed it in a wider context of Mocho ways of speaking.

The use of layers

If Hymes and Tedlock set the translation ball rolling towards the artistic dimension of Native American verbal art, the ethnographers of speaking collected in Sammons and Sherzer (a longer, and fascinating, example is Sherzer 1990) highlight the aspect of art as a social as well as an aesthetic practice. But in this very rich and creative field of translation, not all the current experiments focus primarily on performance. There are many that work with the basic Boasian format of transcription plus translations, but expand it by the use of supplements which together build up a richer, kaleidoscopic view – a method reminiscent of Appiah's 'thick translation', in which the source text is valorized through the accretion of multiple layers of interpretation and debate. The examples we will turn to next demonstrate thick translation in action, and they remind us that alongside its undoubted benefits, thick translation of verbal art carries a special problem in sacrificing the concision of the moment of performance. As Darnell remarks, the need for tedious expansion makes many speakers thoroughly dislike the chore of telling stories to anthropologists: "what is obvious to any civilized Native person has to be stated explicitly to outsiders. To do so is boring and unaesthetic for the Native person" (2001:20). The ethnographically 'layered' approach certainly produces texts far removed from the experience of the telling (though in some cases they aim to keep some record that can be reconstructed in something near its original form); others try to circumvent the problem by keeping 'extraneous' information outside the text in their multiple re-tellings and versions.

The University of Nebraska Press *Studies in the Anthropology of North American Indians* is an important series of long, expensively produced, often multi-volume works that collect and present oral literature with attention to both scholarly and aesthetic dimensions. *Traditional Narratives of the Arikara Indians* (Parks 1991), for example, consists of four volumes, the first two containing transcriptions and interlinear translations, the third and fourth with free translations to allow the reader to "appreciate" the same texts "as historical and literary documents" (Vol III:xix). The third volume includes a 120-page introduction to Arikara oral traditions with a discussion of methodology. Each story is prefaced with a short explanation of the setting of the story, its distinctive features and its source. The overall preface acknowledges the pattern of the early Bureau of American Ethnology collections, considering that this addresses the broadest possible audience including Arikara people, scholars and the general public (Vol I:xiii), and notes that the collection with its accompanying grammar and dictionary largely based on the story corpus will in future be the sole source of information on this now moribund language. In the majority of the stories, the interlinear translation aims for reasonable transparency by omitting morphological information, but one story in each volume includes full detail, including a morphological breakdown (line 2) of the source-language text (line 1). Comparing the third and fourth lines in this translation destroys any illusion that 'literal' translation is a straightforward procedure (Alfred Morsette, "How Summer Came to the North Country", Parks 1991, Vol I:667):

anuú	**naapakúhtu'**		**sinoó**
a +nuu	***naa+pakuht+u'***		***sinoo***
and+then	way+old	+N ABS	yet
Long, long ago			*yet*

kana 'AhnatoxtaakunuuwaáWI
kana+an+na +t +a +ux+raak+hunuu +waa +wi
NEG +EV+MOD ABS+1SUBJ +IN PL SUBJ+AOR +PL +go around +DIST+SUB
when we were not going around

This format allows the reader to follow the translation's analytical tracks. To reach the 'literal' line 3, extensive linguistic interpretation was already required, quite apart from the normalizing process that recasts the source-language units into comprehensible target-language constructions. Including in print the intermediate stages between source and translation unveils the work of the translator – albeit a translator who is a scientist far from access by the lay reader. These lines address an expert readership, but the potential audience is enlarged by the use of separate layers of text, as the third and fourth volumes are free-standing with only 'free' translations of the same texts. The free translation gives the story's opening like this:

> Long, long ago when we people were not yet living on this earth, when the ways on this earth were holy, there was no summer here in this country. (Vol III:129)

In view of the editorial proposals of Hymes and Tedlock, the lack of line breaks is conspicuous. Parks defends his decision not to insert breaks by noting that the stories were not 'staged' but spoken as prose directly to the Arikara-speaking transcribers – it seems that both tellers of the stories and transcribers and translators categorized these events as informational material and not, or no longer, as artistic performances. The significance of source texts, as posited by the source speakers, can change and will contribute to the translation method that is adopted at any one time.

In contrast, another study in the same series comes out of a flourishing language community that still uses its texts regularly, and the translations are presented in a more artistic mode. In a collection of Dene stories, *Wolverine Myths and Visions* (Moore & Wheelock 1990), the Dene transcribers attended tellings addressed to a Dene audience, and the project was initiated by Dene interested in having their traditions recorded for their own children and grandchildren. The presentation of the translation resembles the Parks collection in keeping separate the transcriptions and the free translations, but in this case the free translations come first, shifting the emphasis onto the accessible literary or content component as opposed to the linguistic record. Each of these fluent translations has a short introduction by the teller which prepared the hearers to understand the tale – the introduction's perspective depending on the audience of that particular telling – and each is followed by a longer commentary by the storyteller explaining and elaborating on the lessons to be learnt. The transcription section includes interlinear translations of the introduction, story and commentary in each case. Aside from the introduction and some notes on the language, there is little annotation by the editors in this 'thick' translation.

The speakers' own contextualizations and interpretations, though, are recorded as an integral part of the story, officially inseparable from the story itself as the object of the collection, thus partially dissolving the common division of labour between Art (natives) and Knowledge (anthropologists). The introduction explains:

> The Dene Dháa have a fine sense of etiquette concerning traditional narratives and elders. Elders should not be interrupted or disputed, and the audience must listen attentively throughout a series of narratives. It is inappropriate to pretend to know more than the person who is telling the story, unless the storyteller is younger. [...] Extensive analysis of written stories by academics may violate this protocol by placing the original narrator in an inferior position. Therefore, in this collection notes are used sparingly so as not to displace the voice of the Dene Dháa narrators. (ibid:xxv)

This case highlights a potential problem with the 'thick translation' approach to oral literature. Not only does lengthy exegesis threaten to weaken the aesthetic impact of the texts, but in some cases it could run directly counter to the fundamental principles of the texts' telling and listening, in other words contravening the translation rules of the source language. The fact that the editors of *Wolverine Myths* try to follow the source-culture requirements for translation indicates the presence of a different audience from that of the Boasian 'salvage' collections. More accountability is demanded by the community who sponsored the translation of their own stories. This is reflected in the attribution of authorship: the Dene Wodih Society is credited on the title page as having compiled the collection – though its name disappears on the cover and catalogue data.

Donald Bahr's stereoscopic translations of "Pima Heaven Songs" (1987) take the multi-layered approach to quite some lengths. Bahr offers six different versions of each poem along with annotations. These include an ordinary-language version (in both source and target language) of each song, helping the reader identify what is specifically artistic about the texts, while syllable-matched line-by-line versions isolate one aspect of their aesthetic design which would otherwise disappear in translation. Additionally, two translators' free versions are offered, opening up room for interpretation by the reader. Bahr's method abandons the aim of squashing multiple dimensions of the source text into one translated version. Instead he fans out layers of literary effect into an array of parallel and complementary readings. The immediately obvious disadvantage of this translation technique is the difficulty of reading it – but it is certainly an innovative elaboration of the 'thick translation' tactic. My last example is a widely praised book which combines the layered approach with close attention to authorship. *Yaqui Deer Songs. Maso Bwikam* (Evers & Molina 1987) intersperses contextualizing sections – in a personal rather than an anthropological style – with individual comments on the recording and translating process by the two authors, parallel sections of transcriptions in lines and English translations, endnotes, and below each song an explanation or commentary by the singer. Audio recordings can also be accessed, in a move towards a more multi-media translation style. In the *Deer Songs* authority and perspective is handled with precision: the very fact of layers allows multiple voices to be heard and they are always attributed. Thus the two co-translators, one Yaqui-speaking and one not, set out explicitly the nature of their collaboration, as opposed to appearing as an undifferentiated translator-informant unit (ibid:8-9), and the performers of the songs provide their own interpretations to supplement the bare poetic translations. The illustrations include photos of named singers. The device of giving each chapter and section title first in Yaqui, then in English (though the order is reversed in the book's title) further slants the perspective towards the source language culture, so that overall this translation is clearly directed at an acknowledgement of bilinguality and tries to frame itself in the terms of the source-culture texts.

All these textually oriented 'thick translations' clearly follow the Boasian tradition in placing the once oral text at the centre – although, in contrast to the ethnography-of-speaking approaches, as a textual artefact rather than a sociolinguistic event. They shift slightly the position of the editor/translator and, to varying degrees, leave space for the interpreting voices of the source-language speakers. The results are strongly source-text-oriented translations. The presence of the source text in the translation rules out claims to transparent or objective mediation, since traces of the translation process are visible to all, and especially to those who can read the source language. At the same time, including 'free' translations and emphasizing aesthetic quality calls for an acknowledgement of artistic value and reading for pleasure that crosses the borders of anthropology out into the sphere of literature in general. This combination of educational and aesthetic effect resembles the European tradition of parallel editions, for example poetry in Latin and English – a presentation strategy that gives pride of place to the original and in this respect fulfils Appiah's requirement for the translation of non-Western literary work.

Retranslation

Discussing retranslations, Anthony Pym distinguishes between 'passive' retranslation where the versions do not compete in time and space but respond to the changing requirements of the receiving communities, and 'active' retranslation, where versions are rivals for one cultural space and fulfil different agendas within it (1998:82). We will see that Native American verbal art has generated both types of retranslation, working from written versions – mainly the ethnolinguistic collections of the early twentieth century – that themselves are 'translations' of preceding oral performances. Oral stories hover between ephemerality and permanence, the continuity of oral literature being located in the survival of its users and their memories. Each performance is a one-off in time and, as Tymoczko shows (1990), an intralingual, oral retranslation of the ones before. The marginalized status of oral literature in the West means, though, that successive written translations, following changes in target-culture tastes and ideological requirements, are relatively rare. However, once a text is written down the potential arises for a proliferation of translations if the will is there. I want now to look at two cases of retranslation, the Mayan book known as the *Popol Vuh* and the written versions of the texts collected by Boas and his associates.

The *Popol Vuh*, or 'book of council', is a chronicle of Mayan history, cosmology and mythology in the Quiché language of the Guatemalan Maya. It was first written in a hieroglyphic form accessible only to the very learned, who would unpack the meaning of the glyphs into comprehensible language as they read the book aloud (see Tedlock 1996:30). This unpacked oral version, a translation of esoteric into exoteric language, seems to have taken on a new written form when it was recorded in Latin characters by anonymous Mayan authors in the 1550s. The result was found in the eighteenth century by a Spanish missionary, who copied the Quiché and added a Spanish translation in parallel columns. As the Latin-script 'original' is now lost and its pictogrammatic basis long since burned, it is this paired version that has formed the basis of translations into European languages since the late nineteenth century. The many translations into English have included several from the Spanish side, one from a new Spanish translation of the Quiché side (Goetz & Morley 1950) and another directly from the Quiché by anthropologist Dennis Tedlock in 1985 (revised version 1996) – and no doubt the process will go on.

A prime motivation for retranslators is the feeling that previous interpretations have been factually false and must now be corrected. Such corrections are hampered by the difficulty of understanding texts created in the distant past where the line of traditional interpretation has been severed by violence (Tymoczko discusses this for the case of Old Irish literature, 1999:152). Tedlock had the advantage that modern Quiché is not dramatically distant from its sixteenth-century version, and some of its speakers still possess much of the knowledge needed to make sense of the *Popol Vuh*. This meant he could combine contemporary documents, anthropological context and the expertise of present-day Quiché speakers in his 'ethnopalaeontological' investigation of the text's meanings.

As for the format of his translation, Tedlock keeps the text itself in an integral form, surrounded by an introduction and very extensive endnotes which add interpretive and background information, drawn partly from written sources but mainly from the conversations with his Quiché consultant, Andrés Xiloj. While the book contains little comment on translation method, Tedlock has also written several papers on the process of translating the Mayan document (especially 1987, and chapters 4 and 15 of 1983). In one of these essays, Tedlock experiments with an interpolated form, alternating segments of the translated text with Andrés Xiloj's interpretive comments in a manner similar to Fabian's translation of the "Vocabulaire de ville de Elisabethville" (2002; see Chapter 5). But he also sees his reconstruction of the text's oral delivery, most strikingly as regards pace and contouring (in practice, line breaks), as a dialogical process – a dialogue "with the dead" (1987:173) that brings to life an otherwise lost original.

For translation scholars, the prospect of comparing retranslations is alluring, and may have been sorely missed by readers of Chapter 5. Because of the relative stability of written source texts, the *Popol Vuh* translations allow us to glimpse the ways several ethnopoetic translations set different priorities and pursue different agendas in their content and form. Take this short passage in Goetz and Morley's translation (1950) from Adrián Recinos's Spanish translation, then Dennis Tedlock's (1996 [1985]) from the Quiché manuscript edited by Recinos.

a) Beginning the divination, they said: 'Get together, grasp each other! Speak, that we may hear.' They said, 'Say if it is well that the wood be got together and that it be carved by the Creator and Maker [...]'.

(Goetz & Morley 1950:88; no footnotes to this passage)

b) And they said, as they set out the days:
"Just let it be found, just let it be discovered,
say it, our ear is listening,
may you talk, may you speak,
just find the wood for the carving and sculpting
by the builder, sculptor. [...]".

(Tedlock 1996:70; endnotes cite Tedlock's Quiché consultant Andrés Xiloj and include a photo of a similar ritual in the present.)

Among other things, this short excerpt shows a hint of Christian parallels drawn out by Goetz and Morley ("Creator and Maker"), which is supported in their introduction by references to the Catholic influence on the source text. Tedlock steers clear of the question of colonial contact by choosing terms ("builder, sculptor") which do not directly evoke Christian imagery. The approach to tone and style also differs: Tedlock seems to be aiming for a more lively and contemporary tone while Goetz and Morley stress distance and the ritual moment through the use of archaism ("say if it is well that"). Tedlock's treatment of the divination technique is more specific, through-translating the Quiché wording (see, for example, the endnotes on setting out the days, 1996:231-2). Moreover, in line with his larger project for ethnopoetic translation, Tedlock distinguishes between prose and poem by inserting line breaks (the source record in Quiché has no breaks of any kind; see the facsimile in Goetz & Morley 1950:76). Tedlock's notes draw out the relevance of the ancient text to modern practices and modern Quiché speakers, whereas Goetz and Morley's address philological matters, frequently recording the Quiché word or phrase without further comment – less an explanation than an invitation to scholar colleagues to ponder the accuracy of the translation choice.

To point out the religious sympathies of the older translation is not to denigrate its value as a translation of a Mayan text. Tedlock, after all, is as little a disembodied spirit of objectivity as any other translator, and the claim on his book's cover to be 'definitive' version is surely rather premature. Evidently, the existence of multiple retranslations does not necessarily mean progressively greater faithfulness and accuracy. It does mean, though, that we have access to a usefully layered, knitted multi-text; it proliferates interpretations and, not least, it indicates the fertility of texts as they generate new versions across time and space.

The translation of something designed to exist in written form gives some kind of framework for the task of reconstruction, and Tedlock's work on the *Popol Vuh* additionally benefited from intensive exegetical help by a Quiché expert. In contrast, the originals of the Kathlamet or Tonkawa texts collected in the early years of the twentieth century took place in a spoken language now dead along with its users. Only the dictated record of these poems and stories survives, and the richness of the supplementary information varies widely from one collection to another. While some of the collectors around Boas focused on plot alone and paraphrased what they heard, others put their faith in the exact wording and tried to transcribe it as precisely as possible. In his commentated retranslation of Haida poems, Robert Bringhurst (1999) contrasts the paraphrases, now closed to anything but the narrowest plot-based reanalysis, with the transcriptions, which allow the modern anthropologist and poet to reinterpret at a distance of many decades. However, the Boasian transcriptions are 'thin'. Little or no information is included on oral qualities like tone of voice, changes in pitch, or pauses. As a rule the stories were dictated with stops and starts to a longhand-writing anthropologist, in the absence of the audience and social setting which would normally have defined the performance and its meanings. Dell Hymes has put it harshly: "all the collections that are now in print must be redone" because of their failure to show the poetic structure inherent in the spoken versions. He optimistically continues that this structure is there in the texts, "hidden" within the imposed prose form and "waiting to be seen for the first time" (1987:19).

"For the first time" here means, of course, for the first time outside their home culture. Hymes's project of recuperating the phonic and rhetorical structure of the source texts, about which I will say more below, is one of many that dig up and re-present the early twentieth-century collections for a new audience with different interests. The audience of the Boasian texts was small and specialized, a scientific community of European Americans almost none of whom would be able to understand the transcribed source texts in any one language. The speakers of that language, in contrast, were almost without exception not users of writing, so that the transcriptions had virtually no readers in their day (a point made powerfully by Murray 1991:107). Though many of the languages recorded by that generation of ethnolinguists are now extinct, in some cases the collections can be re-used by a readership of descendants of the source text authors. An example is the collection of Lakota oral tradition by James R. Walker, made in the first decade of the twentieth century and now required by Oglala Sioux organizations as a source of information on the religion, science and philosophy of their forebears (Walker 1980:xxi). The audience changes dramatically upon retranslation: whereas in the first context of the ethnolinguistic publications the inclusion of the source text paired with its translation may have had more rhetorical than practical value except for a tiny number of academic readers, in the new context the same words can be set to the task of enriching and strengthening an anti-hegemonic cultural movement.

A feature of many retranslations of this type is a change in the attribution of authorship. Although early twentieth-century ethnologists did not hesitate to say they had merely taken down the texts from named speakers – indeed, the 'other authors' are the guarantors of the collection's authenticity – these authors or performers are not credited as the copyright owners of the resulting editions. Take the collection of Kathlamet stories discussed above. The introduction gives the title as "KATHLAMET TEXTS. Told by CHARLES CULTEE. Recorded and translated by FRANZ BOAS" (1901:5), and praises Cultee: "The work of translating and explaining the texts was greatly facilitated by Cultee's remarkable intelligence" (ibid:6). Nevertheless, the title page and subsequent bibliographic records name Boas alone as author. Present-day retranslations are more likely to allocate authority to the actual speaker wherever possible, as Darnell notes for the case of a set of texts collected by Edward Sapir and now re-worked and published in consultation with the Kutchin community in Alaska under the name of the original speaker, John Fredson (Darnell 2001:19). This seemingly small change is actually an important one for the professional identity of the anthropologists, who must "become comfortable with the roles of facilitator and translator rather than that of author" (ibid:19). Translation scholars might counter that these roles are less subservient and humble than

Darnell implies – but as we have seen, in the case of ethnographic translation over-humility has never been the problem and there is an urgent need for a more precise delineation of roles which does not eliminate the author in favour of the translator. This is a means of countering excessive generalization and also, importantly for ethnopoetics, of highlighting the component of individual artistry in the production of 'traditional' literature.

Moving to the stylistic aspects of retranslations in this mould, much interesting work has been directed at trying to bring out the "voices" hidden in the transcriptions (Bringhurst 1999:14). Tedlock's translation method cannot be applied to this undertaking, since it requires immediate and tape-recorded performances with the pause patterns created by the speaker him- or herself. However, Dell Hymes, the linguist and anthropologist so instrumental in bringing translation questions to the forefront of discussion, uses a related approach based on the written records. He looks for aesthetic patterning not in physical pauses but in prosodic and semantic aspects: "the form of repetition and variation, of constants and contrasts, in verbal organization" (1965:321). Highly dependent on the precision of the transcribed records, Hymes's translations reinstitute patterns of repetition and articulate the text into lines, stanzas, scenes and acts. Hymes calls for retranslation as a natural component of literary reception. He notes that "any one translation is like a spotlight from one angle, highlighting some features, but shadowing others. A plurality of responsible translations can illumine more and in greater depth" (ibid:335). Indeed, in one paper he offers a counter-translation – an 'active retranslation' in Pym's sense – of one of Tedlock's poems to illumine both their divergence and the element which is, in his opinion, "really there" in the source text. With its highlighted use of repetition, Hymes's retranslation of Peynetsa and Tedlock's "Coyote and Junco" gives a taste of how he prioritizes rhetorical structures over sound structures, drawing on and confirming ethnographic data about, for example, the significance of number patterns in Native American verbal art.

Andrew Peynetsa's "Coyote and Junco"

[i. Coyote meets Junco]

A Son'ahchi.
        Sonti Lo::::ng ago:
    At Standing Arrows,
        Old Lady Junco had her home.

B Meanwhile Coyote,
        Coyote was there at Sitting Rock with his children,
            he was there with his children.

C Meanwhile Old Lady Junco was winnowing,
pigweed and tumbleweed she was winnowing;
with her basket she winnowed these by tossing them in the air,
she was tossing them in the air.

D Meanwhile Coyote,
Coyote was going around hunting,
going around hunting for his children there,
when he came to see where Junco was winnowing.
(Hymes 1997 [1982]:49)

Translating into target-language canons

Hymes's concern with line breaks arises from a change in assumptions about Native American cultures, in earlier decades found 'primitive' and underdeveloped partly with recourse to the evidence of translations of their products. But his positive judgement is also informed by changes in taste in English literature, which can now interpret pared-down, densely symbolic texts as valuable poetry even in the absence of the "familiar acoustic furniture" of rhyming couplets and so on – an absence which led Kroeber to rule out the very existence of a Native American poetry (Bringhurst 1999:363). It was, too, an absence which for some earlier ethnographers prompted a corrective: a 'poetic' translation which claimed a space in the national literary canon as opposed to remaining in the scientific sphere of ethnological information-value. As is the case for literary translations and retranslations in general, the location of these texts in target-language poetic canons has varied over the years. It is a key feature of 'passive retranslation' in Pym's sense that changing tastes demand new versions even if the overall intention and rationale for translating remains similar across time. The translation by Henry Rowe Schoolcraft in 1851 (reprinted in Day's anthology, 1951:28; also cited in Hymes 1965:319) which we will look at now certainly aims to impart the literariness of the text he heard, to defend it from the charge of savage crudeness and bring it into the fold of American Literature. It illustrates how extremely changeable are the fortunes of a translation over time, and how little anthropological confidence can be placed in records of oral poetry that delete the transcription phase and go straight to the English poem:

Chant To The Fire-Fly
(Chippewa original)

Wau wau tay see!
Wau wau tay see!
E mow e shin

Tahe bwau ne baun-e-wee!
Be eghaun—be eghaun—ewee!
Wau wau tay see!
Wau wau tay see!
Was sa koon ain je gun.
Was sa koon ain je gun.

(Literal translation)
Flitting-white-fire-insect! waving-white-fire-bug! give me light before I go to bed! give me light before I go to sleep. Come, little dancing white-fire-bug! Come, little flitting white-fire-beast! Light me with your bright white-flame-instrument—your little candle.

(Literary translation)
Fire-fly, fire-fly! bright little thing,
Light me to bed, and my song I will sing.
Give me your light, as you fly o'er my head,
That I may merrily go to my bed.
Give me your light o'er the grass as you creep,
That I may joyfully go to my sleep.
Come, little fire-fly, come, little beast—
Come! and I'll make you tomorrow a feast.
Come, little candle that flies as I sing,
Bright little fairy-bug—night's little king;
Come, and I'll dance as you guide me along,
Come, and I'll pay you, my bug, with a song.

Incidentally, this translation did not remain confined to an anthropological audience. Longfellow soon adapted it, along with other motifs and personal names, from Schoolcraft's primarily ethnological work into his *Song of Hiawatha*, a version of American Indian life and art which found a much wider popular audience (1855:Book III):

"Wah-wah-taysee, little fire-fly,
Little, flitting, white-fire insect,
Little, dancing, white-fire creature,
Light me with your little candle,
Ere upon my bed I lay me,
Ere in sleep I close my eyelids!"

In Schoolcraft's three-part presentation, the transcription means even an uninitiated reader can spot the slipperiness of the term 'literal' translation as well as the Victorian excesses of the 'literary' one. The use of repetition, for example, is visually accessible and casts into doubt the literal translation, which may (in a charitable interpretation) be aiming to integrate the polysemy of individual items into English without using notes. The combination leaves open the question of whether the song is presented as ethnological information or as art, and it belongs in a tradition ambivalent on the distinction. The 1951 anthology which included the Schoolcraft poem presents itself as gathering Native American poetry in its own right, yet the anthology's construction 'ethnologizes': the poems are preceded by a long introduction, divided into geographical or culture-area chapters, and embedded in explanatory text. Their right to be anthologized is defended in terms of knowledge-gain: "No one who is not familiar with this poetry should presume to make judgments based on his understanding of the 'real' Indian" (Day 1951:xi), an understanding which the fortunate reader of Day can, apparently, access at will. Interestingly, the anthologist deploys evolutionary models very reminiscent of the style of ethnographic monographs. He creates a time-frame where the Indians belong firmly to the past, and recommends that, while "obviously" it would be pointless to compare the best of the collected translations with Dante's *Divine Comedy*, the reader would do well to compare them with, for example, "pagan Greek hymns from the time of Hesiod" (ibid:26). The poems are excluded from the timescale of written European poetry despite the claim elsewhere in the foreword that some of these poems can hold their own as genuine "contributions to American literature" (ibid:x).

Without transcriptions, the translators in an anthology can far more easily steer the reader's perceptions of the works – the reader is, so to speak, at their mercy. In the 1918 collection *The Path on the Rainbow*, the style of the 'Indian' poems is strikingly modern, and this is underlined explicitly in the introduction by Mary Austin. She notes that the reader will remark the likeness with the work of "the Imagists, vers librists, and other literary fashionables" (Cronyn 1918:xvi). This should not be interpreted as evidence that the Imagists are primitive or have unoriginally copied Indian verse, she continues. Rather, the coincidence demonstrates that poetry is shaped by its relationship to the natural environment and that contemporary white American poets are striving to strengthen their connection with the American soil. Thus the likeness which the translations posit between current trends in the dominant culture and the ancient words of the aboriginals "is the certificate of our adoption" (ibid: xvii). The anthology's dedication stresses that none of the songs presented "exhibit the slightest trace of European influence; they are genuine American Classics". Here the role of the translations is to reinforce nationalist claims of the target-language culture by re-writing the ravaged source cultures as harmonious predecessors and ancient pedigrees.

It comes as no surprise to see translations being used to back up the political and poetic agendas of one moment in time – that is a familiar phenomenon in the history of translation. But through their ethnographizing presentation these particular translations carry an especially heavy burden of significance in this respect, since they much more explicitly than other literary translations claim to 'represent' cultures, minority cultures which in some cases have long ago fallen victim to the violence of the target-language dominant culture. The claims of knowledge and representation appear in a much harsher light and the question of accountability becomes paramount.

Accountability versus appropriation is a pressing issue for another branch of ethnopoetics, one less closely related to anthropology or folklore studies and more closely to modernist poetry. The ethnopoets around Jerome Rothenberg – including Nathaniel Tarn, Gary Snyder, and others – translate or retranslate 'native' art in a quest to expand the boundaries of the concept of poetry in English while also bringing the work of non-literate peoples to the attention of the literate world. Rothenberg's 1968 anthology *Technicians of the Sacred* was followed by further collections, and a journal of ethnopoetics, *Alcheringa*, ran from 1970-1980 edited by Rothenberg and Dennis Tedlock. In Rothenberg's collections, the translations are left to stand alone in the body of the text, with a commentary section at the end noting the sources and sometimes associatively discussing style and history. Rothenberg proceeds from the view that 'primitive' poetry is the true poetry and can be accessed by everyone through our human psychic unity; accordingly, his approach is to focus on reconstructing poetic feeling and musicality. Many of the poems are retranslations of ethnolinguistic collections, made without reference to the source language, but some are freshly done by Rothenberg in collaboration with native speakers. A particularly interesting example of the latter is the cycle of "Horse Songs" that Rothenberg translated, with the help of a specialist linguist, from taped performances. The following excerpt from one of the poems anthologized in *Shaking the Pumpkin* (1991:296) shows how Rothenberg tries to represent the marked (that is, 'poetic') language and musical effects of the performances he heard:

THE 13TH HORSE SONG OF FRANK MITCHELL (WHITE)
Navajo

Key: nnnn N N gahn

Some 're lovely N nawu nnnn but some 're & are at my hawuz nawu wnn
N wnn baheegwing
Some 're lovely N hawu nnnn but some 're & are at my howinow N wnn
baheegwing
Some 're lovely N nawu nnnn but some are & are at my howzes nawu
nahht bahyeenwing but bahyeesum nahtgwing

The commentary on this translation (ibid:411-13) refers to Rothenberg's aim of "total translation", as set out in more detail in an essay of that title (Rothenberg 1975). Total translation will account not just – maybe not even primarily – for meaning but for the music, word distortions, and non-word or 'meaningless' syllables, because

> everything in these song-poems is finally translatable: words, sounds, voice, melody, gesture, event, etc., in the reconstitution of a unity that would be shattered by approaching each element in isolation. (1975:306)

This responds to the lack felt by so many ethnolinguists faced with the 'dry' and deadened transcriptions of verbal art, and it promises an accessibility and impact for the target-language reader that is not available in the more hard-core anthropological translation styles. The approach deliberately attacks the radical separation between Western and 'other' poetry. These works of art are brought into the category of 'high literature' by framing them in modernist idioms such as concrete poetry and events; the stated aim is fruitful reciprocity. Rothenberg frames his methods in terms of mutuality and dialogue with the other: "translation, as we have sometimes tried to practice it, is not the reproduction of, or stand-in for, some fixed original, but [...] functions as a commentary on the other and itself and on the differences between them" (1992:65). As Krupat (1992b) points out, this ideal is close to that of Rudolf Pannwitz as quoted by Benjamin, where the aim of translation should be to bend and shape the receiving language through the impact of the source.

On the other hand, the stress on the 'universal' poetic spirit of the pieces also means the voice (collective or individual) of the author may be entirely displaced. In an impassioned attack on another ethnopoet, William Brandon, critic William Bevis accused these writers of jumping on a bandwagon of 1960s and 70s popular interest in Native Americans and passing off freely 'edited' versions of ethnolinguistic documents as authentic poetry, thus oppressing the authors by "putting words in their mouths" (1975:310). Bevis finds that as long as translators claim to provide understanding of Native American culture (which Rothenberg surely does, in the guise of universal human spirituality), they position themselves as a source of knowledge, as opposed to a source of poetic pleasure, and must therefore be judged by more than aesthetic standards alone. Bevis's conclusion is that instead of offering an experience of the foreign, Brandon has pruned and trained the ethnolinguistic texts to fit into "the garden of English verse" (ibid:316). Since the reader has no means of judging what the translator has done, the result is a misrepresentation of the distinct identity of the source texts, an attempt to "shortcut" into alien aesthetic experience (ibid:321) by adapting it to existing expectations. A related criticism comes from Nathaniel Tarn, himself an anthropologist and poet, who notes that gathering poetries from all over the world – "the appropriation of what belongs to others" (Tarn 1984:275) – could be read as a kind of grand-scale exploitation. In view of the limited market for poetry, it would be dangerous if the ethnopoets' 'versions' drove out the work of Native poets themselves, he adds.

The ethnopoets around Jerome Rothenberg would disagree that their translations are shameless appropriations, since the texts they work with are, in their view, first and foremost poems and thus as open to the worldwide flows of literary art as any other piece of literature. Seen this way, the experimental translation of Native American works is an attempt to enliven world literature and to find a fitting place within it for the oral tradition. Indeed, if we judge these translators by the same measure that Descriptive Translation Studies, for example, applies to any other, translations should be studied as legitimate (though not necessarily laudable) products set loose from their sources, and not as aspiring to be the sole mirror and representative of an 'original'. If the Native American poems are considered as literature, we cannot exempt their translators from the right to rewrite. In other words, the argument of 'distortion' falls to pieces in as much as these texts are artistic products waiting to be re-enacted and produced anew in translation. Yet Tarn's criticisms support Niranjana's concerns about the focus in Descriptive Translation Studies on the target text to the exclusion of the effects of translation on the source culture. For anthropologically oriented translators, texts of the oral tradition are more than literary, they are the products and indices of the particularities of real people's lives, and their translations impact back on those people's lives as representations by the dominant culture. As such, they become subject to criticisms of distortion which we might not want to level at pairs of texts in more symmetrical circumstances.

Let's end this chapter with a linguist and ethnographer who rejects the priority given to the 'poetic' by many of the ethnopoets we have discussed and whose goal is "to make texts understandable" by means of extensive annotation. Anthony Mattina (1987; Seymour 1985) describes his approach to translating the style of a Colville narrative: the version was made collaboratively with a bilingual Colville and English speaker, Madeline deSautel, whose spoken translations of the tapes into her own dialect of English formed the basis for the final version. An interlinear version and extensive glossary supplement the continuous translation. Here is a sample, an early section of *The Golden Woman* where the sons are about to set off on their journey:

> 5. And then the youngest one wanted to go along, but he was small. His father told him, "No, you stay home. You're too small, you'd give your brothers something to worry about, you might do something your

> brothers'll be responsible for. You just as well stay here. Take care of us old people. You'll be setting down with us."
>
> But no, he wouldn't listen because a little boy just ain't got no sense. And then he cried.
>
> (Seymour 1985:21)

Mattina admits that the use of what he calls "Red English" risks being read as confirmation of preconceptions that the language of American Indians is 'impoverished' or 'sub-standard', but argues that it is the preconceptions, not the translation style, which need to change. He cites examples of an emerging literary discourse in 'Red English', such as the poetry of Leslie Marmon Silko, into which he wants to hook his translations – a strategy which in effect implements Venuti's call to use translation as a means of valorizing a 'minor' discourse and disrupting the self-confidence of the major language. In contrast to some of the experiments we have been discussing, Mattina's version of the 'foreignizing' approach works not by adding opacity or unexpected typography, but by foregrounding the translating voice of someone outside the dominant discourse of written English (for an interesting defence of a similar approach, see Cruikshank et al. 1990). To this extent, then, the translation corresponds with those ethnographic experiments that try to disrupt the natives' passive state of being-translated. Mattina points towards the growing body of work in English by Native American writers that is itself a many-cultured 'hybrid' in Bhabha's sense (1994), making visible the translatedness of all language and language-art.

If Mattina and deSautel's work was received by some reviewers as an insult to American Indian speech (1987:139), this emphasizes the highly charged political atmosphere surrounding such literary representations. The same problem faces Native American autoethnographers, as Rachel Ramsay (1999) explains. The author she discusses re-told an oral tale in a way that highlighted conflicts among her Gwich'in compatriots, and the story was received by the author's family and friends as a cultural betrayal. They understood the telling not as an individual 'literary' product but as an ethnographic document which could endanger the reputation of the tribe. As Ramsay notes, the non-totalizing account that is called for by the cultural critics might turn out to play a very ambiguous role in the receiving environment: accustomed to totalizing representations of Native Americans, the dominant culture may be unable to let a particular fictionalized perspective stand on its terms and instead insist on seeing it "as representing in a totalizing way what Native Americans are or were" (1999:39). Once again, we are reminded that however experimental and principled the translation, it can never be independent of the existing ideological climate which receives it.

7. Museum Representations

In an essay on anthropological museums, James Clifford suggests that one way of understanding ethnography itself is as "a form of culture collecting". This perspective highlights "the ways that diverse experiences and facts are selected, gathered, detached from their original temporal occasions, and given enduring value in a new arrangement" (1988:231). Like ethnographies, museums construct spaces or slots of meaning inside which other cultures can be made intelligible to the museum visitor, and they give verbal information that answers the visitor's question "What does it mean?" (MacGaffey 2003:255). In these respects ethnographic exhibitions parallel the translation task of written ethnography, and the two also have close institutional and historical links. The ethnographic museum remains an important 'public face' of academic anthropology, though it enjoys an audience far larger and more diverse than written ethnography can dream of. Can museum ethnography, though, usefully be studied in terms of translation? Unlike literary translation there is no preceding physical text, and unlike written ethnography the museum's medium is not primarily words. Yet the ethnographic display shares with written ethnographies the task of 'making sense', in terms intelligible to the receiving culture, of a mass of cultural practices – it is another form of knowledge-sieve through which other people's lives are filtered for presentation inside the receiving discipline of anthropology, the larger institution of the museum, and the surrounding society.

In the study of written ethnography, I argued earlier that searching for an authentic or original 'source text' with which to compare the 'target text' for accuracy was not only impracticable but also based on an untenable assumption that stable, fixed and potentially authentic 'cultures' exist. Instead, we looked at the translations in their own existence as textual representations. Analogously, to study museums as translations is not to evaluate faithfulness but to ask how they work in the world as text-like artefacts themselves, as well as how they impact back onto the places where their artefacts were made. Rather than reading these collections as more or less accurate representations of the other, Virginia Dominguez proposes that

> they can fruitfully be read as referential indices of the Self. Their concrete objects come from other societies, but everything about the collection itself – the way the objects were collected, why they were collected, and how and why they get displayed – points to us [i.e. Euro-American anthropologists]. (1986:554)

This is a reflexive perspective that has been increasingly adopted in recent years by critical museum studies, sometimes referred to as the 'New Museology'. The contributors to Karp and Lavine's important collection *Exhibiting Cultures: The Poetics and Politics of Museum Display* (1991), for example, work with similar questions to those posed by the Writing Culture critics a few years earlier, and the title deliberately echoes that of the Clifford and Marcus volume. They approach museum display as one among many forms of the representation of 'culture', subject to far-reaching query in a postcolonial age.

The museum as translation

Approaching museums as text-like is a method that has gained ground in museum studies over the past few decades. In studies like those collected by Karp and Lavine or the work of Eilean Hooper-Greenhill (e.g. 2000), the museum representation of cultures is described in terms of meaning-production within particular ideological perspectives and as 'written' and 'read' by particular interpretive communities. Analysis along these lines rejects the idea that objects are objective or neutral 'things', and tries instead to understand how the aura of objectivity in museums came about historically and works in the present day. It frequently applies concepts from literary studies, as Bettina Messias Carbonell explains in the introduction to her weighty reader *Museum Studies*, identifying four poetic tropes on which "the rhetoric of museology relies": metaphor (whereby the objects stand for something other than themselves), metonymy (whereby objects conjure up a more complex reality by association), synecdoche (where the object stands as a part for the larger whole), and irony (where objects and other components of the exhibition contradict themselves and each other; Carbonell 2004:6). Especially in the case of ethnographic museums, this kind of approach shares much with the textualizing methods of critical ethnography. Although the 'translation' tag so fashionable in anthropology has up to now been much less popular in museum studies, there are clearly parallel concerns:

> Questions arise about which objects have been collected and why, and what is known about them from which perspective. One critical element in the construction of meaning within museums is the presence or absence of particular objects; a second vital consideration is that of the framework of intelligibility into which collected objects are placed. Objects in museums are assembled to make visual statements which combine to produce visual narratives. (Hooper-Greenhill 2000:3)

Certainly, museums cannot simply be equated with texts. Sharon Macdonald lists the distinctive non-text-like features of museums:

> their authoritative and legitimizing status, their roles as symbols of community, their 'sitedness', the centrality of material culture, the

> durability and solidity of objects, the non-verbal nature of so many of their messages, and the fact that audiences literally enter and move within them. (1996:5)

The museum form differs from writing, yet the aspects which Macdonald lists are the very ones that make museums so interesting for the study of a society's meaning-making – and in our case meaning-making about other 'cultures'. As Macdonald puts it, museums are a kind of "theoretical thoroughfare" (ibid:6) where thinking about identity, knowledge and knowability takes visible shape. Many dimensions have to be factored in here, since the museum offers a polysemiotic combination of visual, verbal, aural and kinaesthetic experiences. For example, a visitor will see an object in a particular setting, arranged and lit in a particular way to seem functional or aesthetically important, typical or unique, positioned with other objects which build up an interpretative context. Thus, an earthenware pot next to many other earthenware pots from around the world asks to be understood differently from an earthenware pot in a reconstructed eighteenth-century potter's workshop, or an earthenware pot next to other cooking utensils, or one set against a large photograph of a landscape or of a person making a pot. The visual context steers the way we will 'read' this object. Interpretative guidance is also provided by the verbal accompaniment to our hypothetical pot, in the form of a label, an introductory panel, the name of the gallery or the exhibition catalogue and other explanatory material. Sound, too, plays its part, whether as musical or other sound-effects incorporated in the display, recorded voices in video or listening stations, or as the silence or background noises brought by the visitors themselves. And the visitor's experience of the pot is affected as well by the physical circumstances – is this pot the last straw for the museum-goer in need of a café break, or is it the gallery's opening flourish; does the display invite visitors to move up close and touch the object or keep them at a distance through glass and alarms?

Even if ethnographic museums are 'more than' text, in this chapter I am going to treat them as cultural translations in two ways: firstly by virtue of their job of representing cultures through the medium of objects – a translation from the originating world of the objects into a new network of meanings and interpretations. This sense is close to the broad sense of translation I have used to describe the transformation from oral to spoken, from experience to academic writing, from one cultural horizon to another. Secondly, I will be looking at the written discourse in the museum and asking how it handles the words that once surrounded the objects displayed. This is closer to the topic of 'native words' as discussed in the previous chapters, although we will see that source-language words are an even poorer cousin in the traditional ethnographic museum than they were in the written ethnographies of the functionalists and their descendants.

Let's start with that former sense: how do objects work in museums? If objects are like lexical items ordered in the "syntax" of the exhibition (Bal 2001:141), they will not be as solid and motionless as they first appear. Just as the meanings of words change in time and specific communicative encounters, collected objects are not static but constantly in flux and subject to multiple interpretations. Although they may seem concrete and individual, displayed objects are called upon to be typical or metonymic, referring to – and guaranteeing the authenticity of – a much larger, anterior reality. Although they seem to belong to a foreign language, in the museum they are retold in the language of the display, a new code which may leave little trace of previous meanings. And although they may seem to be lifeless and non-human, in fact they exist as components of human interaction, including the interactions which brought them to the museum.

If objects are embedded in human action, once in the museum they are also embedded in extensive texts and contexts that accumulate as the years pass. Introducing their interest in objects, Chris Gosden and Chantal Knowles describe a drab-looking piece of barkcloth stored in the Pitt Rivers Museum and show how it is surrounded by text. They cite the notes in the accession book and on the store-room tag, which identify the item as cloth used to bind the head of a newborn and collected in New Guinea on 30 July 1937; the collector's notes in her diary, which include the name of the baby's mother and the price paid; photographs of mother and baby; and cine film of the head-binding process (2001:1). They also outline the historical moment in which the cloth was bought – Beatrice Blackwood collected it during a specific assignment to research head-binding, partly to contextualize displays of elongated skulls and partly as a topic of disapproving fascination to the missionaries and colonial administration. As Gosden and Knowles point out, their own analysis is yet one more "stratum of a series of layered accounts about these objects" (ibid:23). Thus although the barkcloth seems at first sight to be an alien object telling the viewer something about the indigenous people of New Guinea, this is only one way of reading it once inside the Pitt Rivers Museum. Itself recycled from a piece of clothing, the headbinding barkcloth exemplifies the way that objects like this "are always in a state of becoming" whether in their first context of use or after entering the museum (ibid:4).

The 'stories' that an object like the barkcloth is made to tell, and the ways they are told, are what interest narratologist Mieke Bal. In her thought-provoking analysis of the American Museum of Natural History, Bal looks at the museum from a semiotic point of view, as a composition of sign systems – visual, spatial and verbal, frequently contradicting each other – that make up narratives of primitive and civilized, identity and difference. She begins with the topographical significance of two great New York museums facing each other across Central Park as the "preserves of culture and nature", the

Metropolitan Museum of Art and the American Museum of Natural History. The latter contains anthropological exhibits alongside exhibits on the natural world, nature and culture constituting the joint 'other' of the Met (2001:119), and the art of the people displayed in the Museum of Natural History is categorized as not art but nature, as not aesthetically but scientifically interesting. The space of the Museum, says Bal, presupposes a walking tour, "an order in which the dioramas, exhibits, and panels are viewed and read. Thus it addresses an implied focalizer, whose tour produces the story of knowledge taken in and taken home" (ibid:122). Of particular interest from a translation point of view is Bal's analysis of the 'language' of this museum, which she describes as a "truth-speak" able to convince the reader that what she or he is seeing is reality. Truth-speak takes the form of scientific discourse and of 'realism': realism in the literary sense, as a form of fiction where the representational status of what we are seeing disappears behind a third-person narrative that "highlights the object while obscuring the subject" (ibid:126). Thus the museum seems to be all about the others – 'showing' them to us – and nothing about the self – 'telling' a story, with the partiality and the ideological tensions that story-telling involves (ibid:153). Bal advocates a disruption of this realist convention by turning attention to the speaking 'I'. Following Benveniste, she notes that the 'I' of the museum narrative is more authoritative than in a face-to-face conversation:

> in a normal conversation the I-you positions are reversible, while the 'third person' is powerless, excluded. But in the case of exposition, the 'you' cannot take the position of the 'I.' While the I-you positions preside over the 'third person,' the 'I' performs the representation, the gesture of showing, in conjunction with a 'you' who may be real, but who is also imaginary, anticipated, and partly molded by that construction. (ibid:134-5)

Turning explicit attention to the dynamics of such speaking positions can splinter the realist illusion (Bal suggests that mirrors in the exhibition would help) and bring to the fore the other story, "the story of the representational practice exercised in this museum" (ibid:153).

Bal's analysis shows that particular preferred readings are powerfully implemented in the museum. However, the mode of 'reading' museum displays differs from that of reading texts above all because, despite the impact of exhibition 'syntax', material objects are still more open than written texts to disparate and constantly changing interpretations (see Hooper-Greenhill 2000:115). The growing body of work in visitor studies indicates that curators' intentions may bear only a very unpredictable relation to the ways visitors actually use the displays. For example, one study of visitors to a science museum found that far from coming to be informed by the voice of knowledge, families took the interpretive initiative based on their own communicative habits: "mothers do most of the talking in family groupings; they refer to objects as a way of talking about values and family history, rather than talking about the objects per se" (Perin 1992:189). The social surroundings, then – the other people moving around together with the visitor – clearly influence each individual's 'reading'. Not only can the overall aims of the museum be subverted by visitors, but on the level of individual objects the curators' intended interpretations will be only one factor in the reading reached by each visitor. Hooper-Greenhill argues that visitors' interpretations grow from their personal biographies, yet share repertoires with "communities of meaning-making, which establish frameworks of intelligibility within which individual subjects negotiate, refine and develop personal constructs" (2000:119). Her point calls to mind the Bakhtinian perspective applied by so many of the critical ethnographers we looked at in Chapter 5, focusing on the intersection of producer and addressee as the unstable point where meaning comes about, and it lends itself to a perspective where different language frameworks meet and negotiate in the 'third space' of translation.

Shifting contexts

If museums represent cultures in an even partially text-like way, it is clear that they will be subject to change in mode and meaning over time. Not only will the holdings and selection of objects change, but the meaning attached to those objects too will shift, as will the role of the display within larger social and cultural formations. Dusty as some museums may seem to the visitor, not one of them can really remain static, any more than a literary translation can remain unaffected by the passage of time around it. Let's look briefly, therefore, at the paths that European, and later North American, museums have taken over the last five centuries or so.

In her historical survey of European museums, Eilean Hooper-Greenhill bases her chronology on Foucault's identification of successive 'epistemes', or sets of relations which produce knowledge and define rationality (1992:12). Using Foucault's periodization, Hooper-Greenhill begins with a Renaissance episteme that saw divine meaningfulness in things and their hidden relationships with each other. In the apparently jumbled collections of the time, the 'cabinets of curiosities' combining natural and artificial, animal and vegetable and mineral and antique, resemblances between things were to be interpreted for their significance inside a divine cosmos. Synthesizing these meaningful objects was God, or in his stead the powerful patron of the collection, whose ability to amass such treasures was continually reaffirmed by their display. In the classical period from the early seventeenth century, says Hooper-Greenhill, the museum style moved abruptly towards a cataloguing scheme, based on the emerging sciences of botany and zoology and aiming for encyclopaedic coverage. Knowledge now seemed to be potentially "definable and controllable" (ibid:16), and the magical, hermeneutic and multi-faceted experience of the Renaissance cabinet was replaced by a new priority on visual observation, on seeing "a limited number of things in a very systematic way" (ibid:138).

Anthony Alan Shelton locates the 'encyclopaedic' collection somewhat differently, seeing the collections of the mid-sixteenth to early seventeenth century as still importantly informed by the medieval understanding of objects as metaphorical expressions of God's universe. Wonder at curious things belonged to the religious sense of the marvellous (1994:180), while the increasingly important goal of comprehensiveness drew on the centrality of allegory in medieval thought: the collection could represent the universe in a miniature or mirror form. Treasures from the 'New World' arriving in Europe in the sixteenth century were displayed as exemplars of the category of a generalized 'pagan' with little interest in the details of their provenance; Shelton's argument is that the potentially disturbing evidence of high civilization in America, in the form of wonderfully crafted Aztec jewellery and other artworks, was read as a further instance of the marvellous under the guiding hand of a European God.

The late eighteenth century saw the advent of what Hooper-Greenhill calls the 'disciplinary' or 'modernist' museum. She describes the foundation of a public museum at the Louvre Palace in 1793, opening up what used to be the property of royalty and aristocracy to the newly forming democratic public. Administratively attached to the state education system, the Musée Central des Arts was assigned the educational role of "transforming the population into a useful resource for the state" (1992:182), and it gave rise to new subject positions like the professional curator, the guard, or the well-behaved observing layman. As regards the structures of knowledge informing the collection, historical change now became the crucial principle and abstract relationships of underlying structure took over from the visual resemblances that had governed earlier European museum types (ibid:185-6). As Carol Duncan explains, the Louvre's chronological arrangement of its treasures used great historical moments to present a pedigree for the new nation; once "recontextualized as art history, the luxury of princes could now be seen as the spiritual heritage of the nation, distilled into an array of national and individual genius" (1991:95).

Nation-building missions like this were to become a driving force in the development of European and North American museums into the present day. Art museums, with their temple-like architecture, enacted a "ritual of citizenship" (Duncan 1991), while national history museums offered more explicit versions of imagined community for public consumption. Anthropological collections represented exotic others in terms of their immense distance from the domestic audience, and even zoological exhibitions participated in nation-building agendas (see Haraway 1984, discussed below). In fact, the modern museum may be seen as a kind of 'identity factory', reproducing "structures of belief and experience through which cultural differences [and likewise identities] are understood" (Karp et al. 1992:1-2). Images of self and other, thus, were produced and confirmed in the museum in a way not unlike the processes of literary canon formation as described by, for example, Lefevere (1992).

Hooper-Greenhill analyzes one historical moment in these terms. She interprets the establishment of London's National Portrait Gallery in 1856 (2000:ch. 2) as an attempt to define the 'centre' of a sprawling Empire by means of selection and exclusion. The absence of representatives of the 'margin', in other words the bulk of the 200 million people subject to the British Empire at the time of the Gallery's foundation, allowed the definition of the nation as distilled in a small group of illustrious white middle-class or aristocratic men. Likewise, anthropological displays in museums and exhibitions of 'colonial life' in the same period positioned the distant others within a hierarchy of values that placed middle-class British life at the top. The ways of the colonized peoples were represented by objects in the museum, as well as by living actors and mock-up miniature 'villages' along with photos and artefacts in travelling exhibitions. These late-Victorian living exhibitions, set up by commercial operators or missionary societies, worked intertextually with the genre of the colonial adventure travelogue (Coombes 1994:66), and shared with it a "trophy method of display" (ibid:197) that stressed capture and conquest. Such exhibitions gathered momentum and resonance in the late Victorian and Edwardian era "as a site where the myth of national unity was consummated in the public domain" (ibid:187).

But despite the proximity of their content and political context, late nineteenth-century anthropological museums tried specifically to distinguish themselves from the more entertainment-oriented fair tradition. In these products of what is often called the 'Museum Age' in Europe and North America, scientistic principles of taxonomy and hierarchy promised a panoptic mode of knowledge where vision could embrace the entirety of meaningful facts. The classification of the human species was an integral part of the project, carried out through definitions of 'racial types' in the museum cases. The emerging genre of the anthropological museum thus gave pride of place to skeletal evidence, especially skulls, as demonstrations of 'race'. Nélia Dias explains how nineteenth-century French craniology posited racial differences and went on to 'discover' them in the characteristics of the skulls it studied (1998:38). For these differences to be seen, they had to be made visible through a new language of numbers and visual abstractions: "The human body was not directly legible but only offered itself up to the gaze of the scholars by means of rigorous instruments of observation and measurement" (ibid:40). For nineteenth-century museum physical anthropologists, the subjectivity and interpretative scope of verbal language seemed unequal to the task of portraying the reality behind the skulls, of making them into indisputable 'fact'; measuring technologies, statistical models, and diagrams were required (ibid:43). Dias's point here, drawing on the work of historians of science, is that the skulls themselves were not simply 'seen' in some unmediated or natural way, but were offered to a particular form of gaze that made them into facts and, what's more, into facts that proved biological difference. The skulls in the museum, once arranged and interpreted, made it possible both "to visualize difference at all levels, from the general to the particular, and to *naturalize* socially and culturally constructed differences" (ibid:48; Hooper-Greenhill's work pursues a similar argument for museums in general, drawing on Foucault's notion of the gaze; see especially 2000:ch. 1).

The craniological enthusiasm of the period Dias describes did not remain the dominant mode of museum exhibition. Artefacts and images of living people replaced bones as the components of a classificatory approach derived from natural history. This gave a more central role to technology, which could, however, also be presented as itself a factor of 'race', as in the evolutionist representations we will consider below. For our purposes it is important to notice how apparently neutral objects are unintelligible without an interpreting frame which offers the museum visitor a way to read them. In the terms of cultural relativism that we discussed in Chapter 3, the craniological displays worked like a language, conferring a specific and contingent set of meanings on the available mass of reality by processes of selecting and structuring. Though the 'translation stance' of the museum claims to be a difficult but viable movement from the source language of facts to the target language of order and reason, we have seen that the museum translation includes the making of source 'facts' themselves, which come into existence by means of the ordering or translation process.

Compared with written translations of other cultures in the Museum Age, the visible and tangible representations in the museum carried a particular air of truthfulness – seeing is, after all, believing. This was put to use in the strongly educational agenda that drove the development of the anthropological museum in the period. The method of display cases arranged in identical sets was supposed to make large quantities of information easy to absorb, with the cases acting as "punctuation marks" dividing up the content (Hooper-Greenhill 2000:129-30). Like the 'grid'-style approach to knowledge-gathering common in late nineteenth- and early twentieth-century anthropology, inside which the answers to pre-formed questions were sought and found, the categorization offered by the matrix of cases produces and constrains what can be seen and understood. Whatever the objects in the cases once meant in their originating languages, inside those cases they are subject to the external or 'etic' categories imposed by the describing language. In this respect they are 'rewritten' into the language of the museum. But the cases were also designed as a prime means of educating the working-class visitor about the composition of the human world:

> Anthropological museums were intended to provide experiences especially illuminating to the newly leisured and newly enfranchised artisan and lower-middle classes. Anthropologists believed that these classes reasoned in the concrete terms characteristic of the more primitive members of the human species. (Kuklick 1991:108)

Artefacts would be easier for such domestic 'primitives' to grasp than a written tract. The mode of translation here itself posited its readers in a certain way, defining them while it defined the objects of representation, and, in Kuklick's view (ibid:85) along the same dichotomy of 'primitive'-'civilized'.

For these domestic viewers, representations of the colonized peoples had, though, a more affirmative aspect as well, since they were addressed as the victors in a battle for global power. The South Kensington museum that later became the Victoria & Albert is described by Tim Barringer as a "three-dimensional imperial archive" where "the procession of objects from peripheries to centre symbolically enacted the idea of London as the heart of empire" (1998:11). Barringer notes the popular impact of the casts of the Sanchi gateways shipped from India and set up in the central gallery: from the balcony the visitor surveyed the museum's "authority over the cultural terrain of Britain's Asiatic empire as well as the history of Western art and design" (ibid:19). The encyclopaedic claim, culminating in the Colonial and Indian Exhibition of 1886, celebrated the possession of a "commodified" empire (ibid:24) through the visitor's visual possession of the museum's contents.

The complex roles played by objects from the colonized lands, and the interlocking of museological, popular-culture and commercial interests in the period of high colonialism, is something explored in detail by Annie E. Coombes (1994) in her important study of representations of Africa in late nineteenth- and early twentieth-century England. Her central illustration is the fate of a group of 2400 bronze and ivory artworks belonging to the Benin court and looted by British soldiers during a punitive raid on Benin City in 1897. The aesthetically and technically sophisticated 'Benin bronzes' posed a challenge to representations of Africa as 'primitive', opening debate on their origins. Must such art not be derived from Portuguese imports, or could Benin possibly have an ancient and highly developed civilization of its own? And if so, evolution-minded museum anthropologists asked, did that civilization descend from other African traditions or from ancient Egypt, represented in the British Museum as radically distinct from African culture? As Coombes explains, the argument on the origins of the bronzes was motivated not just by conceptions of primitive and civilized, but by professional interests. Curators of the Museum's new, ill-funded Ethnographic Department were in competition for the valuable objects with the well-established and popular Egyptian galleries on whose "drawing power" the Museum so heavily relied (ibid:57-8). The refusal to acknowledge Ancient Egypt as an African society, though loosening in academic Egyptology of the time, remained firm in the division of the galleries, as indeed it does today (ibid:59). The ethnographic curators argued for non-Egyptian provenance and left intact the Museum categorization that continues to help cement popular genealogies of African civilization; the Benin bronzes remained 'freaks', allegedly an anomaly in African art. The 'freak' status, though, brought with it concrete commercial benefits, as it enhanced the objects' rarity value and thus the status of their owners (61; see also Penny 2002:77,95). In the British press the bronzes were treated as sacred relics of a heroic victory of brave English manhood over the savage Edo, with comprehensive and gruesome accounts of the violence said to have prompted the punitive expedition (Coombes 1994:59-60). The fact that German museums were acquiring the new 'possessions' of the British fuelled an anti-German feeling that was quickly mobilized by the Museum in its drive for funding to buy in more of the stolen bronzes (ibid:60), and today an extensive collection of bronze plaques looted in 1897 can still be seen in the British Museum.

The studies by Coombes and by H. Glenn Penny make it clear how multiple institutional, ideological and commercial interests were at work in the collection of ethnographic objects and in their categorization, valuation and display. Ethnographic collections must also be considered from the perspective of disciplinary history: the museum was both the public face of academic anthropology and an integral part of the discipline's formation in the colonial era. Fabian (1998) reminds us that ethnographic collecting in late nineteenth-, early twentieth-century Africa was firmly rooted in the global commercial context. 'Explorers' gained access to African populations through the patronage and interest of giant imperial companies, and ethnographic objects formed part of the currency that mediated encounters between the colonial and the African sides. As we saw in the case of the Benin bronzes, the world market for ethnographic objects themselves also gave financial momentum to collection activities. However, Fabian adds that as well as promising economic and political profit, ethnographic objects served an epistemological purpose in turning "information into knowledge". He applies Lévi-Strauss's famous phrase, coined to describe the use of myths: material objects were "'good to think' – good to label, classify, judge, attribute to, serve as evidence" – and they enabled anthropologists to create records that could be "transported in space as well as in time" (1998:84). To the effect of helping to establish anthropological categories, Penny adds another contribution of collecting to the emergence of the discipline: the identity of the professionalized anthropologist was bolstered by new expectations of scientific collecting, which were held to require a degree of disciplinary expertise not available to the unscientific commercial adventurer. As fieldwork began to distinguish the professional anthropologist, so anthropological expertise began to distinguish the professional collector. Ethnographic collecting thus developed in parallel to ethnography as a genre and discipline, and its trace in the West, the ethnographic museum, is the close cousin of the written ethnographies of the period.

Thinking back to the case of Evans-Pritchard's involvement with the Nuer, this raises again the question of the 'violence of translation'. With what non-consensuality or force were material things 'translated' into the carefully-labelled arrangements of Western museums? We will look below at the ways in which such arrangements imposed meanings that were concerned above all with domestic taxonomies, in a form of assimilative or appropriating translation of concepts. But the issue of ownership or authorship of the objects as 'source texts' indicates a more obvious form of violence. Many of the objects on display in the early anthropological museums, and often still today, were acquired by force, like the art of Benin, or by a degree of duress amounting to force, like the treasures bought at nominal prices from jailed participants after an 'illegal' Canadian potlatch in 1922 (see Clifford 1997, 123-5). The commercial transactions that more commonly brought objects from colonized societies into European museums, though not involving actual theft, also took place in a context of inequality. Gosden and Knowles (2001) reconstruct some specific moments of collecting in Papua New Guinea to show how complex individual transactions were, and how sellers as well as buyers exercised agency. While in some cases massive ethnographic collecting stripped regions of their valuables, in others new life was breathed into genres that could be produced for sale to the collectors or created inter-regional markets in objects previously considered worthless and unusable for trade.

These portraits of the acquisition process, changing the roles of objects within local economies, are a reminder that if Western museums seem to claim their collections silently represent in the target discourse a static originating milieu, in fact they embody a complicated knot of encounters between source and target language which impacted in both directions. As 'translations', thus, the objects in the museum case fit better with notions of translation as a space of negotiation and conflict (as propounded by Bhabha, for example) than to neat pairs of original and reproduction. If that is so, then the 'authorship' is genuinely under dispute: do the source texts still belong to the people who made them?

The question of ownership – and with it, disputes about the repatriation of objects, especially sacred objects and human remains – will be examined in

Chapter 8. For now, we will move on to a specific case of the museum translation of culture to see how the items of material culture removed from their originating locale were re-inserted into different stories – stories of distance in space and, especially, in time.

Ideologies of arrangement: the Pitt Rivers Museum

The Pitt Rivers Museum, founded in the 1880s and still going strong, offers a striking opportunity for present-day visitors to experience a manner of exhibiting ethnographic material that has been partially or radically changed in more modern displays. Of particular interest from the point of view of translation is the Pitt Rivers' distinctive method of arrangement and categorization, remaining largely intact from its origins in nineteenth-century evolutionist thought.

The principles of evolutionist anthropology informed the mainstream of the new anthropological museum-making at the turn of the nineteenth to the twentieth century. Objects were selected and interpreted to demonstrate the theory of gradual evolution from primitive to complex, from savage to civilized, and the arrangement of the displays gave this idea physical shape:

> Moving among the exhibits in intended fashion, visitors were expected to be impressed by the ordered progress of humankind's development from a savage to a superior state. They would observe that examples of each type of artifact, arrayed in a developmental sequence, had been modified very slowly over time. Thus, the act of viewing museum displays would impart a clear political lesson: responsible citizens did not press for precipitous change, but recognized that social evolution was necessarily gradual. (Kuklick 1991:108)

The physical or kinaesthetic experience described by Kuklick was designed specifically to address the new lower-middle class who, as we have seen already, were thought to be in need of education but themselves still too undeveloped to grasp a written account (ibid). The form of representation seemed well suited to the task of taming the potential savagery of the domestic audience just as it helped to portray the savage abroad as an underdeveloped creature.

The explicitly evolutionist arrangement, where objects were presented as if in chronological sequence, was not the only or even the dominant one in late nineteenth-century European museums. Classification by place of origin was widely practised, but in most cases the geographical arrangement too rested on evolutionist assumptions: in the 1860s the large ethnological collections in Paris, Berlin, Dresden and especially Leiden were mainly arranged geographically to illustrate 'racial' groupings and with the aim of reconstructing humankind's 'past' (Chapman 1985:24). In the United States, anti-evolutionist

Franz Boas pushed for an arrangement focusing on cultural wholes, in order to highlight the specificity of the group being presented: "the main object of ethnological collections", he argued in 1887, "should be the dissemination of the fact that civilization is not something absolute, but that it is relative, and that our ideas and conceptions are true only so far as our civilization goes" (1887/2004:142). To achieve this, artefacts must be shown in context, not as exemplars of a synthesizing theory – as indeed Boas's form of written ethnography, discussed in Chapter 6, gave preference to specificity over synthesis. To complement the cases of ordered artefacts in the museum he curated, Boas made use of life groups, large glass cases with models of people using the artefacts against a painted backdrop.

As Michael Ames (1992:52) notes, Boas's contextualizing life group arrangement also reflected the anthropological concern to present the 'native point of view' (to be sure, without any active involvement of those 'natives'). But there were pitfalls involved. Thus, the great popularity of the life group or 'diorama' among the public turned out to be inspired more by admiration for the technology of the lifelike displays than by interest in their contents. Deploring this distraction from content by form, Boas argued that the exhibit should draw attention to its own artificiality and avoid "ghastly" waxwork effects (Jacknis 1985:102-3). Consciousness of artificiality seems not to be enough to spoil the effect of dioramas, however, which in Bal's view work through the willing suspension of disbelief like the reading of fiction (2001:126,151-3). In her influential study of early twentieth-century zoological dioramas, Donna Haraway (1984) shows that the story told by the diorama form is one of natural hierarchies and perfectibility. By using only representative, unblemished and typical specimens of animals, the exhibits she discusses mediated a systematized, unified version of nature which appealed to the viewer as an incontrovertible demonstration of evolutionary categories. In anthropological dioramas, human beings were brought into a similar zoological framework – while it contextualized artefacts, the diorama decontextualized human beings themselves. Focusing on physical attributes, and frequently built from casts of actual people, the diorama extracted thoughts, language, actions and interactions and left an objectified body on show. As the curator of a 1996 exhibition about representations of the Khoisan comments, the "Bushmen Diorama" in Cape Town's South African Museum continued a white tradition of representing Khoisan people as "physical type or specimen", devoid of words and individuality (Skotnes 1996:20; the diorama, using life casts made in 1912, was dismantled in 2001).

Discussing the use of dioramas and live actors to illustrate ethnographic artefacts in action, Barbara Kirshenblatt-Gimblett distinguishes between "in-situ" and "in-context" representations in a way which evokes target- and source-orientated translation strategies (1991, especially 388-90). The in-situ or mimetic style exemplified by the diorama creates an illusion of completeness and authenticity, draining away the viewer's own interpretations and consciousness of the artifices of representation. Even though the diorama highlights alterity, as a translation strategy it depends on the illusion of transparency, or in Venuti's terms 'fluency', effacing the work of the translators themselves. Kirshenblatt-Gimblett adds that the furthest extension of the in-situ approach is the inclusion of living people as illustrations or interpreters of the exhibits in 'living' or open-air museums (ibid:389). In contrast to the illusionistic in-situ display Kirshenblatt-Gimblett sets the more cerebral, but also more contestable 'in-context' style, which uses explanatory text to provide theoretical frameworks for viewers. Though it exerts "strong cognitive control" over the objects, this form reduces control over viewers' responses by openly admitting the ordering principles that have been applied to the artefacts on display.

In the Pitt Rivers Museum the diorama format stayed strictly in the zoological galleries, and the anthropological collections were arranged as series of evidence in cases. A particularly enthusiastic proponent of the evolutionary approach to material culture and its display, archaeologist and military officer A.H.L.F. Pitt Rivers (1827-1900) posited a ladder of human development at whose pinnacle stood modern Western European Man. Not only people of the chronological past, but contemporaries of Pitt Rivers could stand lower on this scale: Irish and Australian Aborigine people he considered to be in a state of "arrested development", fixed in an earlier point in time, and thus capable of illustrating the lives of their distant predecessors (cited in Chapman 1985:31). While other contemporary collectors saw skeletal remains as the ultimate evidence of racial development (see Dias 1998), for the collector Pitt Rivers artefacts were the most important traces of this evolutionary ladder or 'tree'. They could, he thought, demonstrate the development from prototypical to highly complex forms of, for example, a weapon or a fish hook (Figure 4 shows a sketch by Pitt Rivers of the development of the throwing-stick). Again, one of the lessons Pitt Rivers expected to be drawn from displaying the evolution of artefacts was that sudden change, revolution, was unnatural for both objects and living creatures, and this was the principle he used in a small museum housing some of his considerable ethnological collections and set up for the local rural population in Farnham, Dorset. In lectures on the ideal museum, Pitt Rivers called for an arrangement of concentric circles of display cases, showing artefacts evolving from simplicity to sophistication (Chapman 1985:40-1) with the geographical component indicated by 'pie wedges' dividing up the main developmental thrust. In the centre would be the relics of original Man, "when he is discovered" (cited ibid:41). Though we might expect 'evolution' to imply historical change, the 'history' here is not chronologically but racially defined; 'we' are of the present while 'they' are of the past, in line with what Fabian (1983) calls the "denial of coevalness" in written anthropology. The objects in the Pitt Rivers collection, apparently static because taken out of their context of use, seemed ideally suited to represent settled stages in humanity's past. He interpreted the objects through the prism of a "principle of continuity" (Chapman 1985:20), and wanted them arranged to give visual expression to precisely that principle.

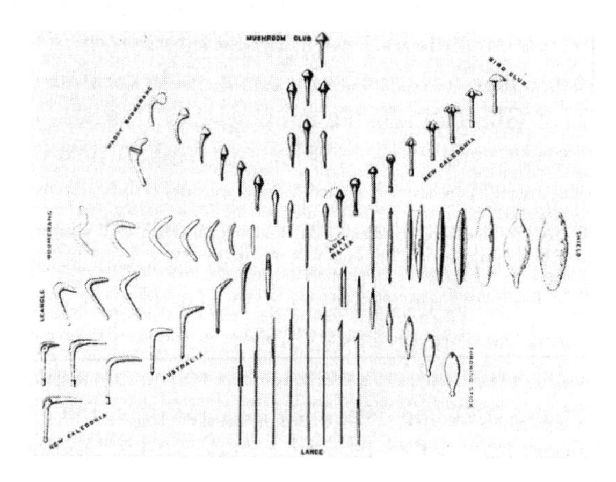

Figure 4. "Clubs, Boomerangs, Shields and Lances", from A.H. Lane Fox (=Pitt Rivers), 'The Evolution of Culture', 1875, facing p. 513

When Pitt Rivers donated the bulk of his collection to Oxford University in 1884, thus establishing what is now the Pitt Rivers Museum, his typological principles were laid down in the deed, although, to his chagrin, they were not carried out as strictly as he had hoped (ibid:39). Still, the museum today retains more or less the original format (with additional labelling, to which I will return below), and is arresting in its arrangement by functions rather than the geographical categories that are more standard today. Figure 5 shows the gallery as it looked in the 1880s, and the general impression is not dissimilar today.

As the Museum's most recent introductory leaflet explains, in the galleries "objects are grouped according to their purpose or use to show how people of different cultures have responded to the same problem. At times they have done so in very similar ways, but sometimes their solutions are poles apart". Thus, the need for light and different technologies used to fulfil that need are illustrated by a case full of candlesticks and lamps, collected from all over the world (relatively unusually for an ethnological collection, this includes European 'folkloric' objects). The items retain their original small, handwritten original labels, but more recent texts have been added to the cases and wall displays as well. Along with the texts of the website and leaflets, these additions shift the interpretation away from the 'primitive to civilized' trajectory so powerful at the Museum's inception, and towards a 'shared human

Figure 5: The Pitt Rivers Museum c 1910
(courtesy of the Pitt Rivers Museum, Oxford)

needs' perspective. The combination makes the Pitt Rivers a particularly rich 'translation', where layers of different interpretation co-exist and make quite different claims. To visit this museum is to experience almost physically the oscillation between 'otherness-oriented' and 'sameness-oriented' translation strategies that we have seen in written ethnographic forms.

Whereas the original display highlighted primarily the difference between the European visitor and the exotic others who produced the artefacts in the cases, the re-framing partially negates this by asking the visitor to 'read' the artefacts as co-temporal and functional, responding to a common reality. Both frameworks order the objects and make sense of them within specific narratives, but there are other reading strategies on offer as well. Perhaps the most distinctive feature of the Pitt Rivers is the sheer mass of objects and their immense variety, piling up layers of examples rather than selecting 'typical' or metonymical ones designed to guide the reader's interpretation along one path around the world on display. Even the Pitt Rivers audio-guide does not take the form of a synoptic guided tour around the galleries; instead, it offers comments on individual numbered cases to be picked at will. The somewhat anarchic aspect of the museum with its thicket of display cases and their crowded contents seems to be appreciated by visitors. Indeed, the audio-guide narrator, David Attenborough, introduces the Pitt Rivers as a "rich plum-pudding of a museum". Children in particular go in search of juicy raisins, and an educational activity sheet lists their 'Top Ten' most popular objects: a set of travelling pistols; Bast, the Ancient Egyptian cat god; miniature ballerinas made of flies; a set of stocks from Oxford; a model ship used as a pattern for potential customers; the African power figure Mavangu; a Sussex witch in a bottle (or, at least, the bottle); an Egyptian mummy; the totem pole; and, top of the list, shrunken heads from South America. There are evidently other selection criteria here than either the ordered march of evolution or the recognition of common practical needs – the visitors' sense of wonder and their own narratives have space to move around the sensual, potentially chaotic, resolutely non-mimetic setting of the Pitt Rivers cases.

The original, nineteenth- and early twentieth-century labels do little to control this variety of responses. They are small and for the most part very terse, noting the object, source location or 'tribe', date of collection, name of collector or donor, and an identification number. Although some add unobtrusive evaluative comments ("Peculiar dismantling pricket candlestick. JAPAN. Coll by A.S. Hewlett, Pur 29.1.1934 (S.G: Hewlett)"), little is offered in the way of synthesis or explicit interpretation. Instead, the visitors bring their own taxonomies of interest and interpretation, and it is not even necessarily the objects themselves which catch their imagination. One woman I overheard was telling her daughter that this museum was just like the museums of her youth in Australia. For her, the visit was to a museum of museums, in Mieke Bal's formulation a 'meta-museum'.

The meta-museum displays both the others and itself; it "points to its own complicity in practices of domination, while continuing to pursue an education project that, born of those practices, has been adjusted to accommodate new concepts and pedagogical needs" (Bal 2001:121). The reflexive element of the Pitt Rivers as a meta-museum is one being actively pursued by a group of researchers on the "Relational Museum" project (www.history.prm.ox.ac.uk), which investigates the history of the Museum's collections. The project views "museums as trans-cultural artefacts composed of relations between the museum and its source communities". The same approach informs the dual labelling strategy within the galleries, where the juxtaposition of the original and more recent labelling styles robs the interpreting voice of its claim to a monopoly on knowledge. It points out that interpretations change over time; the result could be to ironize all the labels and deny final authority to any of them. As a translation strategy, this recalls a palimpsest style which tries to retain different and potentially conflicting versions within one text – though, as we will see, the new labels are rather non-confrontational in their form. On a larger scale, the retention of the complete original layout and labelling more or less intact, along with the research project on the history of the collections, accords with Gosden and Knowles's suggestion that instead of seeing a museum as an incomplete representation of a complete reality, we should use it as a full representation of an incomplete moment – a moment situated in time, place and class with its specific assumptions and agendas, as "complete, although particular, outcomes of individual sets of colonial practices" (2001: xix). The majority of the labelling in the museum prompts precisely this approach, since the main information regarding date and ownership relates to the museum acquisition, not the originating settings. In this respect the 'source text' disappears behind the 'translation'. Attention is diverted to the making of the representation in a similar way to the reflexive written ethnography.

Bal warns, however, that if the reflexive element remains peripheral to the museum it risks being more an "apology" than a real disruption (Bal 2001:142). Although the research projects behind the scenes at the Museum are vital, they are not yet fully integrated into the public display. The distinctive dual labelling approach distances the reader from both sets of labels, but the content of the newer labels seems to avoid fully exploiting the opportunity to throw the museum's history into relief. Apart from an introductory panel, the new labelling does not explicitly address its predecessors but simply offers a more legible, familiar and in fact more synthesized explanation than they do.

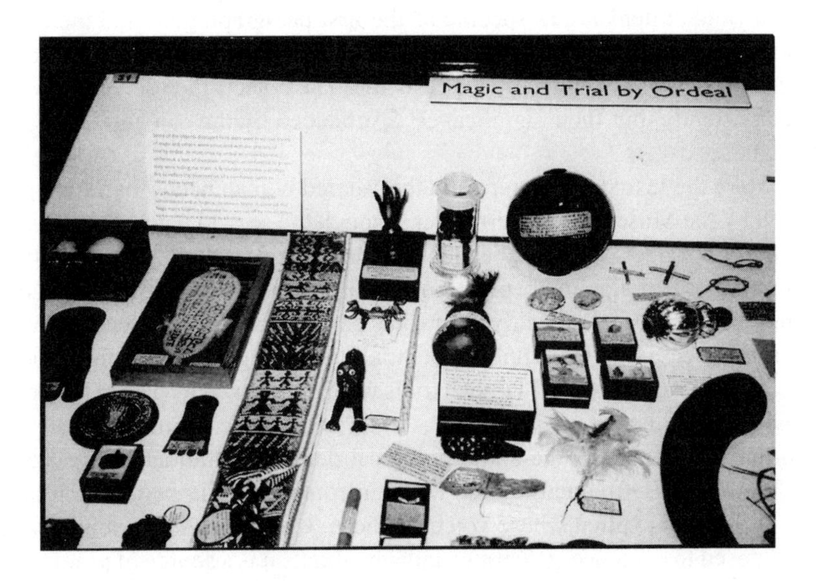

Figure 6: 'Magic and Trial by Ordeal' case, Pitt Rivers Museum (courtesy of the Pitt Rivers Museum, Oxford)

Figure 6 shows part of the case entitled 'Magic and Trial by Ordeal'. The case includes not only the beans and the fingertip referred to in the explanatory label, but also the popular witch-in-a-bottle and a range of amulets and charms. The label runs as follows:

> Some of the objects displayed here were used in various forms of magic and others were associated with the practice of trial by ordeal. In most

> trials by ordeal an accused person undertook a test of divination, strength, or endurance to prove they were telling the truth. A favourable outcome was often felt to reflect the intervention of a non-human agent or other divine being.
>
> In a Madagascan trial by ordeal, poisonous nuts might be administered and in Nigeria, poisonous beans. In contrast the Naga man's fingertip exhibited here was cut off by him to attest to his reliability as a witness to adultery.

There are two aspects of this text which seem to connect it to the genre of 'classical' ethnographic writing as discussed in Chapter 4. One is the impersonal tone, especially striking being the use of passive constructions. In the first sentence, for example, the claim is made that certain objects "were used" for certain purposes. The object is shown; the purpose is named – but the subject is not, in this sentence not even in the guise of the anonymous collective subject familiar from the "the Nuer believe" ethnographic format. "Some", "most" and "often" are as specific as the first paragraph gets, and the effect is to collapse the multifarious objects into the common denominator of their general function as defined by the case title. The objects themselves draw the eye insistently, but their significance is produced by the categorization and the label text.

Here the text strongly supports the 'shared human needs' narrative proposed by the Museum's modern layer. Though the second paragraph narrows the focus considerably, the label does not thematize conflicting cross-cultural definitions of 'magic' or explain how trial by ordeal fits into the category. While trial by ordeal is tacitly defined as part of magical practices by inclusion in the case, the text applies potentially anti-magical terms in its coolly Evans-Pritchardian report that such trials were undertaken by people "to prove they were telling the truth". 'Proof', 'truth' and 'magic' combine forces in a shorthand reminder of the anthropological debates on rationality discussed by Tambiah (1990), and they can do so uncontroversially because the label does not make explicit whose voice is whose: who thinks the trial is 'magic' as opposed to evidence-gathering, and who thinks it is a source of proof more reliable than the spoken assertion?

The conflation of different 'others' into a portmanteau passive construction is reinforced by a conflation of different times into a generalized past tense. Eliding historical specificity, the first paragraph creates a composite people in a composite or non-existent time, while the second paragraph moves towards a very specific, single moment – the moment when the particular man cut off the particular fingertip we see before us – but does not name that moment, only notes that it existed. The generalizing move is fundamental to the project of making objects objective, the translation from chaotic surface appearances to orderly underlying patterns which Asad describes as the goal of British functionalist anthropology. At the same time it offers an interpretation of the 'beliefs' as distanced and closed away in the past, an interpretation which accords well with the earlier story told by the Pitt Rivers Museum, where primitive artefacts and practices belong to an era now in essence overcome, even if their makers and proponents physically exist in the same time as the writer. For the museum-goer, the physical presence of the objects in the case is sternly disputed by the textual explanation which places them outside the present, at a mysterious distance.

Unspecified past-ness in this museum label, then, works in a somewhat similar manner to the "ethnographic present" discussed by Fabian (1983), and in fact museum labels often use a generalized present tense to similar effect. In Clifford's example from the American Museum of Natural History, the present tense is used in the caption to a photograph of an Australian Arunta woman and child taken around 1900 – Aborigines, he comments, "apparently must always inhabit a mythic time" (1988:202). From Fabian's perspective the present tense in such cases is a refutation of contemporaneous existence in the world by means of an attribution of timelessness to the others, timefulness to ourselves. Clifford connects the use of generalized tenses to the claim of authenticity, about which I will say more below: the authenticity of the objects on display, he argues, is produced by extracting them from their historical situation and thus putting a full stop to their movement through history (ibid:228). In this respect the display case on 'Magic and Trial by Ordeal' offers a visual and textual experience of the absence of the others and their difference from the visitor's own here-and-now.

Art or ethnography?

Much of the above has assumed that the experience of visiting the Pitt Rivers is one of following an evolutionist trail through banks of knowledge. But in fact classifying the objects in the cases as knowledge-deliverers – 'specimens' that illustrate a background scientific reality – obscures the competing classification as aesthetic objects, as 'art' (we have seen that visitors may prefer yet another classification, as wondrous 'curio' or marvellous, inexplicable one-off phenomenon). Despite the Pitt Rivers Museum's research-oriented mission, there is a strong aesthetic appeal in the serried ranks of artefacts, backed up by the relatively small labels and audio commentaries that focus on the beauty of individual items. Still, the Museum's arrangement announces its collections as ethnographic evidence, packing them closely in imperfectly lit cases in strong contrast to the spacious presentation and boutique lighting that signals 'art' in Western museums.

The crucial, yet sliding, distinction between art and ethnography is one discussed by several writers, including James Clifford in two chapters of

The Predicament of Culture. Clifford argues that twentieth-century Western collecting of non-Western objects has taken meaning from a particular set of oppositions:

> Since the turn of the century objects collected from non-Western sources have been classified in two major categories: as (scientific) cultural artifacts or as (aesthetic) works of art. Other collectibles – mass-produced commodities, 'tourist art,' curios, and so on – have been less systematically valued; at best they find a place in exhibits of 'technology' or 'folklore.' (Clifford 1988:222-3)

Using a Greimasian semiotic square, Clifford shows how definitions as 'masterpiece' versus 'artefact' and 'authentic' versus 'inauthentic' assign value and meaning to collected objects (ibid:223-4). The attributions make up an initial framework for translation that fits exotic objects into domestic taxonomies of meaning (what we called 'cognitive economies' in Chapter 3). Whereas 'civilized'/'art' is produced by an individual, 'primitive'/'folklore' or 'ethnographic object' is produced by a collective, and while 'art' speaks for itself, 'ethnography' has to be explained. In this way, the distinction between art and artefact by museums has distinguished subjects of artistic expression from objects of scientific scrutiny. It is inextricable from the classic distinction between 'civilized' and 'primitive', like the distinction between 'literature' and 'folklore' in verbal art, and Penny (2002:86) argues that it must also be seen as a constitutive part of disciplinary history. In his view, a key condition for the art–ethnography distinction was the drive by the discipline of anthropology to establish its monopoly on interpretation of the exotic. Museum anthropologists of the turn of the century claimed that ethnographic objects were not, like art objects, interesting for being unique but for being representative. Unlike art, they could not do without translation – by means of labels, treatises, expert guides – in order to become readable, and the role of translator of invisible truths was one only the newly professionalized anthropologist could satisfactorily fill.

Importantly, Clifford points out that objects can and do move between categories; the generation of meaning takes place within a system that for the historical moment remains largely stable overall while changing constantly as regards the detail of its attributions. Among many examples of such mobility, he notes that "things of cultural or historical value may be promoted to the status of fine art" (1988:224). Items formerly considered primarily beautiful may later be reclassified as exemplars of an interesting, superseded historical trend, while certain 'tribal objects' may travel from ethnological displays to canonization in the temples of high art.

Clifford looks in detail at one example of this latter movement, the emergence of the category of 'primitive art' in the early twentieth century when European modernists 'discovered' and reworked African art they saw in museums like the Trocadéro in Paris. His chapter 'Histories of the Tribal and the Modern' is an extended commentary on a 1980s Museum of Modern Art exhibition claiming "affinities" between 'tribal' and modern art. That affinity, Clifford argues, should rather be called an appropriation, disguised by denying the historical dimension of the contact between African and European works of art in colonial relationships. Clifford's approach here is reminiscent of translation critiques that decry 'domesticating' appropriations. His preferred exhibition would "question the boundaries of art and of the art world, an influx of truly indigestible 'outside' artifacts" (ibid:213).

One more translation-related motif is relevant here, the notion of untranslatability as proposed by Wyatt MacGaffey in discussing the location of a genre of African art in the European art–ethnography system. In nineteenth-century museums, he explains, the 'primitiveness' of African art was a crucial contrast helping to create a white, European identity as civilized. The representation of the colonies as timeless, static, collective and absent threw into relief a self-representation of the colonizing societies as historical, dynamic, individual and present:

> Much of the talk about what art is and what it means uses the idea of art to campaign for particular definitions of what it is to be civilized. The idea of art, like that of the rational, has always been most clearly defined by what it is not or, more accurately, by whatever lack in other people explains the assumed absence of civilization among them. [...] Primitives, motivated solely by impulse and emotion, were supposed incapable of abstraction and lacked any sense of history. Instead of art, they produced forms that were either grotesque (lacking discipline) or at best ornamental (lacking narrative). There was nothing there to translate, if by translation we mean to express in our own terms the significance of the objects to those who produced and used them. (2003:249-50)

In other words, nineteenth-century anthropological collections used their exhibits to demonstrate thinness and absence of meaning, in contrast to the dense meaningfulness of European art. The objects could usefully illustrate evolutionist hypotheses but, even in their later interpretation as anonymous items of 'folk' or 'traditional' art, not function as objects of primarily aesthetic value. The categorization, still in force if in a modified form, is readable in the different institutions which house the items, in different modes of exhibiting, and in the more or less comprehensive explanatory stance taken by curators. Like Clifford, MacGaffey notes that it can change over time, and he traces one such change in the case of the *minkisi* 'power objects', also known as 'fetishes', made and used by Bakongo people of Western Congo (MacGaffey 1998). Europeans encountering these objects in the sixteenth century interpreted them as graven images, idols to be burned. With the rise of ethnographic collecting in the nineteenth century they were read as "evidence of Otherness". When museums began to display the Kongo *nkisi*, for example, it was positioned in the company of other examples of its originating culture, pointing to a greater cultural whole of which it was part, or else with other 'fetishes' from other places, pointing to a greater pattern of religion that connected all the non-civilized world. "In each case, an implicit message is conveyed that has nothing intrinsically to do with the object itself but recalls and confirms elements of the museum-goer's world view" (ibid:224).

This is the sense in which the 'idol' has been retranslated into 'ethnography', and the further retranslation into 'art' entails removing both the indigenous context of the *nkisi*, its meaning inside Kongo culture, and the anthropological context which made sense of it as 'example of Kongo culture' or as 'example of fetishes' in the ethnographic setting (ibid:225). To support the new categorization, museum interpretations needed to identify in the source-culture objects the accepted attributes of 'art' in the receiving-culture system – having aesthetic and non-practical functions, for example, or being produced by autonomous creative individuals. MacGaffey sums up: "if Africans were to have art, its institutional matrix and creative motivation had to be much like ours" (ibid:228). Like textual translation, this process entails problems of category match and mismatch, as discussed in Chapter 3: the museum presentation of exotic art squeezes its objects into the cognitive categories of the receiving 'language' to make them both less unintelligible and less specific to themselves.

Faithfulness and authenticity

In the Pitt Rivers Museum the objects that crowd the cases could individually be read as works of art, banalities of everyday life, or vital maps to hinterlands of knowledge; as we have seen, the reading we choose is guided by frameworks and categories offered by the translating curators over the past 130 years. Structurally and institutionally, objects made by colonized people are supposed to be read in their capacity as representing a way of life, and not as pieces of art sufficient to themselves. The museumized object is a piece of evidence of the source culture, and as such its validity depends on its authenticity. In terms of translation, authenticity here refers to both the genuineness of the source 'text' and the faithfulness of its representation, because the collected object is in a way both original and translated even before the additional layers of interpretation (classification systems, labels, and so on) kick in. As Kirshenblatt-Gimblett puts it, ethnographic objects are "artifacts created by ethnographers. Objects become ethnographic by virtue of being defined, segmented, detached, and carried away by ethnographers" (1991:387).

Despite the multiple translatedness of such objects, though, their originality, or authenticity, is a key claim of conventional ethnographic museums. Spencer R. Crew and James E. Sims (1991) define the authenticity of objects as founded not on ontological truth but on their authority; the museumized object is a kind of 'authorized version' which can't be circumvented, only commented on. They describe how a reconstructed room in an American history museum had been quite considerably altered from the state of its first production and the period it was supposed to illustrate, but the new décor complied with popular ideas of what such a room ought to look like (ideas that themselves draw on previous museum representations). Disclaimer labels explaining the alterations proved ineffective, "outshouted" by the aura of authenticity that the museum setting – combined with the audience's pre-existing expectations – produced, and visitors praised the room as satisfyingly authentic. The aura of originality is fuelled by the object's claim to be the real thing, not merely a representation. A copy is no competition here, and the translatedness of museum displays must be hidden if the objects' claim to authenticity is to remain undamaged.

Of course, the ethnographic museum claims to display not individual artefacts but the larger culture they stand in for. Conventionally, in order to be authentic and thus worthy of display, this culture itself must be definable as homogeneous, distant and untouched. Hence the reluctance (now gradually changing) to include Western cultures in ethnographic displays; they risk muddying the waters of exhibited primitivism. Hence, too, the 'one-tribe-one-style' convention in ethnographic exhibition (identified and demolished by Kasfir 1984), which lays down that distinct tribes can be identified by their unique styles of art. The notion of 'tribes' as small, coherent and manageable cultural units was a crucial term for the colonial-era anthropology that fed nineteenth-century ethnographic museums, and it underpinned the static, timeless representations of other cultures discussed in Chapter 4. In this model of culture no change is possible, and if there is a present day it must be either identical with the past or else a sad falling-off from the more genuine reality of times gone by. In this view the interaction of different groups is a sign of decadence; modernization a melancholy process of loss. Nor is individuality a virtue, in stark contrast to the evaluation of Western artworks: the ideal traditional object is typical, demonstrating the collective nature of traditional in contradistinction to modern culture. The object's authenticity is located not in its uniqueness and the personal authority of its maker, but in its originating society. It is there to show us the 'real thing' behind the real thing.

Today many ethnographic galleries are still divided by named cultural group, selecting those objects that seem unique to that group and representative of its unchanging core, the 'essence' that distinguishes one culture from another. It tends to be only more recent exhibitions that highlight change, modernization and hybridity in their representations of non-Western cultures. Clifford describes the 1993 exhibition "Paradise: Continuity and Change in the New Guinea Highlands" at the Museum of Mankind, London, which presented a conscious challenge to before/after narratives of traditional, authentic past followed by modernizing decay. Instead, "Paradise" focused on changing tradition and the "entanglement" of Wahgi artefacts in "regional, national, and international forces" (1997:154). The use of new materials like metal ring-pulls or plastic shells in traditional ornamentation, for example, is presented as a matter of fashion rather than the death of authenticity (ibid:151). For the curator, the approach cast doubt on the selection of items to 'represent' contemporary Wahgi life: he notes that when the crates of artefacts arrived from New Guinea, their contents were carefully stowed in tissue paper while the crates themselves – "no less carefully" made and decorated – were designated as trash; the museum's traditions of collectability prevailed (O'Hanlon cited ibid:169). Still, the focus on change achieved by an exhibition like "Paradise" opens up the directionality of the display. Instead of offering a separate 'other' to be contrasted with a homogeneous 'self' in a source text/target text dichotomy, this kind of museum translation tries to display intercultural encounters and invites Western museum-goers to see themselves as contemporary with the people behind the display-case glass.

The inclusion of newly commissioned work is another way of disrupting conventional museum assumptions of timeless stasis. Although sometimes accompanied by assertions of authenticity in the sense of unbroken continuity with the past ('This coat was made using traditional methods and materials'), new works mean cutting through the museum's claim to hold the real (old) thing. They foreground personal authorship, since newly commissioned articles normally carry the name of their makers (as opposed to generalized 'tribes') and details of how they came into existence (as opposed to arising naturally from a generalized past). At the same time, they introduce new, and significantly more equitable, kinds of commercial relations into the history of museum acquisition.

As the idea of fixed cultural otherness falls into disrepute among ethnographers, so that "self-other relations are matters of power and rhetoric rather than of essence", as Clifford puts it (1988:14), 'authenticity' is bound to be thrown into doubt as well. However, the notion of authenticity is not simply a colonial remnant in retrograde Western museums. On the contrary, claims of authentic cultural identity are often key to the self-representations of decolonizing societies, whether as the basis for land claims (as in North America and Australia) or as a counter to colonialist cultural depredations. Clifford notes that "hybrid exhibits like 'Paradise' might not appeal to many cultural activists for whom the recovery of an indigenous past, a tradition relatively clear of the West, is a crucial political stake" (1997:176). In the sphere of written anthropology, Jocelyn Linnekin (1991) traces heated debates that arose in New Zealand when anthropologists thematized European influence on Maori traditions and their representation. Though in postmodern terms it was a model of 'reflexivity' and 'hybridity', many Maori considered this type of work to be yet another colonialist attack on their integrity as a people and on the struggle for political rights underway at the time. The anthropologists defended a model of culture as "an ongoing human project" as opposed to something dependent on unchanging essence – 'authenticity' – but the example makes clear that understandings of authenticity are bound to be politically contentious in the context of decolonizing societies (see also Kylie Message's discussion of disputes over the "representational responsibilities" of New Caledonia's national museum, 2006:13).

Museums, tourist performance and 'heritage', as narratives of nationhood, are important tools in cultural activism of this kind, as Adrienne Kaeppler's paper on contemporary Pacific museums explains. The museum institution itself is alien to many of the settings she describes – for example, in New Guinea treasures have traditionally been put on display, but not to all-comers, and in Vanuatu objects are not considered something worth preserving across time (1994:21,40). However, the old institution can lend itself to new uses, and museums and cultural centres are being deployed for particular political goals. Thus Papua New Guinea's national museum has designed displays that assert cultural similarity between the nation's many different groups, following a unifying agenda set in other political arenas (ibid:35), while the New Caledonia Museum's mission is "to act as an instrument of cultural reappropriation" by controlling the export of artefacts and using them to educate the population towards a New Caledonian cultural identity (ibid:38). Clifford's study of two 'tribal' museums on the Northwest coast of Canada (1991) also illustrates the political potential of the museum form for anti-colonial agendas. Museums of this kind highlight family relationships and local history, issues which majority museums "subsume in the patrimony of Art or the synthetic narrative of History" (ibid:232). But museums like the U'mista Cultural Center at Alert Bay do not simply stick to local significance; they use the museum effects of the majority-based institution and turn them to the purpose of gaining recognition in the majority world, as actively oppositional interventions. The U'mista Cultural Center directly addresses identity and history, claiming "the power to reclaim and recontextualize texts and objects 'collected' by outside authorities" (ibid:236; for example, the museum shows creation stories that are based on Boas and Hunt's 'salvage' collections in *Kwakiutl Texts*). The use of quotations and individual testimonies refutes generalization, and specific moments in the history of encounter between Kwakwa̲ka̲'wakw and the Canadian government are highlighted through installations and lengthy text as much as through individual objects.

In this kind of context the label 'museum' risks sounding rather narrow. In fact, forms of identity-building cultural display take place in a wider range of institutions than only the classic temple of the arts. Processes and performances as opposed to objects may be exhibited in cultural centres (see Kaeppler 1994:40-1), festivals preserve and demonstrate traditional crafts and rituals (see Part 4 of Karp & Lavine 1991), and the 'heritage' agenda museumizes built spaces as well – Richard Handler (1985) describes how the notion of *patrimoine* in Quebec makes buildings, streets and furniture into indices of cultural authenticity, to be carefully chosen, interpreted and preserved for Québécois collective ownership. The Québécois case recalls Annie Brisset's work on the search for cultural identity in the linguistic practices of Canadian translation (2000), suggesting that studies of textual translation can benefit greatly from cross-reference to a much larger range of representational practices.

Displays of heritage are not, of course, directed only inwards to the community they try to represent. They are inextricable from national politics in the Quebec case, and in many others from the tourist industry's attempts to represent the local population to outsiders. Although small-scale museums and heritage parks may be created locally, tied up in networks of local interests, they reveal the duplicity of the term 'self'-representation: such displays are crucially influenced by the need to fulfil paying visitors' practical and ideological expectations. Particular versions of the area's 'culture' are offered for visitors' perusal, and much work in the study of tourism addresses, if indirectly, the translational aspect of these processes. In a paper on guided tours in Ireland, for example, Annette Jorgensen points out the translating role of the guides' commentaries: "A foreign country, experienced in a 'raw' state, as a jumble of sounds, sights, smells and tastes, cannot be 'understood', that is, given coherence and narrative, without some form of mediating, of interpretation" (2003:142). The coherence and narrative, a kind of textualization of the tourist experience, comes in Jorgensen's case from the Irish guides' presentations, but it is intertextually informed as well by a wealth of pre-existing images mediated through news coverage, political stereotypes and international touristic discourse on Ireland. The guides select aspects of the passing landscape, ignoring others, and interpret them in a way that accumulates into an image of Irishness that is serene and friendly, lovable if untrustworthy, rooted in the past with little relation to the present. Jorgensen's analysis of the tours is an interesting exercise in 'reading' touristic discourse, but her key point is that this discourse is not monolithic, and nor is the 'dominant' meaning offered the only one that the tourists take away. Instead, her interviews show that while some tour participants responded directly to the content of the tour presentation and accepted its content, others took what she calls a "post-touristic" stance and evaluated the form of the presentation ('theatrical', 'skilful', 'entertaining') apart from, and sometimes in contradiction to, their evaluation of the content. As we saw above, the 'consumers' of cultural displays are active participants, and their concurrence in the intended readings can by no means be taken for granted.

Ambivalent and even starkly conflicting receptions of cultural displays come to the fore in the case of 'ethnographic' tourist performances like dance spectacles or displays of 'natives' pretending to go about their daily business in staged villages. Nick Stanley's study of performances of this kind, *Being Ourselves for You*, focuses on the ways that local agency interacts with tourist expectations to produce an 'authenticity' that does its job as a declaration of identity, yet simultaneously undermines the fiction of a pure, unchanging tradition diametrically opposed to contaminated modernity. Once a performance is staged for tourists it ceases to be 'authentic' or fully effectual in its previous way (1998:105), like a ritual object inserted into a museum; on the other hand, such performances demonstrate the elasticity of 'tradition' and its capacity for deployment within a global economy. The problems of cultural translation in this case relate to different, and perhaps irreconcilable, sets of audiences and skopoi, as government programmes of cultural recovery meet the tourist industry's use of performance to generate income (ibid:107).

Stanley discusses staged 'village life' in theme parks as sometimes overlapping with a Disney-style representation of odd but ultimately unthreatening others. Such scrutiny from behind the safety barrier dates back to nineteenth-century ethnographic displays designed for entertainment, showing 'genuine savages' in miniaturized street or village settings. In fact, Kirshenblatt-Gimblett notes that the practice of putting on show living people from colonized regions began in England as early as 1501, when Eskimos were exhibited in Bristol, and the practice continued for centuries "in taverns and at fairs, on the stage [...] in zoos and circuses, and, by the latter half of the nineteenth century, at world's fairs". The mode of presentation of these people could be either zoological (analogous to natural history exhibits) or theatrical (analogous to the circus or freak show performance), but both approaches served to produce "wildness" and exoticism (ibid:402-3). The living exhibits were shown 'going about their daily life' or participating in rituals for the wonderment of audiences, who were invited to look and project their own imaginations from a safe distance. This kind of display blurs the boundaries between 'performance' and 'demonstration', to use a distinction applied by Richard Bauman and Patricia Sawin apropos of folklife festivals (1991:297): performance here is the doing of the action on its own terms and with reference to an audience constituted as unmediated and original, while demonstration is doing the action out of its usual context as a way of showing a new, secondary audience how it's done. The distinction parallels that between an 'original' or non-translated text and its 'derived', translated version. If you look at the original hard enough, it already becomes a translation, while if you look at the translation hard enough, it becomes a new original.

As we saw in Chapter 5, 'self'-representation does not *per se* solve the political dilemmas of cultural translation. Apart from anything else, the definition of what is 'self' will always be subject to fierce dispute: "the struggle is not only over what is to be represented, but over who will control the means of representing" (Karp 1991:15). In the tourist industry representations of culture are set about with different interests and mix innovative with historically familiar modes of display. As forms of translation, tourism and travel offer a salutary complication of linear producer–translator–recipient models, something which is just beginning to be explored by translation studies (see, for example, Polezzi 2006).

Verbal interpretation in the museum

So far we have been focusing on the selection and arrangement strategies that give meaning to the museum's contents visually. But as translation scholars we are bound to have a special place in our hearts for the verbal mode. Can museum objects speak, and if so in what tongues? In their essay on authenticity, Crew and Sims are unambivalent: "The problem with things is that they are dumb. [...] And if by some ventriloquism they seem to speak, they lie" (1991:159). Let's begin by looking at this figure of the mute object spoken through by a hidden translator.

Words and silence

The museum as a whole participates in giving a voice to its collections, providing the institutional and political context which credits them with significance and educational value, as windows onto the world. Curators make some objects 'speak' through arrangements, juxtapositions and definitions, while relegating others to the silent basement, but they also provide verbal interpretations which guide the visitors' interpretation. In fact, words and objects seem almost to vie for status in the exhibition: is it the object alone which can truly be 'real', at most shadowed by unreliable text, or does the object only serve to illustrate the text written by the didactically minded curator, a text which contains the 'actual' reality of the object (see Kirshenblatt-Gimblett 1991:394-5)? The practice of most contemporary ethnographic museums is at neither of these poles, but written text is certainly a crucial component of the museum display.

That begins with the title of an exhibition, defining the context within which the collected objects are to be deciphered, and proceeds through the titles for individual galleries or sections and the texts of introductory panels, right down to individual exhibit captions; it includes, too, accompanying material, catalogues and school resource packs. Texts like these are not written individually but are the collaborative outcomes of discussion with what may be a very wide range of stakeholders. As Ames points out, though the curators of anthropological collections are scholars, their mode of writing differs from scholarly writing in that it is checked and rechecked, streamlined to be readable from a crowd, shortened to fit the design criteria, simplified to cater to an assumed reading age of ten to twelve years old (1992:33). In this intralingual translation of research results into accessible language, the norm is not a singular, let alone a single named, translating figure.

The anonymity of the translator in this case is not, though, just a practicality. By remaining anonymous – an invisible translator – the label writers do not diminish their agency but on the contrary become absorbed into the Voice of Science, an institutionally powerful speaking position and one that brooks little dissent. The anonymous label allows the words only one possible source, the museum institution. This reflects a traditional division of labour in the museum whereby artefacts belong to the cultural others, but verbal interpretations solely to the curators: the object is silent while the subject speaks. Colonial-era curators, in common with their fellow anthropologists in the field, believed that the words of the 'natives' could not be trusted. Coombes cites an 1896 injunction to collectors to use photographs, not verbal accounts, as a source of documentation for their treasures because

> by these means the traveller is dealing with facts about which there can be no question, and the record thus obtained may be elucidated by subsequent inquirers on the same spot, while the timid answers of natives to questions propounded through the medium of a native interpreter can be but rarely relied upon, and are more apt to produce confusion than to be of benefit to comparative anthropology. (1994:136)

In this nineteenth-century view, the owners of the objects have no authority to interpret – they are 'intimidated' by the collector and the truth of their statements is further clouded by the intrusive, probably corrupting presence of a language-mediator because they do not speak the language of the anthropological collection. Better by far to subordinate them to silent, thus objective, witnesses like the photograph, and have Western experts give cogent verbal form to the raw material collected.

In a modern setting, such a belief in the reliability of anthropologists' photography and capriciousness of native explanations can no longer be officially sustained. Nevertheless, that has not yet overturned the mode of verbal interpretation across ethnographic museums. It is common to see labels that synthesize curatorial views into a neutral-sounding, impersonal and anonymous commentary – the modern label in the Pitt Rivers Museum discussed above is an example. The authority of that label was undermined by the historicizing presence of previous labels; still, the ensemble gathers the voices of generations of curators and remains inside the academy.

In a study at the Natural History Museum in London, Paulette McManus found that groups of visitors responded to the labels as a substitute for the interpreters' "speaking presence" and brought these disembodied guides into their own conversations at the display case, recapitulating and commenting on the label's words as if it were a speaking participant (1991:39,40). This casts an interesting light on the dynamic of source and translation in the museum setting: even though the 'source text' (the artefact) is physically present, unlike the source text of written translations, it seems that the conversation between label-translator and visitor-reader could take place above the head of the objects themselves. What is clearly missing in this constellation is the verbal participation of the people who made, owned or used the objects on display.

Not only do the objects' previous owners have little say in the interpretation, but material traces of their words in cultural objects are missing too. The remit of anthropological departments of Western museums has traditionally excluded writing-based cultures: Chinese, Indian or Arabic artefacts conventionally belong in the Orientalist galleries. The Pitt Rivers is more eclectic, but the writing it includes is displayed as pictures. Untranslated, the inscribed ceramics or ivories in the 'Writing and Communication' case lose their writtenness and become ornamentation for the great majority of visitors. The physical object 'text' is there, but not linguistically, only artefactually – a failure of translation indeed. To be sure, the museum is not a library; still, the absence of language as an object of study intensifies the silence of the people being represented. This aspect of verbal museum texts is one that is being increasingly challenged by new museum displays, as we will see in Chapter 8. In particular, it is becoming more common to integrate audio resources, spoken language offering a more immediate marker of voice than can be achieved in written texts. Other senses remain at the margins: touch is reserved for children's 'hands-on' sessions, while taste and smell are more or less entirely banished. As Kenneth Hudson (1991:461) complains, the restriction to sight and, as a poor second, sound makes ethnographic museums "anaemic" and unnaturally severed from the surrounding world. Even so, the physical presence of the 'reader' is extremely to the fore in the experience of museum-going compared to the reading of written words, where the reader is limited to a pair of eyes or set of fingertips alone, and the paths being taken by museum outreach to schoolchildren, involving eating and making and dancing (examples can be found in the advertising of most major museums), may eventually be extended to those more serious creatures, adult museum-goers, as well.

Label texts

As a genre, labels are charged first and foremost with making explicit the implicit categorizations that order the exhibits and give them their museum meaning. On the larger scale this means dividing the museum into different regions or themes, and the individual galleries into segments by function, place of origin or another classification. These titles provide the interpretive scaffolding below the level of the institution as a whole ('if it's in here, it must be educational, ethnographic, and authentic') and above the level of individual cases and items. The explanatory texts attached to cases or sections of the gallery give more detailed guidance on how to interpret the objects on display. The Pitt Rivers explanatory label I quoted earlier, for example, asks the reader to find an inherent connection between things that could all too easily look like a heap of unconnected bits. The connection, or anthropological 'context' in Dilley's terms (1999), is magic and trial by ordeal, apparently a single unit of significance. The text, as we saw, adds more detail to the classification and defines the objects as distant in space and time even though we can see them physically present.

Individual items in a museum case are traditionally captioned in a way that confirms their membership of pre-decided geographical regions and 'tribes'. A classic label will include, for example, object; material; tribe; region; date in centuries; date of acquisition; name of donor. It will be noticed that the maker of the object is not an individual but a cultural group; the time not a date but a range of several centuries. Like the titles of functionalist ethnographies, this naming device goes a long way to 'producing' the culture under study for the discipline. In fact, Enid Schildkrout and Curtis A. Keim contend that "it is in the search for labels for artifacts that much of the contemporary map of Central Africa was drawn" (1998:5) – in order to fill the spaces in the interpretive grid that labelling required, places of origin themselves had to be defined in a framework usable for the museum. Even in newer museums, these provenance labels often remain untouched. They bear witness to the taxonomic drive of nineteenth-century museum culture, which hoped to assign facts from all over the world to manageable categories in a similar manner to the appropriative or domesticating translation that subordinates source-language systems of meaning to the target-language cognitive economy. The attribution of meaning to the exhibit, finally, may be elaborated in individual exhibit labels giving more or less detailed information which helps translate the object into the terms of the overall display strategy. Michael Baxandall discusses labels in this frame, pointing out that the label in an ethnographic museum aims to actively *explain* the object. It does not describe the object but "describes the exhibitor's thinking about it" and thus integrates it into the didactic message of the exhibition as a whole (1991:38).

If ideally the different levels of labelling form an explanatory ensemble, the Pitt Rivers case and item labels do not cooperate in this way – they diverge in style and intent, and may even seem puzzling (how does the Hampshire witch in a bottle relate to trial by ordeal, and was it 'used in various forms of magic'?). The availability of different sign systems in the museum is a source of instability, as Bal notes: "The sign system of the verbal panels constitutes precisely the museum's luck: it provides the latitude to change" (2001:124). While the collections held by the big European ethnographic museums mainly date from high colonialism, alterations to the verbal commentaries allow the exhibits to be retranslated by succeeding generations. Retaining successive translations side by side, as the Pitt Rivers does, is an ironic strategy which highlights contradiction, and irony can also be used to contrast objects and verbal interpretations. Thus the Royal Ontario Museum's controversial exhibition "Into the Heart of Africa", discussed by Henrietta Riegel (1996), juxtaposed colonial images and labels in an attempt to criticize the museum's own past. However, the power of the racist images turned out to be greater than the understated critical dimension, and the exhibition was attacked as sustaining colonial representations of Africa. Ironic labelling requires a solid basis of consensus from which to distinguish the ironic statement, and for this among other reasons the exhibition failed in its retranslation of older labelling (another key reason apparently being a failure to collaborate with African Canadians in the exhibition design).

Baxandall's essay discusses another aspect of the museum label which is of interest to a translation studies perspective, the relationship between translator and target-language reader. To be sure, for museum practitioners the concept of 'the target-language reader' must seem like pie in the sky, faced as they are with a potential readership that stretches from scholars to toddlers, from native speakers to people who can just get by or not at all in the language of the label. As McManus (1991) points out, some of these readers want to check every word and consult the catalogue, others to ignore the labels and provide their own commentaries in conversation with friends or family. The label's context and its voice of authority addresses them all more or less as one group, as potential or desirable recipients of Museum Knowledge, but the way visitors actually read labels cannot be controlled. Rather than deploring this room for manoeuvre, Baxandall calls for it to be exploited much more fully. He notes the three-way nature of the communication between the makers of the object, the theorizing exhibition-maker and the visitor, each with their different purposes and interests, and advocates enlarging the space between exhibit and label so that the viewers can examine the relationships they find there – a kind of translation criticism, where the reader interprets less the object than the translator's translation of the object. Exhibitors, says Baxandall, "cannot *represent* cultures" but can offer minimal "tactful and stimulating" prompts that require visitors to think themselves about the object on display and in particular its difference from the receiving culture (1991:40-1).

This raises the issue of how much contextualization a label should carry. Baxandall's proposition is for minimal explication, but this carries the danger that without explicit contextualization the object may be experienced only as confusing or meaningless, thus fitting and confirming existing categories of scarily irrational culture. In an attempt to at least indicate the relativist assumption that different cultures have their own rationalities, Baxandall advocates the use of source-language terms in the text as an index of cultural difference. Wyatt MacGaffey also values the use of native words but, in contrast to Baxandall, wishes he could include hugely extensive contextualization in the labels for his objects of study, the Bakongo *minkisi* mentioned above. As MacGaffey admits, even his short sample of some of the knowledge necessary for Western visitors to understand a *nkisi* takes up more space than a conventional label – or a museum-goer's patience – could possibly sustain. He explains that *minkisi* are themselves textual in nature, composed of words spoken in their making, formulae prompted by their use, and linguistic puns that motivate the choice of some of their components (such as the *kazu*, or kola nut, included so that the *nkisi* may *kazuwa*, bite off, witchcraft; 1998:231). Any attempt at a full 'translation', or contextualization, of the *minkisi* is bound to meet both the physical limits of the label format and the substantive question of where the limits of 'context' should be drawn (see Dilley 1999, discussed in Chapter 5). MacGaffey is faced with the promises but also the limitations of Appiah's "thick translation", which as we saw in Chapter 5 will have to remain partial in view of the immense denseness of taken-for-granted meanings that surround any cultural articulation. What MacGaffey's version of thick translation usefully adds to Appiah's is the expectation that a label of this kind should, in addition to illuminating the object on display, also explicitly address the categories into which it has been placed – as art, as ritual, as magic or artefact – and thereby challenge the receiving language's concepts of genre and meaning (1998:230).

All the above assumes that museum labels will be offered in English only, with no concession either to other languages living in the museum's catchment area or to visiting tourists. Monolingual labelling is the norm in English-speaking museums, and anglophone museum studies has paid little attention so far to translated labels, as Robert Neather (2005) notes. Neather discusses bilingual labelling in a Chinese temple, though mainly from a 'translation deficit' perspective which outlines the failures of the English translations. As he points out, the linguistic translation from Chinese to English adds another layer of refraction and another audience, and like the Chinese text it works not simply in verbal terms but also intersemiotically, in (another) relation to the total surrounding. From the other perspective, Neather mentions Bal's experience of non-translated labels. Visiting a Czech museum, she faced exhibits that were for her purposes unlabelled, and she found that "plain looking" did not help: "I automatically looked for a clue, a direction that would turn the random set of objects into a 'text,' a whole in which the various objects had their place" (Bal 1996:81). Looking without verbal guidance opened up new possibilities for interpretation – not synecdochic (where the objects would have stood "for the culture they came from") but metaphorical ("standing for aesthetic choices made by the curators", ibid:82). These were probably not the interpretations intended by the exhibition, but then that may be no bad thing. It does, at least, fulfil Baxandall's requirement that the museum label should indicate the exhibit's otherness and mutability of meaning, and it is a productive example of non-translation generating new sets of readings through more dedicated exploitation of the other signifying systems on offer.

Museums as contact zones

Quoting Mary Louise Pratt, Clifford describes museums as potential 'contact zones' between cultures. Pratt's concept of the contact zone is the "space of colonial encounters, the space in which peoples geographically and historically separated come into contact with each other and establish ongoing relations, usually involving conditions of coercion, radical inequality, and intractable conflict" (Pratt 1992:6). As Clifford notes, the emphasis on relationship is what makes this notion so relevant to museums: the museum becomes a "power-charged set of exchanges" (Clifford 1997:192) and thus a space where different languages meet and struggle to be heard. As a model of translation in the museum, this usefully keeps in view the continued existence of the 'voices' of the people on display, despite the power of the museum's authoritative discourse. As we will see in the next chapter, the multiplicity of voices in a museum can be enhanced and, as in the U'mista Cultural Center, the history of exchanges itself can be made a central object of display.

For translation studies, the notion of the museum as a contact zone is a useful one because it encourages us to question the model of source texts and target texts facing each other across a divide bridged by a heroic translator figure. Instead, the directionality of translation in museums is much more confusing and richer, within and between the cultures participating (willingly or not) in the display. We see the dialogue between translations and their audiences as well as the intervention of source-text makers, and the museum also implies the ricochet effect of translations on their source cultures – representations are, as Rabinow reminds us (1986), "social facts" that impact on geopolitical realities. Secondly, the multimediality of museum representations might encourage us to expand our view from verbal translation alone and take more account of the interrelations of different forms of translation in representing cultural others. Ethnographic film and photography suggest themselves for study in this immediate context. And finally, the example of anthropological museum offers different translation styles – the familiarized, the shockingly alien, the search for affinities, the claim of radical difference, and various permutations of all these – in a particularly visceral, impressive way. Stephen Greenblatt proposes a pair of terms to describe museum viewing that in many ways echo translation debates, but perhaps can lead us away from the familiar poles of domesticating and estranging approaches. He defines "resonance" and "wonder" as follows:

> By *resonance* I mean the power of the displayed object to reach out beyond its formal boundaries to a larger world, to evoke in the viewer the complex, dynamic cultural forces from which it has emerged and for which it may be taken by a viewer to stand. By *wonder* I mean the power of the displayed object to stop the viewer in his or her tracks, to convey an arresting sense of uniqueness, to evoke an exalted attention. (1991:42)

As Greenblatt points out, these two modes are not mutually exclusive, though museums can favour one or the other by stressing context (for example through heavy labelling) or uniqueness (for example through dramatic 'boutique' lighting). The 'resonance' model has much in common with thick translation, but while Greenblatt admits this is the preferred approach of his own academic habitat, he extols the virtues of 'wonder', an "enchanted looking" (ibid:49) at the sheer particularity of someone else's treasure. The respect and admiration which, in Greenblatt's view, this style of looking can promote is surely also relevant for both ethnographic and literary translation. By taking the further step required by Greenblatt, historicizing our own sense of wonder as a mutable cultural habit, such translation might be able to respond to the problem of how to "present the objects of an 'other' without replacing their view of how an object means with ours" (Karp & Lavine 1991:19).

8. Ethical Perspectives

This chapter will not try to pick a systematic path through the ethics of translation. Instead, I am going to apply to the museum context two main clusters of ethical issues that have recurred throughout the discussion so far. These are questions of ownership and authority to speak, and questions of dialogue and difference.

Ownership and authority

We saw in the previous chapter that a large proportion of the objects housed in Western ethnographic collections arrived there in the wake of colonialist transactions. Clifford asks, "Why has it seemed obvious until recently that non-Western objects should be preserved in European museums, even when this means that no fine specimens are visible in their country of origin?" (1988:221). The question raises the spectre of an unethical translation practice that robs the source culture or destroys the source text instead of multiplying it through supplementary layers.

Debates about the rightful ownership of museum objects have been heated, nowhere more so than the issue of human remains on show in museums. It could be argued that displaying human remains as museum objects is a very particular act of translation, one that defines certain human bodies outside the category of 'human' (with its meanings of 'not-zoological', 'subject to funerary rites' and so on). As the commentators on the Cape Town exhibition *Miscast* point out, human remains were frequently obtained in contexts of violence – the South African Museum collection included body parts taken from executed prisoners (Skotnes 1996:18), and many mummies, human skeletons or shrunken heads came from archaeological excavations that could also be termed grave-robbing. Protests by the descendants of people whose bodies were 'collected' have led to the widespread removal of human remains from display especially in North America and Australia, though Moira Simpson suggests that the process has been driven not by ethical considerations alone but also by changing tastes among visitors, whose tolerance for the gruesome has declined since the nineteenth century (Simpson 2001:177-82).

Sacred objects face museums with another controversial problem. A Navajo medicine bundle, for example, is subject to conflicting definitions:

> To the non-Navajo they are ethnographic artefacts, owned by an individual or displayed in public collections. To the Navajo, they have power, they are living entities which are passed on through the generations, and belong to the tribe as a whole: no individual has the right to sell a medicine bundle. (ibid:195)

The category mismatch here arises from conceptions of property which 'do not translate' across cultures and a redefinition of the objects into Anglo-American terms. It has in many, though not all, cases been successfully disputed by Navajo, who have demanded the right to access these objects and control how they are conserved and displayed, using them ceremonially or for education (212; see also Message 2006). This may involve physical repatriation, like the return of the potlatch items acquired by coercion in 1920s Canada to a cultural centre run by local inhabitants (detailed in Clifford 1991). Or it may mean changing the terms of 'ownership' to approximate more closely the terms applied in the originating language. Thus in New Zealand, Simpson reports, museums "have custodianship of Maori *taonga*" or historical treasures, but "the Maori retain spiritual ownership" (2001:204).

As the fortunes of the Maori taonga show, the ethical handling of museum objects is complicated by the question of who exactly should be considered the individual or collective 'author' of the object as source text. The exhibition "Te Maori", which displayed the taonga in New York, generated intense debate on authority and appropriate display among the Maori co-curators and the community (traced by curator Douglas Newton, 1994). For example, while some Maori argued that traditional values ruled out the display of weavings and featherwork "because they had had too much bodily contact with the ancestors", others criticized the omission because it excluded the major art of women from the exhibition (1994:281). Some people felt that the exhibition was just another theft of Maori culture, others that it could augment the cultural power of Maori internationally and at home. In cases where no clear line of inheritance can be retraced, often due to genocide, disputes over cultural copyright may be much more complex still (see Clifford 1988:248).

The authority to display activates claims and counter-claims around self-definition, in the course of which the notion of cultural property becomes a powerful political tool. As Handler (1985) shows, to be capable of owning property is to be a politically viable cultural entity, so that the high-profile demonstration of reclaimed ownership can be a crucial move in postcolonial nation-building (an issue explored by the essays in Kaplan 1994). Accordingly, Western museums have not been eager to relinquish the power to own and to display that ownership. Many of the famous Benin bronzes held by the British Museum, for example, remain in London despite repeated calls for their return to Nigeria. Coombes notes the "unyielding possession and flagrant display" (1994:223) of a set of bronze plaques in a highly visible position on the Museum's main staircase, which can be "understood, in part, as the manifestation of an unconscious desire – the fantasy of a continued British sovereignty" (ibid:224). Cultural icons like these, she continues, have always been "repositories" (220) of conflictual social and political encounters, and aside from the obvious responsibility to return stolen items when requested,

Western museums also have the responsibility to display those conflictual encounters instead of disguising them in the robes of universal artistry or 'world heritage'. Coombes further comments that current museum interest in displaying hybrid or 'transculturated' objects – such as the Nigerian Princess Diana puppet displayed in London's Horniman Museum – risks mystifying the actual power relationships that underlay the transculturating contact. Although the hybrid object usefully disrupts ideologies of purity and primitivism (see Clifford 1997 on the "Paradise" exhibition), it may promote an "assumption that all players are equal in the global arena" (1994:218). Coombes calls for museum displays to address meaning-making itself, as a process of differentiation that can "reproduce the experience of multiple, but specific, forms of social and political disempowerment – and conversely, empowerment" (ibid). This will extend the effectiveness of 'hybridity' as the new museum ideal:

> Hybridity so often remains a term which primarily describes the culture of the 'margins'. In these exhibitionary narratives, it rarely disturbs the equilibrium of the culture of the 'centre'. We need [...] to recognise the hybridity of all cultures and to explore the specific conditions of this hybridity – the *how* and the *who* of it – which might then dispel the monolithic repetition [...] of hybridity as an encounter between the West and its 'Other' and the ultimate reassertion of a Manichean model. (ibid:221)

In terms of translation, this indicates a reflexive style which would track processes of meaning-making instead of claiming to represent referentially stable objects. However, anthropology's criticisms of reflexivity, as outlined in Chapter 5, should not be forgotten. Chief among them was the concern that the reflexive representation can come alarmingly close to being a mirror of the self, with no outlook onto other people's lives. An exclusive attention to the context of collecting and display would edge out the artefacts' indigenous contexts, amounting to "an extreme form of cultural appropriation" (Peirson Jones 1992:235). For this reason I'd like to look now at a museum which tries to disrupt one-sided ethnographic authority not so much by directly attacking the receiving culture's truth claims as by according space to the truth claims of the source cultures.

Interpretative authority at the Horniman Museum

Aside from the physical custody of valuable objects, authority in museum translation may involve the right to 'tell' objects: to present source-language interpretations and propose target-language circumlocutions. In terms of an ethics of translation, this implies a demand on the majority target language to cede some of its power to the originating language, holding back and allowing the source language more space to speak. However important it is to consider museum translations of culture as a document of the receiving culture, the loop that makes both target text and presumed source text into components of the target discourse excludes the people who made the objects on display; those people become shadows in the wings of the real translation action. Undermining realist translation is therefore not enough, certainly not in a museum practice that aims to serve more diverse and democratic publics in the West, nor for one that aims to serve publics in postcolonial regions. The other step is to break through self-reference and change the distribution of voices in the translation process. This is the route taken by London's Horniman Museum in its permanent exhibition "African Worlds", which opened in 1999.

The Horniman Museum was established in 1901 as an educational institution to serve the working and lower-middle classes in search of betterment. In its early days the Museum produced extensive labelling and detailed handbooks, backed up by public lectures, in the hope of leaving as little of visitor interpretation as possible to chance (Coombes 1994:157). If the early twentieth-century administration complained of "irresponsible and frivolous" visitors using the Museum "as a promenade" (cited ibid:248), today this is less of a damning critique, and the Museum positively entices noisy children to visit. But the "African Worlds" gallery has another shift of audience in mind: it aims to address London's diasporic African communities, and this changed readership of the museum 'translation' has meant considerable rewriting of the collected objects, many of which were acquired in the colonial era. I will focus here on the labelling techniques that support this policy.

Although the style of the labels in "African Worlds" varies, the one pictured in Figure 7 is reasonably typical. Perhaps its most immediately striking aspect is the inclusion of a photograph of one of the commentators. The maker of the mask is named and the explanatory text defines a historical and political context, two moves against the attribution of African artefacts to generalized 'tribes' living outside the time-world of the receiving culture. The authors of the label itself are named, a specific attribution of the interpreting voice which enables accountability and opens up the hermetic Voice of Science, or what Bal calls "truth-speak". This is backed up by the inclusion of different sources in a polyphonic, desynthesizing form. At the same time, the device gives authority to a different kind of expertise about the object. Instead of the anthropologists – here both European and Nigerian – being the sole reliable witnesses, members of the communities who use or used the object offer their own comments. The proverb presents a contextualizing frame that comes from the source-language culture (in a wide sense), selected but not formulated by the museum academy, and a present-day Yoruba Londoner takes the 'we' away from the exclusive use of the curator-experts. While this label keeps intact the

YORUBA EPA MASK - NIGERIA

"Aye l'ajo, orun n'ile."
"The world (life) is a journey, the otherworld (afterlife) is home."
Yoruba proverb

"So, in the olden days, we didn't have ... a camera or anything like that. The only way we could remember our warriors or kings was to carve a mask, looking like him when he was alive."
Ayan Ayandosu, hereditary talking drummer. London, 25th June 1998.

Epa masks come from the northeast part of Yoruba territory in modern day Nigeria. Historically, this area was subject to foreign invasions and large movements of different populations, which helped the northeastern Yoruba build a unique cultural heritage still found in their religious and ceremonial observances. *Epa* masks are an important part of this heritage. They are crowned with skilfully carved figures and weigh up to 25 kgs. Young men wear them to demonstrate their strength and balance in ceremonies to commemorate their ancestors and promote the fertility and wellbeing of the community. Since the 1930s, the *epa* mask has become a symbol of 'Eliti Parapo', a strong nationalist movement within Nigeria. The *epa* mask shown here was made in the early twentieth century by Fasiku Alaye, a master carver who lived in the village of Ikerin in the region of Opin.

Emmanuel Arinze, Kathryn Chan, Joseph Eboreime, Keith Nicklin, Anthony Shelton

Figure 7. Label to Yoruba Epa mask, © Horniman Museum

three-way model of exhibit, exhibitor and reader, with the exhibitor giving voice to the silent exhibit for the benefit of the willing reader, the roles are occupied by a different set of people. The producers and users of the object are 'represented' in the parliamentary sense, by people who identify with them, more than in the textual sense of portrayal by an outside speaker.

In this label, the language of the museum too is pushed off-centre by the statement in Yoruba followed by its translation. This differs from the inclusion of 'native words', which is practised in other exhibits in a comparatively mild way, for example in the panel on the Haitian vodou altar. There, an italicized Haitian term is used after the English, "spirits *(lwa)*", and no extra information is given as to what distinguishes the source-language concept from the one-word English 'equivalent'. Like native words left standing in written translations as a token of otherness (or as Tedlock calls them, souvenirs with explanatory placards, 1983:324), these items seem to add not so much content as evidence of the authenticity of the represented habit or artform. For the Epa mask label, in contrast, the Yoruba line is not primarily indexical – reminding us that the foreign language exists – but, a complete proverb, also stands for itself as a work of verbal art, addresses Yoruba speakers in the audience, and governs the subsequent text in a way that isolated lexical items cannot. Its location at the top of the label and its large font forces the English translation into a subordinate position, in line with the traditional Western concept of the original–translation relationship rather than with those ethnographic interpretations which attribute fullness to the translation and insufficiency to the source text. The translation's hesitant use of bracketed alternatives adds to the downgrading of the English vis-à-vis the Yoruba text.

Figure 8. On left: Bronze plaque of Ekpenede, Iyase of Benin, c. 1570-1590, with label by Joseph Eboreime, © Horniman Museum

The principle of dispersing ethnographic authority is also applied in the display of the Horniman's collection of Benin bronze plaques, cast in the 1520s to 1640s and acquired by Frederick Horniman in the international buying frenzy that followed the British looting raid of 1897. The Horniman's bronzes are now re-displayed in the "African Worlds" gallery (see Figure 8). According to curator Anthony Shelton, the new display meant "returning the voice of interpretation, if not the disputed objects, to the Bini people themselves" (2000:11), namely by commissioning Joseph Eboreime of Benin's National Museum to research the iconography of the individual plaques and decide how they should be presented. Eboreime's exegeses of the plaques are detailed in a 2000 paper and summarized in the explanatory labels in the gallery. The makers of the plaques intended the images to invoke stories and historical memories, and Eboreime sets out to reconstitute those meanings for museum-goers, with reference to modern uses by the descendants of the plaques' creators. Some of the multiple layers of meaning embodied in the artworks, he notes, are open to the general Bini public but others are reserved for those initiated "into the hierarchies of the palace association" (2000:64); the source-culture expert is the one to filter acceptable degrees of knowledge for the London public, and in this respect some kind of restitution of authority has indeed occurred. The style of Eboreime's labels mixes the didactic with less easily accessible material (Horniman Museum, 1999):

> ***EKPENEDE, IYASE OF BENIN, C. 1570-1590 – NIGERIA***
>
> *"Omu egbe vbe n' Ozolua mu egbe okuo.*
> *No Y' Oze yo' ese Eghodin I' wi ye okuo erhen."*
>
> *"He is as battle-ready as Oba Ozolua the conqueror. Whoever puts on the leaded body armour need not be afraid he should be confident because the falcon does not perish in a war of fire, however fierce it may be."*
>
> *Benin aphorism.*
>
> Commanders-in-chief of the Benin army were known as *Iyase*. Ekpenede was the *Iyase* in Oba Orhobua's reign from 1550 to 1578. He successfully led the Benin troops against the Oyos to the west and the western Igbo chiefdoms to the east of Benin. Oba Ewebo created the office of *Iyase* to stem the opposition of the elders of state. *'Iyase'* is the shortened version of *I' Yo Na Se'Uwa* which literally means 'to demonstrate my power over you'.
>
> The *Iyase* became the head of the town chiefs, whose main function was to check the excesses of the pre-dynastic elders of state, the *Uzama*. It became customary to give the title to one of the members of the Oba's military corps and he also enjoyed the privilege of marrying the Oba's first daughter, Uvbi N'Okhua, the princess royal.
>
> *Joseph Eboreime*

Whereas the classic label would prioritize artefactual over linguistic aspects, here the object is presented as wholly enmeshed with words – whether the descriptions and proper names of the people it represents, the condensation that makes up the defining term *Iyase*, or the contextualizing 'aphorism', a genre outside the conventional repertoire of an English-language museum. The specificities of ways of speaking are made present by the text, almost edging out 'information' as the most important value. For outsiders, the aphorism asks for an evocative rather than a directly educational reading – in Greenblatt's terms, an element of 'wonder'.

The kaleidoscope of explanation in the "African Worlds" labels matches the gallery's refrain of diaspora and syncretism. The introductory panel presents the contributors to the reworked exhibition as including "curators from Nigeria, Trinidad and the United Kingdom with support from scholars in American and the European mainland. Members of Black communities have shared the personal meanings and their feelings about the objects on show". This is a claim to authorial credibility in the ideological context of multiculturalism, but it is also a statement of cross-national affiliations, and important sections of the exhibition support the strategy of refuting homogenized, monolingual cultures. Three vodou shrines, from Haiti, Benin and Brazil, directly address the impact of African cultural histories in the diaspora. In his paper on one of the shrines, curator Phil Cope describes Haitian vodou as a translation of Catholic and secular Western icons into the imagery of African deities. He lists correspondences between the taxonomies and argues that Haitian vodou syncretism is not a hotchpotch "but a structured, intentional and powerful form of resistance to white colonial rule" (2000:56). The exhibit itself, a newly commissioned Haitian installation, juxtaposes familiar and unfamiliar to embody an attack on conventional museum dualities like 'here/there', 'Europe/non-Europe', 'authentic/impure' or 'authentic/contemporary' – and the three shrines also blur another boundary, that of art and artefact, or in this case art installations and scientific evidence. This kind of approach tries to present cross-cultural 'affinities' not as abstract universalizations, like the art-historical exhibition criticized by Clifford (1988, ch.9), but as concrete, historically situated meetings and clashes. To this extent the Horniman's shrines represent culture and translation as polyphonic and conflictual; translation is envisioned as a process of multiplication within the object and between museum and object, not solely as a process of ordering imposed by the museum text *on* the object.

The Horniman's attempt to re-translate its collections is intended to be an intervention in the city's political and social texture via translation – translation in a panoramic and politicized version, which is driven on by the presence of a vocal and active diasporic community in the city. As Clifford points out, the urgency of Western museums' sense of responsibility towards the people they represent (portray) depends on the particular constituencies they represent (speak for and to). When nobody is on the spot to complain, the museum's accountability fades, so that, for example, the Wahgi people who sent artefacts and expertise to London for the "Paradise" exhibition had no real chance of implementing their views on how the show should be arranged (Clifford 1997:173). In culturally diverse urban Britain the calls for greater involvement in representation cannot so easily be brushed over, and pressures grow for a devolution of the museum's power (see Simpson 2001).

The curators of the Horniman evidently consider their task as translators to be an eminently ethical one: to rewrite colonial histories, to present alternative interpretations, to open up a public arena for voices that were silenced by the previous display strategies. The process is highly constrained by the demands of the funding authorities and models of public service to majority populations, and Ames suggests that such constraints make it unrealistic to hand mainstream museums the tasks of minority advocacy and political debate (1992:7). Nevertheless, museums as translators of culture may try to move beyond the 'do no harm' principle that guides codes of ethics (see www.aanet.org/committees/ethics/ethcode.htm) and actively open up more dialogic forms.

Dialogue and difference

In the collection *Museums and Communities* (Karp et al. 1992), John Kuo Wei Tchen describes one such dialogic project, the Chinatown History Museum in New York. The project set out to ask how the museum institution can respond to "these 'new' publics who have not traditionally been a part of 'We the People'" (Tchen 1992:287) and consequently to redefine the 'we'. Like other museums of this kind, the Chinatown project faced the difficulty of representing a 'community' without squashing its members into pre-formed definitional boxes. As we saw in Chapter 5, the 'native anthropologist' is not a singular, uncontested figure – who exactly appoints him or herself to speak for a particular group's culture, who defines the borders of the 'community', and who is to decide what it requires in terms of ethical representation in the museum? Nima Poovaya Smith (1991) shows how consultation with community representatives threw up different and contradictory answers to the question of whether the labels in a Bradford exhibition of South Asian jewellery should be written in English only. The advisory panel was adamant that offering translations would be a waste of time, since any non-English speakers visiting were likely to be either accompanied by an English-speaker and/or illiterate in any language – while separate market research indicated that many Bradford citizens would be reluctant to attend an exhibition with incomprehensible, because untranslated, labels. The information needed to be translated into Bengali, Punjabi, Urdu or Hindi in order to attract the visitors the museum was in fact aiming for.

Secondly, like autoethnographies, community-curated museum displays necessarily engage intertextually with existing representations within majoritarian society, whether it be to refute them, to re-direct and exploit them, or to celebrate them in romanticized nostalgia. Moving through the thicket of previous translations can be a politically fraught activity. The Chinatown museum tried to address this head-on by making the very multivocality of Chinese America its guiding principle (1992:286). The curators hoped their critical approach would help visitors "become active in identifying the differences and similarities in their experiences with one another and with people who have not lived their experience. At this point more critical insights begin to challenge simple nostalgia" (ibid:293). The argument is for a reflexive style of translating, but this time a reflexivity based less on the translators than on the readers, who are asked to bring to the table their own representations of themselves and others. The plan for staff to engage in discussion with visitors at the exhibits and at follow-up appointments (309) is the logical extension of an inevitable dialogic aspect of museum-going touched on in Chapter 7: visitors come to the museum bearing their own biographies, interests and narratives, and pit these against the museum's proffered interpretations in ways both unpredictable and productive (see also Dicks 2000).

Like it or not, the populated museum is a multivocal place, but this multivocality can be amplified or dampened by institutional processes. In terms of accountable representation, the mode of construction of the Chinatown museum was important: not top-down from experts to lay people, but in collaboration between different groups (scholars, museum professionals, different Chinese American community groups), including the provision of training in museum skills (Tchen 1992:300). The ideal of collaborative translation in this 'dialogic' museum can be found in some written ethnographies as well. *Piman Shamanism and Staying Sickness (Ká:cim Múmkidag)* (Bahr et al. 1974) is an interesting example. In this study of theories of disease, the anthropologist, shaman, interpreter and editor are all named as co-authors, their contributions specified in the introduction and highlighted by the use of extensive commentated quotes (see also Clifford 1988:51-2). Both the jointly written ethnography and the community-run museum remind us that a translational 'dialogue' is not the conversation between two isolated, decontextualized individuals (or cultural entities) but actually a multiply oriented polylogue. This rules out any notion of 'complete' or 'adequate' translation: an ethical translation cannot record in full, but must point out its own partiality.

Difference in museum translation

Nathaniel Tarn, anthropologist and poet, has described anthropology's fascination with difference as a "thrust towards the other" that pushes people onward, preventing stasis and atrophy. But, he warns, there is a razor-sharp line between "love and appropriation", because "the more one's gaze fixes on the other, the more the other becomes a mirror in which one sees one's own reflection: the better he or she is known, the closer the other looks like the self" (1984:279). In this respect, the museum translation faces similar dilemmas to those of written ethnography: how much should it focus on distance, how much on proximity?

We have seen that the nineteenth-century ethnographic museum, like its written-language cousin, combined a strong sense of difference and the exotic with a strong claim to translatability. The value of objects for exhibition, though not necessarily for researchers, lay to a large degree in their visible strangeness; if the pot in the glass case was just the same as the pot at home, how would it be an 'ethnographic exhibit'? But the artefacts of the others were not only distant and unintelligible, they were also within the viewer's grasp, capable of being made intelligible by the authoritative voice of anthropological expertise (translatable into categories of evolutionary progress, for example). It is the combination of these two facets, rather than distancing alone, which made traditional ethnographic exhibits a form of imperialist translation – failing to deal with cultural difference in the way advocated by, for example, Antoine Berman. Berman (in Venuti's translation) argues for a 'trial of the foreign' in two senses: as an 'experience' that establishes a relationship between the self and the foreign by trying to "open up the foreign work to us in its utter foreignness", and as a trial for the foreign text itself, which is uprooted from its own soil (2000:284). Decrying assimilating forms of translation, Berman finds that the good – that is, ethical – translation should "shake with all its might the translating language" (ibid:285). If we assume that 'language' is used here in a wide sense, as the cultural universe of the receiving language, then this is indeed part of the mission of a contemporary ethnographic museum, as like anthropology it tries to defamiliarize home truths by confronting them with others.

At the same time, there is a strand of museum practice that focuses more on shared ground. Children, especially, are addressed along lines of commonality in the British museums we have looked at. Thus the Pitt Rivers school worksheet commentates the 'Top Ten' favourite shrunken heads as follows: "Did you know? The shrunken heads come from the Jivaro Indians in South America. In Britain the heads of traitors were stuck on posts in medieval times, and we still talk about 'headhunting' in business". Here explicit connections to home are drawn, facilitating particular orderings of the alien object within the readers' terms. The redesigners of the ethnographic exhibits in the Birmingham Museum and Art Gallery, too, made a conscious decision to highlight common ground for educational purposes. The gallery, described by its curator Jane Peirson Jones (1992), centres on a set of panels posing direct, often personal questions about social practices. "Why do we celebrate certain events in our lives?", "How did you gain your position in society?" the panels ask, and the cases propose answers across cultural boundaries by mixing the nineteenth-century collections with modern artefacts including items from everyday British life. The museum education services are using anthropology's potential to enlarge the bridgehead of understanding, discussed in Chapter 3, as a resource to expand the field of mutually accessible meanings across the city's communities.

Because Birmingham's ethnographic gallery explicitly sets out to make positive representations of cultural diversity, a risk arises of conflict being minimized and majority assumptions left untroubled. As Peirson Jones points out, the most popular and requested topics for a gallery of this kind are the "icons of diversity" considered harmless by majority culture: food, festivals, music, dance (1992:229, and see Kirshenblatt-Gimblett [1991:421] for a related discussion of representations of diversity as "spice of life"). The focus on shared values can be a form of appropriative translation that fails to 'shake up' the target language in Berman's sense, since in contrast to minoritized readers, majority readers can feel reassured in their world-view and need not fear their own specificities getting lost in the harmonious generality (Lavine in Karp et al. 1992:155). The ideal of mutual accessibility which accompanies museum multiculturalism could thus end up favouring only some of its constituents. Spivak warns that accessibility is something taken as a natural entitlement "in the house of power" (1993/2000:410) and calls for much more awkward and demanding forms of translation – though museum educators might respond in terms of the youth and inattentiveness of their translations' target audience.

Where does the ethical translator-curator stand in this debate? If we applied a spectrum based on target-language versus source-language orientation, the poles would be public servant to the receiving culture and advocate for the sending cultures. However, as we have seen, the hybrid nature of contemporary museum-using societies in the West digs the ground from under that polarity. Neither are 'sending' and 'receiving' cultures separate and opposing entities, nor are the people represented in the museum amenable to being 'spoken for'. Karel Arnaut describes the museum curator as, instead, a 'broker' who negotiates between different interests on all fronts (2000:17): Arnaut is referring chiefly to the modalities of artefact acquisition, but the metaphor can be taken further if we view the museum as a site of translation. As Bachmann-Medick (forthcoming) shows, the space of translation as cultural brokerage is one that involves conflict, misunderstanding and bargaining for power as well as compromise, engagement and rapprochement. In this model, translators 'represent' in the sense of lawyers or agents rather than either of the Marxian senses discussed in Chapter 1, while Michael Ames calls for the ethical museum not to "represent" at all, but to "report on" the views of other people (Ames 1992:6).

9. Conclusion

I hope this brief trip through anthropological and museological writing on translation will have shown that translation studies need not be defensive about working with translation 'in the narrow sense'. It may be a narrow sense, but it surely isn't a narrow *thing* or object of study. Translation in the narrowest sense is inextricable from an immense range of complex problems that go right to the heart of cultural difference. Yet neither do we need to shy away from translation 'in the wider sense'. Not only are some of the wider senses less distant from interlingual translation than they might first appear, but the more abstract uses of the term can themselves be fertile sources for our thinking on translation narrow or wide. Let me retrace my steps to list some of the areas that I believe could be fruitful for translation studies.

To begin with, anthropology's thorough-going investigation of the notion of 'culture' offers routes out of some rather sclerotic translation dilemmas that have arisen from our traditional conception of pairs of fixed and monoglossic languages. Ethnographic studies have shown how languages live in constant and mutually altering contact, and do so not on equal terms but under the pressure of dominant language-cultures. They indicate, as well, that no fixed 'object' of study pre-exists its representation. To resist essentializing and monologizing accounts, we need more, and more multiply oriented, translation in both a metaphorical and a practical sense, and anthropological thinking can help us consider what that translation should look like.

Another area of relevance to translation studies is the discussion of 'difference' in anthropology and museology. Roy Dilley notes that anthropological questioning of generalization and relativization has produced not an impasse but a "theoretical dialectic that is the motor of disciplinary debate" (1999:9), and this is desirable for translation studies too. Not only does this debate inform textual translation strategies, but it draws the issue away from strict polarities. The stark contrast of source and target language as two opposing realities has been eroded by anthropological theory and the potential arises to compare "polythetically", as Appadurai puts it in a thought-provoking essay, along "several configurations of resemblance and contrast" (1988:46). Furthermore, instead of agonizing about translatability versus untranslatability, translation studies like ethnography can benefit from accepting that, despite difference, translations are made, they have effects in the real world, and those effects can be evaluated in terms of bringing us together or keeping us apart or revealing our own denied translatedness.

This brings me to a third area of interest, which is the translator's power. Ethnographic practice, as we have seen, can cast a rather garish light on discussions of the translator's stance vis-à-vis the source language and its products – as visible or invisible, servant or master. The example of museum translation, in particular, emphasizes that translation does not occur in a vacuum but is forced to take a particular standpoint within networks of cultural representations and of power relations. As Said (1989) insists, there is no space of objectivity outside our own practices, so that translations need to address their own partiality and power. How to do this is another question for which ethnography has proposed practical solutions, for example the leaving of traces or the dispersing of authority. As Natrajan and Parameswaran conclude, accountable representations can be achieved by "interrogating our own stake in what we produce, considering how our knowledge will be used, and acknowledging our responsibilities to the people we write about" (1997:53).

In all the heated debates among ethnographers about modes of representation, few are prepared to propose non-translation (though Fabian [1990] discusses the strategic withholding of writing). From the point of view of the target culture, "anthropology is our one chance of escaping the sheer tedium of our own thought" (Hobart cited in Dilley 1999:9). Marcus and Fischer (1986) go further, stressing the potential of anthropology to mount fierce critiques of the receiving culture – a project with close connections to Berman's vision of a defamiliarizing, innovative translation practice that shakes and radically alters the receiving language. Finally, Nancy Scheper-Hughes makes her point from a different but not unrelated perspective: ethnographic translations, done with a sense of responsibility, can be "acts of solidarity. Above all, they are the work of recognition. Not to look, not to touch, not to record can be the hostile act, an act of indifference and of turning away" (1995:418).

I'd like to finish on an optimistic note. Anthropological translation, says Clifford Geertz, "is not a simple recasting of others' ways of putting things in terms of our own ways of putting them", but involves "displaying the logic of their ways of putting them in the locutions of ours; a conception which [...] brings it rather closer to what a critic does to illumine a poem than what an astronomer does to account for a star" (1983:10). Like riding a bicycle, Geertz concludes, it is easier done than said.

Bibliography

** = key texts*

Abu-Lughod, Lila (1991) 'Writing Against Culture', in Fox (ed), 137-62.

Ames, Michael M. (1992) *Cannibal Tours and Glass Boxes*, Vancouver: UBC Press.

Anzaldúa, Gloria (1987) *Borderlands/La Frontera: The New Mestiza*, San Francisco: Aunt Lute Books.

Appadurai, Arjun (1988) 'Putting Hierarchy in its Place', *Cultural Anthropology* 3:1, 36-49.

------ (1996) *Modernity at Large: Cultural Dimensions of Globalization*, Minneapolis: University of Minnesota Press.

* Appiah, Kwame Anthony (1993) 'Thick Translation', *Callaloo* 16:4, 808-19 (reprinted in Venuti, ed, 417-29).

Arnaut, Karel (ed) (2000) *Re-Visions: New Perspectives on the African Collections of the Horniman Museum*, London: The Horniman Museum and Gardens & Museu Antropológico da Universidade de Coimbra.

* Asad, Talal (1986) 'The Concept of Cultural Translation in British Social Anthropology', in Clifford & Marcus (eds), 141-64.

------ (ed) (1973) *Anthropology and the Colonial Encounter*, Atlantic Highlands: Humanities Press.

* Bachmann-Medick, Doris (2006) 'Meanings of Translation in Cultural Anthropology', in Hermans (ed), Vol. 1, 33-42.

------ (forthcoming) 'I+1=3? Intercultural Relations as a Third Space', trans. K. Sturge, in Mona Baker (ed) *Critical Concepts: Translation Studies*, London: Routledge ('I+1=3? Interkulturelle Beziehungen als "dritter Raum"', 1999).

Bahr, Donald M. (1987) 'Pima Heaven Songs', in Swann & Krupat (eds), 198-246.

------, Juan Gregorio, David I. Lopez & Albert Alvarez (1974) *Piman Shamanism and Staying Sickness (Ká:cim Múmkidag)*, Tucson: University of Arizona Press.

Bakhtin, Mikhail (1981) *The Dialogic Imagination: Four Essays*, trans. Caryl Emerson & Michael Holquist (selections from *Voprosy literatury i estetiki*, 1975).

Bal, Mieke (1996) *Double Exposures*, London: Routledge.

* ------ (2001) 'On Show: Inside the Ethnographic Museum', in *Looking In: The Art of Viewing*, Amsterdam: OPA, 117-60 (an earlier version of this essay is 'Telling, Showing, Showing Off', *Critical Inquiry* 18:3, 1992, 556-94, reprinted in Bal 1996).

Barber, Karin (1991) *I Could Speak until Tomorrow:* Oriki, *Women, and the Past in a Yoruba Town*, Edinburgh: Edinburgh University Press.

Barringer, Tim (1998) 'The South Kensington Museum and the Colonial Project', in Tim Barringer & Tom Flynn (eds), *Colonialism and the Object: Empire,*

Material Culture and the Museum, London: Routledge, 11-27.

Bauman, Richard & Joel Sherzer (1989) *Explorations in the Ethnography of Speaking*, 2nd ed. (first edition 1974), Cambridge: Cambridge University Press.

------ & Patricia Sawin (1991) 'The Politics of Participation in Folklife Festivals', in Karp & Lavine (eds), 288-314.

Baxandall, Michael (1991) 'Exhibiting Intention: Some Preconditions of the Visual Display of Culturally Purposeful Objects', in Karp & Lavine (eds) 33-41.

Behar, Ruth (1993) *Translated Woman: Crossing the Border with Esperanza's Story*, Boston: Beacon Press.

------ (1995) 'Writing in my Father's Name: A Diary of *Translated Woman*'s First Year', in Behar & Gordon (eds), 65-82.

------ & Deborah A. Gordon (eds) (1995) *Women Writing Culture*, Berkeley: University of California Press.

Benjamin, Walter (2000) [1968] 'The Task of the Translator', trans. Harry Zohn, in Venuti (ed), 15-25 ('Die Aufgabe des Übersetzers', 1923).

Berman, Antoine (2000) 'Translation and the Trials of the Foreign', trans. Lawrence Venuti, in Venuti (ed), 284-97 ('La Traduction comme épreuve de l'étranger', 1985).

Bevis, William (1975) [1974] 'American Indian Verse Translations', in Chapman (ed), 308-23.

Bhabha, Homi K. (1994) *The Location of Culture*, London: Routledge.

Boas, Franz (1887) 'Museums of Ethnology and Their Classification', *Science* IX:228, reprinted in Carbonell (ed), 2004, 139-42.

------ (1901) *Kathlamet Texts*, Washington, DC: Government Printing Office.

------ (1911) 'Introduction', *Handbook of Indian Languages*, Part I, Washington, DC: Government Printing Office.

Brettell, Caroline B. (ed) (1993) *When They Read What We Write: The Politics of Ethnography*, Westport: Bergin & Garvey.

Brightman, Robert (1995) 'Forget Culture: Replacement, Transcendence, Relexification', *Cultural Anthropology* 10:4, 509-46.

Bringhurst, Robert (1999) *A Story as Sharp as a Knife: The Classical Haida Mythtellers and their World*, Vancouver: Douglas & McIntyre.

Brisset, Annie (2000) [1996] 'The Search for a Native Language: Translation and Cultural Identity', trans. Rosalind Gill & Roger Gannon, reprinted in Venuti (ed), 343-75.

Brown [i.e. Radcliffe-Brown], A.R. (1922) *The Andaman Islanders: A Study in Social Anthropology*, Cambridge: Cambridge University Press.

* Carbonell, Bettina Messias (ed) (2004) *Museum Studies: An Anthology of Contexts*, Oxford: Blackwell.

Chamberlain, Lori (2000) [1988] 'Gender and the Metaphorics of Translation', reprinted in Venuti (ed), 314-29.

Chapman, Abraham (ed) (1975) *Literature of the American Indians: Views and Interpretations*, New York & Scarborough: New American Library.

Chapman, William Ryan (1985) 'Arranging Ethnology: A.H.L.F. Pitt Rivers and the Typological Tradition', in Stocking (ed), 15-48.

Cheyfitz, Eric (1991) *The Poetics of Imperialism: Translation and Colonization from The Tempest to Tarzan*, New York & Oxford: Oxford University Press.

* Clifford, James (1988) *The Predicament of Culture: Twentieth-Century Ethnography, Literature, and Art*, Cambridge MA: Harvard University Press.

------ (1991) 'Four Northwest Coast Museums: Travel Reflections', in Karp & Lavine (eds), 212-54 (and reprinted in Clifford 1997).

------ (1997) *Routes: Travel and Translation in the Late Twentieth Century*, Cambridge, MA: Harvard University Press.

* ------ & George E. Marcus (eds) (1986) *Writing Culture: The Poetics and Politics of Ethnography*, Berkeley: University of California Press.

* Coombes, Annie E. (1994) *Reinventing Africa: Museums, Material Culture, and Popular Imagination in Late Victorian and Edwardian England*, New Haven: Yale University Press.

Cope, Phil (2000) 'When Ghede met Barbie: Syncretism in Haitian Vodou Culture', in Arnaut (ed), 47-59.

Crapanzano, Vincent (1980) *Tuhami: Portrait of a Moroccan*, Chicago: University of Chicago Press.

------ (1986) 'Hermes' Dilemma: The Masking of Subversion in Ethnographic Description', in Clifford & Marcus (eds), 51-75.

------ (1992) *Hermes' Dilemma and Hamlet's Desire: On the Epistemology of Interpretation*, Cambridge, MA: Harvard University Press.

Crew, Spencer R. & James E. Sims (1991) 'Locating Authenticity: Fragments of a Dialogue', in Karp & Lavine (eds), 159-75.

Cronyn, George W. (ed) (1918) *The Path on the Rainbow: An Anthology of Songs and Chants from the Indians of North America*, New York: Boni & Liveright (the introduction by Mary Austin is reprinted in Chapman, ed, 266-75).

Cruikshank, Julie, in collaboration with Angela Sidney, Kitty Smith, and Annie Ned (1990) *Life Lived Like a Story: Life Stories of Three Yukon Native Elders*, Lincoln: University of Nebraska Press.

Darnell, Regna (2001) *Invisible Genealogies: A History of Americanist Anthropology*, Lincoln: University of Nebraska Press.

Davis, Kathleen (2001) *Translation and Deconstruction*, Manchester: St. Jerome.

Day, A. Grove (1951) *The Sky Clears: Poetry of the American Indians*, New York: Macmillan.

Dias, Nélia (1998) 'The Visibility of Difference: Nineteenth-century French Anthropological Collections', in Sharon Macdonald (ed) *The Politics of Display*, London: Routledge, 36-52.

Dicks, Bella (2000) 'Encoding and Decoding the People: Circuits of Communication at a Local Heritage Museum', *European Journal of Communication* 15:1, 61-78.

Dilley, Roy (1999) 'Introduction', *The Problem of Context*, New York & Oxford: Berghahn, 1-46.

Dingwaney, Anuradha & Carol Maier (1995a) 'Translation as a Method for Cross-Cultural Teaching', in Dingwaney & Maier (eds), 303-19.

------ (eds) (1995b) *Between Languages and Cultures: Translation and Cross-Cultural Texts*, Pittsburgh: University of Pittsburgh Press.

Dominguez, Virginia R. (1986) 'The Marketing of Heritage', *American Ethnologist* 13:3, 546-55.

Dryden, John (1997) [1697] 'Dedication of the *Aeneis*', reprinted in Douglas Robinson (ed) *Western Translation Theory*, Manchester, St. Jerome, 174-5.

Duncan, Carol (1991) 'Art Museums and the Ritual of Citizenship', in Karp & Lavine (eds), 88-103.

Dundes, Alan (1980) 'Texture, Text, and Context', in *Interpreting Folklore*, Bloomington: Indiana University Press, 20-32.

Duranti, Alessandro & Charles Goodwin (eds) (1992) *Rethinking Context: Language as an Interactive Phenomenon*, Cambridge: Cambridge University Press.

Dwyer, Kevin (1982) *Moroccan Dialogues: Anthropology in Question*, Baltimore: Johns Hopkins Press.

Eboreime, O.J. (2000) 'Recontextualizing the Horniman's Collection of Benin Bronzes', in Arnaut (ed), 61-72.

Ellis, Roger (ed) (1989) *The Medieval Translator: The Theory and Practice of Translation in the Middle Ages*, Cambridge: D.S. Brewer.

Evans-Pritchard, E. E. (1940) *The Nuer: A Description of the Modes of Livelihood and Political Institutions of a Nilotic People*, Oxford: Oxford University Press.

Evers, Larry & Felipe S. Molina (1987) *Yaqui Deer Songs: Maso Bwikam, A Native American Poetry*, Tucson: University of Arizona Press.

* Fabian, Johannes (1983) *Time and the Other: How Anthropology Makes its Object*, New York: Columbia University Press.

------ (1990) 'Presence and Representation: The Other in Anthropological Writing', *Critical Inquiry* 19:4, 753-72.

------ (1998) 'Curios and Curiosity: Notes on Reading Torday and Frobenius', in Schildkrout & Keim (eds), 79-108.

------ (2002) 'Virtual Archives and Ethnographic Writing: "Commentary" as a New Genre?' *Current Anthropology* 43:5, 775-86.

Feleppa, Robert (1988) *Convention, Translation, and Understanding: Philosophical Problems in the Comparative Study of Culture*, Albany: SUNY Press.

Feuchtwang, Stephan (1973) 'The Colonial Formation of British Social Anthropology', in Asad (ed), 71-100.

* Fine, Elizabeth C. (1984) *The Folklore Text: From Performance to Print*, Bloomington: Indiana University Press.

Finnegan, Ruth (1992) *Oral Tradition and the Verbal Arts: A Guide to Research Practices*, London: Routledge.

Foley, William A. (1997) *Anthropological Linguistics: An Introduction*, Oxford: Blackwell.
* Fox, Richard G. (ed) (1991) *Recapturing Anthropology: Working in the Present*, Santa Fe: School of American Research Press.
* Geertz, Clifford (1973) *The Interpretation of Cultures*, New York: Basic Books.
------ (1983) *Local Knowledge: Further Essays in Interpretive Anthropology*, New York: Basic Books.
------ (1988) *Works and Lives: The Anthropologist as Author*, Stanford: Stanford University Press.
Goetz, Delia & Sylvanus G. Morley (1950) *Popol Vuh. The Sacred Book of the Ancient Quiché Maya*, English by Delia Goetz & Sylvanus G. Morley, from the Spanish translation by Adrián Recinos, Norman & London: University of Oklahoma Press.
Gosden, Chris & Chantal Knowles (2001) *Collecting Colonialism: Material Culture and Colonial Change*, Oxford: Berg.
Greenblatt, Stephen (1991) 'Resonance and Wonder', in Karp & Lavine (eds), 42-56.
Handler, Richard (1985) 'On Having a Culture: Nationalism and the Preservation of Quebec's *Patrimoine*', in Stocking (ed), 192-217.
Haraway, Donna (1984/85) 'Teddy Bear Patriarchy: Taxidermy in the Garden of Eden, New York City, 1908-1936', *Social Text* 11, 20-64.
Hermans, Theo (1999) *Translation in Systems: Descriptive and System-Oriented Approaches Explained*, Manchester: St Jerome.
------ (ed) (2006) *Translating Others*, 2 vols, Manchester: St. Jerome.
Hill, Jane H. (1995) 'The Voices of Don Gabriel: Responsibility and Self in a Modern Mexicano Narrative', in Tedlock & Mannheim (eds), 97-147.
Hollis, A.C. (1905) *The Masai: Their Language and Folklore*, Oxford: Clarendon.
Hooper-Greenhill, Eilean (1992) *Museums and the Shaping of Knowledge*, London: Routledge.
* ------ (2000) *Museums and the Interpretation of Visual Culture*, London: Routledge.
Huang, Yunte (2002) *Transpacific Displacement: Ethnography, Translation, and Intertextual Travel in Twentieth-Century American Literature*, Berkeley: University of California Press.
Hudson, Kenneth (1991) 'How Misleading Does an Ethnographical Museum Have to Be?', in Karp & Lavine (eds), 457-64.
Hymes, Dell (1965) 'Some North Pacific Coast Poems: A Problem in Anthropological Philology', *American Anthropologist* 67:2, 316-41.
------ (1981) '*In Vain I Tried to Tell You...' Essays in Native American Ethnopoetics*, Philadelphia: University of Pennsylvania Press.
------ (1987) 'Tonkawa Poetics: John Rush Buffalo's "Coyote and Eagle's Daughter"', in Sherzer & Woodbury (eds), 17-61.

------ (1997) [1982] 'Narrative Form as a "Grammar" of Experience: Native Americans and a Glimpse of English', in Karl Kroeber (ed) *Traditional Literatures of the American Indian: Texts and Interpretations*, Lincoln: University of Nebraska Press, 43-67.

Inghilleri, Moira (ed) (2005) *Bourdieu and the Sociology of Translating and Interpreting*, Special Issue of *The Translator* 11:2.

Jacknis, Ira (1985) 'Franz Boas and Exhibits: On the Limitations of the Museum Method of Anthropology', in Stocking (ed), 75-111.

Jacquemond, Richard (1992) 'Translation and Cultural Hegemony: The Case of French-Arabic Translation', in Lawrence Venuti (ed) *Rethinking Translation: Discourse, Subjectivity, Ideology*, London: Routledge, 139-58.

Johnson, Douglas H. (1982) 'Evans-Pritchard, the Nuer, and the Sudan Political Service', *African Affairs* 81, 231-46.

Jones, Todd (2003) 'Translation and Belief Ascription: Fundamental Barriers', in Rubel & Rosman (eds), 45-73.

Jorgensen, Annette (2003) 'Power, Knowledge and Tourguiding: The Construction of Irish Identity on Board County Wicklow Tour Buses', in Michael Cronin & Barbara O'Connor (eds) *Irish Tourism: Image, Culture and Identity*, Clevedon: Channel View Publications, 141-57.

Kaeppler, Adrienne L. (1994) 'Paradise Regained: The Role of Pacific Museums in Forging National Identity', in Kaplan (ed), 19-44.

Kaplan, Flora Edouwaye S. (ed) (1994) *Museums and the Making of 'Ourselves': The Role of the Objects in National Identity*, London: Leicester University Press.

Karp, Ivan (1991) 'Culture and Representation', in Karp & Lavine (eds), 11-24.

* ------ & Steven D. Lavine (eds) (1991) *Exhibiting Cultures: The Poetics and Politics of Museum Display*, Washington: Smithsonian Institution.

* ------, Christine Mullen Kreamer & Steven D. Lavine (eds) (1992) *Museums and Communities: The Politics of Public Culture*, Washington: Smithsonian Institution.

Kasfir, Sidney Littlefield (1984) 'One Tribe, One Style? Paradigms in the Historiography of African Art', *History in Africa* 11, 163-93.

Kavanagh, Gaynor (ed) (1991) *Museum Languages: Objects and Texts*, Leicester: Leicester University Press.

Keesing, Roger M. (1989) 'Exotic Readings of Cultural Texts', *Current Anthropology* 30:4, 459-79.

Kirshenblatt-Gimblett, Barbara (1991) 'Objects of Ethnography', in Karp & Lavine (eds), 386-443.

* Kuklick, Henrika (1991) *The Savage Within: The Sociology of British Anthropology, 1885-1945*, Cambridge: Cambridge University Press.

Kulick, Don (1998) *Travesti: Sex, Gender, and Culture among Brazilian Transgendered Prostitutes*, Chicago: University of Chicago Press.

Krupat, Arnold (1992a) 'On the Translation of Native American Song and Story: A Theorized History', in Swann (ed.), 3-32.

------ (1992b) *Ethnocriticism: Ethnography, History, Literature*, Berkeley: University of California Press.

Lambert, José (1991) 'In Quest of Literary World Maps', in Harald Kittel & Armin Paul Frank (eds) *Interculturality and the Historical Study of Literary Translations*, Berlin: Erich Schmidt, 133-44.

Lane Fox, Col. (=A.H.L.F. Pitt Rivers) (1875) 'The Evolution of Culture', *Notices of the Proceedings at the Meetings of the Members of the Royal Institution of Great Britain* VII (1873-1875), 496-520.

Lefevere, André (1992) *Translation, Rewriting, and the Manipulation of Literary Fame*, London: Routledge.

Lévi-Strauss, Claude (1981) *The Naked Man (Introduction to a Science of Mythology 4)*, trans. John & Doreen Weightman, London: Jonathan Cape (*L'Homme nu*, 1971).

Lewis, Ioan (1973) *The Anthropologist's Muse: An Inaugural Lecture*, London: LSE.

Linnekin, Jocelyn (1991) 'Cultural Invention and the Dilemma of Authenticity', *American Anthropologist* 93:2, 446-9.

Lumley, Robert (ed) (1988) *The Museum Time Machine*, London: Routledge.

Lutz, Catherine A. (1988) *Unnatural Emotions: Everyday Sentiments on a Micronesian Atoll and their Challenge to Western Theory*, Chicago: University of Chicago Press.

Macdonald, Sharon (1996) 'Introduction', in Macdonald & Fyfe (eds), 1-18.

------ (1997) 'The Museum as Mirror: Ethnographic Reflections', in Allison James, Jenny Hockey & Andrew Dawson (eds) *After Writing Culture: Epistemology and Praxis in Contemporary Anthropology*, London: Routledge, 161-76.

------ & Gordon Fyfe (eds) (1996) *Theorizing Museums*, Oxford: Blackwell.

MacGaffey, Wyatt (1998) '"Magic, or as we usually say, Art": A Framework for Comparing European and African Art', in Schildkrout & Keim (eds), 217-35.

------ (2003) 'Structural Impediments to Translation in Art', in Rubel & Rosman (eds), 249-67.

Mafeje, Archie (1971) 'The Ideology of "Tribalism"', *Journal of Modern African Studies* 9:2, 253-61.

Maier, Carol (1995) 'Toward a Theoretical Practice for Cross-Cultural Translation', in Dingwaney & Maier (eds), 21-38.

Malinowski, Bronislaw (1930) [1923] 'The Problem of Meaning in Primitive Languages', in C.K. Ogden & I.A. Richards (eds) *The Meaning of Meaning*, rev. ed., New York: Harcourt & Brace, 296-336.

------ (1935) *Coral Gardens and Their Magic*, 2 vols, especially vol. 2, *The Language of Magic and Gardening*, London: Allen & Unwin.

Mannheim, Bruce & Dennis Tedlock (1995) 'Introduction', in Tedlock & Mannheim (eds), 1-32.

Maranhão, Tullio & Bernhard Streck (eds) (2003) *Translation and Ethnography:*

The Anthropological Challenge of Intercultural Understanding, Tucson: University of Arizona Press.

* Marcus, George E. & Dick Cushman (1982) 'Ethnographies as Texts', *Annual Review of Anthropology* 11, 25-69.

------ & Michael Fischer (1986) *Anthropology as Cultural Critique: An Experimental Moment in the Human Sciences*, Chicago: University of Chicago Press.

Martin, Laura (2000) 'Parallelism and the Spontaneous Ritualization of Ordinary Talk: Three Mocho Friends Discuss a Volcano', in Sammons & Sherzer (eds), 104-24.

Mattina, Anthony (1987) 'North American Indian Mythography: Editing Texts for the Printed Page', in Swann & Krupat (eds), 129-48.

McClaurin, Irma (2001a) 'Theorizing a Black Feminist Self in Anthropology: Toward an Autoethnographic Approach', in McClaurin (ed), 49-76.

------ (ed) (2001b) *Black Feminist Anthropology: Theory, Politics, Praxis, and Poetics*, New Brunswick: Rutgers University Press.

McGee, R. Jon (1990) *Life, Ritual and Religion among the Lacandon Maya*, Belmont, CA: Wadsworth.

McManus, Paulette (1991) 'Making Sense of Exhibits', in Kavanagh (ed), 35-46.

Message, Kylie (2006) 'Contested Sites of Identity and the Cult of the New: The Centre Culturel Tjibaou and the Constitution of Culture in New Caledonia', *reCollections: Journal of the National Museum of Australia*, 1:1, http://recollections.nma.gov.au.

Messick, Brinkley (2003) 'Notes on Transliteration', in Rubel & Rosman (eds), 177-96.

Moore, Patrick & Angela Wheelock (eds) (1990) *Wolverine Myths and Visions: Dene Traditions from Northern Alberta*, Lincoln: University of Nebraska Press.

Muhawi, Ibrahim (2006) 'Towards a Folkloristic Theory of Translation', in Hermans (ed), Vol. 2, 365-79.

Murray, David (1991) *Forked Tongues: Speech, Writing and Representation in North American Indian Texts*, Bloomington: Indiana University Press.

Myerhoff, Barbara (1978) *Number Our Days*, New York: Simon & Schuster.

Narayan, Kirin (1997) 'How Native is a "Native" Anthropologist?' in Louise Lamphere, Helena Ragoné & Patricia Zavella (eds) *Situated Lives: Gender and Culture in Everyday Life*, London: Routledge, 23-41.

Natrajan, Balmurli & Radhika Parameswaran (1997) 'Contesting the Politics of Ethnography: Towards an Alternative Knowledge Production', *Journal of Communication Inquiry* 21:1, 27-59.

Neather, Robert (2005) 'Translating the Museum: On Translation and (Cross-) Cultural Presentation in Contemporary China', in Juliane House, M. Rosario Martín Ruano & Nicole Baumgarten (eds) *Translation and the Construction of Identity*, Seoul: IATIS, 180-97.

Needham, Rodney (1972) *Belief, Language, and Experience*, Oxford: Blackwell.

Newton, Douglas (1994) 'Old Wine in New Bottles, and the Reverse', in Kaplan (ed), 269-90.

* Niranjana, Tejaswini (1992) *Siting Translation: History, Post-Structuralism, and the Colonial Context*, Berkeley: University of California Press.

Ortner, Sherry (1991) 'Reading America: Preliminary Notes on Class and Culture', in Fox (ed), 163-89.

* Pálsson, Gísli (ed) (1993) *Beyond Boundaries: Understanding, Translation, and Anthropological Discourse*, Oxford: Berg.

Parks, Douglas R. (1991) *Traditional Narratives of the Arikara Indians*, 4 vols, Lincoln: University of Nebraska Press.

Peirson Jones, Jane (1992) 'The Colonial Legacy and the Community: The Gallery 33 Project', in Karp, Kreamer & Lavine (eds), 221-41.

Penny, H. Glenn (2002) *Objects of Culture: Ethnology and Ethnographic Museums in Imperial Germany*, Chapel Hill: University of North Carolina Press.

Perin, Constance (1992) 'The Communicative Circle: Museums as Communities', in Karp, Kreamer & Lavine (eds), 182-220.

Polezzi, Loredana (ed) (2006) *Translation, Travel, Migration*, Special Issue of *The Translator* 12:2.

Poovaya Smith, Nima (1991) 'Exhibitions and Audiences: Catering for a Pluralistic Public', in Kavanagh (ed), 121-34.

Pratt, Mary Louise (1986) 'Fieldwork in Common Places', in Clifford & Marcus (eds), 27-50.

------ (1992) *Imperial Eyes: Travel Writing and Transculturation*, London: Routledge.

Pym, Anthony (1998) *Method in Translation History*, Manchester: St Jerome.

Quine, Willard V.O. (2000) [1959] 'Meaning and Translation', reprinted in Venuti (ed), 94-112.

Rabinow, Paul (1977) *Reflections on Fieldwork in Morocco*, Berkeley: University of California Press.

------ (1986) 'Representations are Social Facts: Modernity and Post-Modernity in Anthropology', in Clifford & Marcus (eds), 234-61.

Rafael, Vicente L. (1988) *Contracting Colonialism: Translation and Christian Conversion in Tagalog Society under Early Spanish Rule*, Ithaca: Cornell University Press.

Ramsay, Rachel (1999) 'Salvage Ethnography and Gender Politics in *Two Old Women*', *Studies in American Indian Literature* 11:3, 22-41.

Rattray, R. Sutherland (1916) *Ashanti Proverbs (The Primitive Ethics of a Savage People)*, Oxford: Clarendon.

Riegel, Henrietta (1996) 'Into the Heart of Irony: Ethnographic Exhibitions and the Politics of Difference', in Macdonald & Fyfe (eds), 83-104.

Robinson, Douglas (1997) *Translation and Empire: Postcolonial Theories Explained*, Manchester: St. Jerome.

Rosaldo, Renato (1986) 'From the Door of His Tent: The Fieldworker and the

Inquisitor', in Clifford & Marcus (eds), 77-97.
Rosman, Abraham & Paula G. Rubel (2003) 'Are Kinship Terminologies Translatable?' in Rubel & Rosman (eds), 269-83.
Rothenberg, Jerome (1975) [1969] 'Total Translation: An Experiment in the Presentation of American Indian Poetry', in Chapman (ed), 292-307.
------ (1985) *Technicians of the Sacred*, rev. ed. (first ed. 1968), Berkeley: University of California Press.
------ (1991) *Shaking the Pumpkin: Traditional Poetry of the Indian North Americas*, rev. ed. (first ed. 1971), Albuquerque: University of New Mexico Press.
------ (1992) '"We Explain Nothing, We Believe Nothing": American Indian Poetry and the Problematics of Translation', in Swann (ed), 64-79.
* Rubel, Paula G. & Abraham Rosman (eds) (2003) *Translating Cultures: Perspectives on Translation and Anthropology*, Oxford: Berg.
Rushdie, Salman (1983) *Shame*, London: Jonathan Cape.
* Said, Edward (1978) *Orientalism*, New York: Pantheon Books.
------ (1989) 'Representing the Colonized: Anthropology's Interlocutors', *Critical Inquiry* 15:2, 205-25.
* Sammons, Kay & Joel Sherzer (eds) (2000) *Translating Native Latin American Verbal Art: Ethnopoetics and Ethnography of Speaking*, Washington, DC: Smithsonian Institution.
Scheper-Hughes, Nancy (1995) 'The Primacy of the Ethical: Propositions for a Militant Anthropology', *Current Anthropology* 36:3, 409-40.
Schildkrout, Enid & Curtis A. Keim (eds) (1998) *The Scramble for Art in Central Africa*, Cambridge: Cambridge University Press.
Sewell, William H. (1999) 'The Concept(s) of Culture', in Victoria E. Bonnell & Lynn Hunt (eds) *Beyond the Cultural Turn: New Directions in the Study of Society and Culture*, Berkeley: University of California Press, 35-61.
Seymour, Peter J. (1985) *The Golden Woman: The Colville Narrative of Peter J. Seymour*, ed. Anthony Mattina, trans. Anthony Mattina & Madeline deSautel, Tucson: University of Arizona Press.
Shelton, Anthony Alan (1994) 'Cabinets of Transgression: Renaissance Collections and the Incorporation of the New World', in John Elsner & Roger Cardinal (eds) *The Cultures of Collecting*, London: Reaktion, 177-203.
------ (2000) 'Preface', in Arnaut (ed), 9-12.
Sherzer, Joel (1990) *Verbal Art in San Blas: Kuna Culture through its Discourse*, Cambridge: Cambridge University Press.
------ & Anthony C. Woodbury (eds) (1987) *Native American Discourse: Poetics and Rhetoric*, Cambridge: Cambridge University Press.
Shostak, Marjorie (1981) *Nisa: The Life and Words of a !Kung Woman*, Cambridge, MA: Harvard University Press.
Siegel, James T. (1986) *Solo in the New Order: Language and Hierarchy in an Indonesian City*, Princeton: Princeton University Press.
Simpson, Moira G. (2001) *Making Representations: Museums in the Post-Colonial*

Era, rev. ed. (first ed. 1991), London: Routledge.
Skotnes, Pippa (ed) (1996) *Miscast: Negotiating the Presence of the Bushmen*, Cape Town: UCT Press.
Socolovsky, Maya (1998) 'Moving Beyond the Mint Green Walls: An Examination of (Auto)Biography and Border in Ruth Behar's *Translated Woman*', *Frontiers* 19:3, 72-97.
Spivak, Gayatri Chakravorty (1988) 'Can the Subaltern Speak?' in Cary Nelson & Lawrence Grossberg (eds), *Marxism and the Interpretation of Culture*, Urbana: University of Illinois Press, 271-313.
------ (2000) [1993] 'The Politics of Translation', reprinted in Venuti (ed), 397-416.
Stanley, Nick (1998) *Being Ourselves for You: The Global Display of Culture*, London: Middlesex University Press.
Stocking, George W. (1983) 'The Ethnographer's Magic: Fieldwork in British Anthropology from Tylor to Malinowski', in *Observers Observed: Essays on Ethnographic Fieldwork*, Madison: University of Wisconsin Press, 70-120.
* ------ (ed) (1985) *Objects and Others: Essays on Museums and Material Culture*, Madison: University of Wisconsin Press.
Strathern, Marilyn (1987) 'The Limits of Auto-Anthropology', in Anthony Jackson (ed) *Anthropology at Home*, London: Tavistock, 16-37.
Sturge, Kate (1997) 'Translation Strategies in Ethnography', *The Translator* 3:1, 21-38.
Sturrock, John (1990) 'Writing Between the Lines: The Language of Translation', *New Literary History* 21, 993-1013.
* Swann, Brian (ed) (1992) *On the Translation of Native American Literatures*, Washington, DC: Smithsonian Institution.
------ & Arnold Krupat (eds) (1987) *Recovering the Word: Essays on Native American Literature*, Berkeley: University of California Press.
Tambiah, Stanley Jeyaraja (1990) *Magic, Science, Religion, and the Scope of Rationality*, Cambridge: Cambridge University Press.
Tannen, Deborah (1995) 'Waiting for the Mouse: Constructed Dialogue in Conversation', in Tedlock & Mannheim (eds), 198-217.
Tarn, Nathaniel (1984) 'Dr Jekyll, the Anthropologist Emerges and Marches into the Notebook of Mr Hyde, the Poet', *Conjunctions* 6, 266-81.
Tchen, John Kuo Wei (1992) 'Creating a Dialogic Museum: The Chinatown History Museum Project', in Karp, Kreamer & Lavine (eds), 285-326.
Tedlock, Barbara (1995) 'Works and Wives: On the Sexual Division of Textual Labor', in Behar & Gordon (eds), 267-86.
Tedlock, Dennis (1978) [1972] *Finding the Center: Narrative Poetry of the Zuni Indians,* translated by Dennis Tedlock, from performances in the Zuni by Andrew Peynetsa and Walter Sanchez, Lincoln: University of Nebraska Press.
* ------ (1983) *The Spoken Word and the Work of Interpretation*. Philadelphia: University of Pennsylvania Press.

------ (1987) 'Hearing a Voice in an Ancient Text: Quiché Maya Poetics in Performance', in Sherzer & Woodbury (eds), 140-75.

------ (1995) 'Interpretation, Participation, and the Role of Narrative in Dialogical Anthropology', in Tedlock & Mannheim (eds), 253-87.

------ (1996) [1985] *Popol Vuh: The Definitive Edition of the Mayan Book of the Dawn of Life*, trans. Dennis Tedlock, rev. ed., New York: Simon & Schuster.

* ------ & Bruce Mannheim (eds) (1995) *The Dialogic Emergence of Culture*, Urbana & Chicago: University of Illinois Press.

Toolan, Michael (1992) 'The Signification of Representing Dialect in Writing', *Language and Literature* 1:1, 29-46.

Toury, Gideon (1995) *Descriptive Translation Studies and Beyond,* Amsterdam & Philadelphia: John Benjamins.

Trouillot, Michel-Rolph (1991) 'Anthropology and the Savage Slot: The Poetics and Politics of Otherness', in Fox (ed), 17-44.

Tymoczko, Maria (1990) 'Translation in Oral Tradition as a Touchstone for Translation Theory and Practice', in Susan Bassnett & André Lefevere (eds) *Translation, History and Culture*, London: Routledge, 46-55.

------ (1999) *Translation in a Postcolonial Context: Early Irish Literature in English Translation*, Manchester: St Jerome.

Van Maanen, John (1988) *Tales of the Field: On Writing Ethnography*, Chicago: University of Chicago Press.

Venuti, Lawrence (1995) *The Translator's Invisibility: A History of Translation*, London: Routledge.

------ (1998) *The Scandals of Translation: Towards an Ethics of Difference*, London: Routledge.

* ------ (ed) (2000) *The Translation Studies Reader*, London: Routledge.

Vinay, Jean-Paul & Jean Darbelnet (2000) [1995] 'A Methodology for Translation', trans. Juan C. Sager & M.-J. Hamel, reprinted in Venuti (ed), 84-93.

Vincent, Joan (1991) 'Engaging Historicism', in Fox (ed), 45-58.

Walker, James R (1980) *Lakota Belief and Ritual*, edited and partly translated by Raymond J. DeMallie & Elaine A. Jahner, Lincoln: University of Nebraska Press.

Watson, Graham (1991) 'Rewriting Culture', in Fox (ed), 73-92.

White, Hayden (1973) *Metahistory: The Historical Imagination in Nineteenth-Century Europe*, Baltimore: Johns Hopkins University Press.

Wikan, Unni (1993) 'Beyond the Words: The Power of Resonance', in Pálsson (ed), 184-209.

Wolf, Michaela (2002) 'Culture as Translation – and Beyond: Ethnographic Models of Representation in Translation Studies', in Theo Hermans (ed) *Crosscultural Transgressions: Research Models in Translation Studies*, Manchester: St. Jerome, 180-92.

------ (ed) (2006) *Übersetzen – Translating – Traduire: Towards a 'Social Turn'?* Münster: LIT

Index